ONE SPECK OF HUMANITY

This is the story of a boy who had but one ambition — to see the world, in the days when a trip from London to Southend was a big event. Then fate — or chance — took over; Syd Metcalfe joined the Army and spent four adventurous years in India. He returned to England just before the outbreak of the Second World War and was immediately 'called up', being posted to France and then to West Africa, India and Burma. After the war, he joined the Merchant Navy and visited many other countries. Eventually, he 'paid off' in Australia and stayed for eleven years. Later, he lived for many years in New Zealand, but now he is back where he belongs — in England, with his many memories.

SYD METCALFE

ONE SPECK OF HUMANITY

Complete and Unabridged

CHARNWOOD
Leicester

910.4092

First published in Great Britain in 1995 by
Syd Metcalfe

First Charnwood Edition
published 2000

The moral right of the author has been asserted

British Library CIP Data

Metcalfe, Syd
    One speck of humanity.—Large print ed.—
Charnwood library series
    1. Metcalfe, Syd—Journeys
    2. Voyages and travels
    3. Large type books
    I. Title
    910.4'092

    ISBN 0–7089–9130–0

Published by
F. A. Thorpe (Publishing) Ltd.
Anstey, Leicestershire
Set by Words & Graphics Ltd.
Anstey, Leicestershire
Printed and bound in Great Britain by
T. J. International Ltd., Padstow, Cornwall

This book is printed on acid-free paper

The author, on leave in Karachi.
Hence the happy smile.

Foreword

In the dim light of the early morning the old man was sweeping down the pavement in front of the building of which he was caretaker. A nondescript character, with no outstanding feature, soon he will have finished and will have disappeared into the murky bowels of the building. With an eye on the more important members of the work-force hurrying by his broom goes jerkily towards the gutter. He is part of the daily scene, this old chap, a regular feature, like the pigeons searching for scraps in the roadway, watching all the time for the occasional bus passing by.

Not that his constant appearance on the pavements has aroused any interest in those who bother to notice him, and certainly no-one will stop to consider what his past life might have been, what might have led up to his present position. If a young man were to cast him a casual glance it would be to see in return an innocuous old fellow coming to the end of his days, a picture of a wasted life.

Should the young man pursue the matter he might well imagine that nothing would ever induce him to finish his days in the same way. It would be hard for him to see that the old boy was ever trim and alert, dressed in the fashion of the day, perhaps even athletic. It would be harder still for the youngster to imagine him as

1

once able to command a modicum of attention from the girls of his day.

Yet so it was. For, as with us all, his present indifferent appearance tells only a fraction of his story. And the least interesting at that. For the whole story we need to go back to the very beginning and work our way slowly through.

That way I hope would show what it is that makes a man finish his days sweeping the pavements down while others pick their way past him on their way to work.

The story is mine, for I am the old boy at the end of the broom whom every young man is sure he will not emulate.

But does one need to end up a figure of national importance to have a story to tell, to have lived a life filled with interest? Were my loves any less tender, any less passionate because I am unheard of? Were my dreams as a child any less real, my idealism any less sincere because of my lowly beginnings?

Fate takes no account of stature or status. What it holds in store is on offer to all — only some venture to take a little more freely of it than others.

As for the times we live in, I am sure that opportunities for adventure and excitement were greater then than now. What young man of today, for example, can ever hope to find himself passing four or five years of his life on the North West Frontier of India, the target of resentful tribesmen? Why, even the name no longer exists. It is unlikely too that he will ever be stranded for two days on Dunkirk beach, struggling to find a way off, while the skies are filled with enemy planes. He might well say, 'Well, who wants to?' But it was these things that gave life an intensity and colour that makes a story worth telling. This plus the movement and the variety of activity that was on the streets of those times.

We were simpler then. And just as a child in its innocence finds all that's happening around it terribly real and awfully important so did we in our ignorance incline to be more easily affected by what happened around us. It made for a life of higher peaks and lower troughs of emotion, which left less time for the boredom that seems to be around today.

So let us go back to those simpler times, to as far as my memory will take me and from there I shall proceed in the order in which my life unfolded.

Myself, I make no apology for writing of my life in the order in which I lived it. I was born and developed in a certain order. It is because certain events happened that others followed. It is because of these happenings that I became what I am. Let us see then this development take place knowing what led to what. Let us see what goes to make ONE SPECK OF HUMANITY.

SYD METCALFE.

3

1

My Father Meets My Mother

Nobody seemed interested in how I felt about the matter under discussion on that day when our whole family was ensconced in a horse-drawn carriage, en route to a large North London cemetery for the purpose of laying my little sister to her final rest. Not that she had done anything else but rest from the very day of her birth for now she was dead before she had ever learned to stand on her own feet.

The only association that there was between her and me came at the odd moments when I would lift up the net that covered the top of her pram and gaze in upon her. What effect she had upon me, whether I admired her, felt any affection for her or whether she left me completely unmoved, at this stage could be no more than conjecture, but I do know that that day when we were being conducted towards the cemetery *en famille* my interest was mostly taken up by the behaviour of the people we passed on the way. For some reason or other everyone chose to stop and wait until we had passed on before they continued on their way. Some went so far as to remove their hat and stand there bareheaded a while. Why they should want to do this I could not even guess, and in response to my, 'Oh, look, mum,' there was only complete silence.

The whole world seemed sad on that ride there. Except me. I felt all right. I was quite enjoying the ride. My very first, in fact, but I wish they would go a bit faster.

The atmosphere in that carriage was distinctly gloomy. Even my mother, who was normally irrepressible was quite subdued.

Two men were standing on the back of our carriage and even they seemed to be affected by the occasion for they couldn't muster a smile between them. 'Why should they be sad, they were nothing to do with our family?'

Then we came to the cemetery gates. Massive they were. The largest gates I had ever seen, although if one should see them now they have shrunk. I have seen them frequently since. But that day they were twice the size they are now.

Inside I was captivated by the glorious array of flowers and monuments. I liked it there. Then we all descended and there followed quite a bit of useless standing around. I was directed to 'Stand still and keep quiet,' which I did, even though there didn't seem to be any earthly reason for doing so.

After a while we took our places in the carriage again and headed for home. For some unaccountable reason the whole attitude of everyone had now changed. Mum and dad talked freely and animatedly, while even I was allowed to chatter without being told to shush. The two men on the back had now come to life and no longer seemed to be affected by the occasion. The horses too sensed the relaxation of tension for they were now trotting. Ah, this was better, now we were moving at a lively pace and the clatter of the horses' hooves on the road gave off quite a merry sound. Neither did anyone on the pavements seem any longer to be concerned by our passing. All these things I noted and wondered about.

On our arrival back at the house the drivers and the men who had stood on the back were all invited in and the room was alive with chatter as they all stood around with their glasses of beer and sandwiches.

As far as I know that little girl who was interred that day was never mentioned again. If she had lived long enough to be christened her name was never spoken in my presence. But child mortality was so common then and usually there were so many children left over at the final count that the loss of the odd one here and there on the way didn't really matter much. It was as though this elimination process whereby only the stronger ones survived was accepted as a perfectly natural state of affairs. Families were built up in this fashion, with so many defunct and so many living.

When the possibility of any further additions being made to our family had been eventually dismissed we children numbered three, my young sister, my older brother and myself. I was sandwiched in between the two and there I remained, well and truly hemmed in.

The lot of a middle child can be a most unfortunate one. Unless the parents are most careful he can very soon be made aware of the fact that he has no outstanding qualities in their eyes, being neither the eldest nor the youngest. Neither their first-born nor their baby. And if this same middle child happens to be a boy between an elder brother and a younger sister then he is in double jeopardy — for then he can be told, when he enquires as to why he isn't receiving equal treatment with the others, one of three things. He can be told, 'Well, he's the eldest', or 'Well, she's the youngest' or even, 'Well she's a girl'.

This, I think, had a serious, even pernicious effect upon my character. It made me feel unimportant at all times, even outside the family atmosphere and had a restrictive influence right through my growing life. There was always within me a small voice warning me not to feel quite equal to others in case I should be put in my place. Dad's 'Keep quiet, you' was always niggling away at the back of my head.

But there was no sense of under-privilege in my mind on the return from the cemetery that day. All that concerned me then was my glass of lemonade and the difficulty that I had in tipping it at such an angle that I could drink it in comfort. As it was it would keep dripping down my chin and on to my brand new vest.

Neither did I feel badly treated or unloved when some short while after that I was securely perched upon the broad shoulders of my father watching the soldiers march by.

The scene was a happy one with the crowd cheering, flags waving and the soldiers laughing and waving back to the crowd.

The 1914 – 1918 war had just broken out and they were off to give the Germans a short sharp lesson and then back again. Nobody would have dared prophesy that it would be four years before they would march back sadder and wiser, with their ranks torn to pieces. Nobody would have said that within a year those two broad shoulders on which I felt so safe would be 'over there' caught up in the most ghastly war of all time.

Certainly my father had no thoughts of following them over as we stood watching that day. For up till then all wars had been fought by the Regular Army. Conscription was a word as yet unknown to the masses. Soon it was to become familiar to everyone.

That was a happy day for me for it was a rare treat to be taken out alone by my father. I can remember no other until I was a man. Many years had passed and my father was now elderly, lonely and in need of comfort.

But as I sat with my legs dangling over his chest as the soldiers went gaily by there was no thought in my mind that he would ever be anything to me but a source of strength and security.

Yet I wonder how his thoughts were running at that time. For already there were portents that his future was not too rosy.

He was the eldest son of a master builder and he worked for his father as a painter and decorator. A good one too for he had learned his trade the hard way, having been compelled by his dad to come up through the ranks. He received no favours and had started working in his father's business as 'the boy'. As such he was expected to do anything that was asked of him. And he did it, for he lived at a time when a son paid his father the greatest respect, even if through his mind ran the most rebellious thoughts. Later on, as he progressed, having passed through the various branches of the trade he settled for the decorating side of the business as it was considered a little more respected.

As a teenager he had played football for Clapton Orient and in a photograph of the team that was a part of our household for many years one could see him as a fair-haired, thick-set rather serious looking young man. Not unhandsome, yet not the most outstanding member of the team.

He was destined to live a most miserable life, but that lay way ahead on the day that that photograph was taken.

Many, many years later, with my dad buried in a grave we could no longer find, Clapton Orient, now renamed Leyton Orient, won their way into the First Division. This was a momentous event in the club's history. They had never been in the First Division before. My brother and I were both there to watch when they won the decisive game, the last of the season. It was the winning of this game that finally decided whether they had won promotion or not. As soon as the referee's whistle blew the crowd, or the more agile of those there, went over the rails and rushed the team to congratulate them.

When I say the more agile of the crowd, there were two 'old boys' who clambered over the rail and went with them. That was my brother and I, both well turned fifty. Of course by the time we reached the centre of the pitch all the young element had beaten us to it and there was already a large crowd clustered around the players. We could only stand at the back and look on. But we were there, that was all that mattered. Once I looked at Arthur and was glad that he was not looking at me for we were both struggling to hold the tears back. We were thinking of our dad.

At a local dance one day he had met a girl who had made him want to see more of her.

A gay young thing she was. Full of life. It was this that appealed to him for he was by nature somewhat quiet. Her lively behaviour had made him feel quite jolly that night, and they were going to meet the next evening. He had promised to take her to a show.

The next evening, dressed in his best suit, eagerly anticipating another happy three or four hours in her company dad waited for her for three quarters of an hour but she did not show up. Through his mind ran the thought that perhaps she was waiting somewhere else. Perhaps she had not heard him rightly when he had said 'outside the front of the station.' He wandered around to the back, but, no, she was not there. Finally he left and went home, full of misgivings and doubts.

Not that he doubted her sincerity. She seemed too nice for that. Something must have happened to prevent her from keeping that appointment. He must see her again and find out what it was. He knew where she worked, she had told him. Today he would have phoned her up but in his day telephones were a rarity and most ordinary folk were afraid to use them. Instead he finished work early the next day and was waiting outside the clothing factory where she worked when she came out. As usual she was the centre of attraction — some of her workmates were there alongside her as he came down the steps laughing as she recounted the happenings of the night before. When they broke up, each going their separate way dad caught up with her and said, 'Hello, do you remember me?'

She wasn't particularly interested but he refused to acknowledge this. In fact so point blank was his refusal that he eventually persuaded her to marry him. And so was created the first step towards my appearance on earth.

The day that my father announced to his parents that he intended to marry his factory girlfriend there was an unholy row. Both the parents pleaded with him to show more sense and finally when my dad proved immovable in his intention his father said in melodramatic fashion, 'Well, I don't ever wish to see her or any of your children in this house.' So, even before we arrived we were barred from the home of our paternal grandparents. And things were no better after our arrival for we never did see them, nor they us.

Yet my dad was kept on with the business

and continued as a painter-decorator.

Whatever was on his mind the day that he hoisted me to his shoulders there is no way of ever knowing now but it could well have been concern for the way his marriage was going, for he and his lively wife had already parted once some time before. They had parted while my mother was pregnant with me. It was, in fact, my arrival that brought my dad back again. He was curious. But they continued to remain a most inharmonious couple. I have wondered since whether perhaps this didn't have something to do with his dislike of me for things went from bad to worse in their relationship until, unable to take any more my dad eventually left.

2

The War Years and Our Mum

When dad went off to do battle with Kaiser Bill he left his wife and three young children behind in a flat situated over a sweet-shop somewhere in North London. One evening after mother had put us all to bed and we were all soundly asleep a Zeppelin came over with its cargo and when almost directly above our sweet-shop it let go a string of fire bombs. One dropped directly in front of the shop setting the window alight and the next dropped in our back garden starting a huge bonfire.

So that when mother leaned across my bed and shook me awake saying, 'Get up quickly the house is on fire,' I awakened to find a blaze of light pouring into the room from both back and front.

Now, at four years of age one does not panic, but there was, however, a full recognition of the urgency in mother's voice, and so, while still pulling on my knickers I allowed myself to be bundled out of the room and down the stairs. The passage below was filled with smoke and the ominous crackle of burning wood could be distinctly heard.

As we emerged from the passage door onto the pavement we were suddenly caught up in a jostling crowd and I became separated from my

14

mother and the others. This started me crying and it was then that someone took me by the hand and led me across the road. What my thoughts were at that time I have clean forgotten but what happened next will live with me to my very last day. I trod with my bare feet into a heap of still wet and warm horse-dung.

This nauseated me. I can sense it yet. I was defiled. From that moment on I could think of nothing else. The house was on fire, I had lost trace of my mother and the others, my clothes were still in the burning house, but all I could think of was the fact that I had sunk my bare feet into that heap of mire.

I don't know whether I would have remembered the occasion at all were it not for that one fact. So strangely works the mind of a child. For there is no pattern to the memories that one retains. We forget things of the utmost importance while remembering trivialities.

Now, with our dad no longer around the house our mother became the dominating influence in our lives. Not that she hadn't been the one all along with whom we had closest contact, but I was a little boy and to me the one that held most interest was my father. But now, with him playing the role demanded of a man in war-time — a warrior — now we were under the sole auspices of our mother.

This doesn't mean that we now saw more of her. One would have thought so. And with a normal mother, thrown on her own resources, with her man away at the war it would most certainly have been so. But our mother was not normal. She was still the girl who left my dad standing on the corner. She was still the girl who came down the factory steps with half the staff hanging on her words. She loved life. She loved gaiety. She loved crowds, company, variety.

Hers was a frivolous nature that could not be held down. Three young children meant no sense of deprivation to her. The uppermost thought in her mind was that with my dad out of her way she was now free to do just whatever she liked.

And what opportunities there were. London was full of soldiers, from all parts of the world, all out for a good time. All looking for someone with whom they could enjoy their leave, for, who knows, these could be their last days.

She loved a drink and she loved the pub atmosphere. Mind, one does not find that too hard to understand when they realise that the pubs of those days were filled with merry-makers at all hours, all out to enjoy themselves. It was an odd pub that didn't finish up at 'turning out' time with a bar full of customers all joining together in singing the songs of the day.

My recollection of this comes from the many hours I spent standing outside waiting for our mum to feel that it was time she left and came home to where her family was waiting to be fed. But those pub-door vigils came later. At the time that I now write of there was no sense of injustice, or mourning the absence of our fun-seeking mother. We were free to play in the streets. Other boys' mothers were ordering them in to dinner. We were lucky, we

16

were free to play until mum appeared at the top of the street with her latest boy-friend. Always a glamorously uniformed soldier or sailor, for mum treated both services alike. Then we would run to meet them for we knew that always there would be sweets for us from the boy-friend, to be followed by pie and mash, or fish and chips, which mum had brought home for our dinner. These would be laid out on plates with all the ceremony of a banquet celebrating some special occasion.

Then the brain-washing would start, 'Here you are, now get this down you. This will do you good. What do you think of my three lovely children? Look at them' — this to the uniform — 'don't you think they are lovely?'

At that time I allowed myself to be hoodwinked into believing that we were indeed lucky to be blessed with such a thoughtful mother. But later on, when years of this sort of behaviour had allowed us to have second thoughts on the matter, when sometimes we had even gone to bed without our dinner and mum had woken us up on her arrival home at midnight to eat an infernal pie. Then as she started her chanting, 'Don't say I don't think of my lovely children' I would sense something phoney about it all. By then I had seen other children in our street sitting down to a real dinner, at a real dinner-time and I knew that mum was trying to fool us, trying to pacify her own elusive conscience.

She also had a knack of not seeing that which she had no wish to see. Anything that was unpleasant was simply put aside. 'Live for today, for tomorrow never comes' that was her motto and she would say with all the emphasis in the world as she was sending me out to buy something she specially liked with the last of her money, 'Bugger tomorrow, we'll meet that when it comes'.

When I was young I thought she was marvellous. She was so gay, so amusing, and she brought such sparkle into the home but as I grew older so I came to recognise her shortcomings. How could it be otherwise when they concerned me so? I have gone to bed early ravenously hungry when mum was out somewhere enjoying herself. I have come home from school at midday for a meal, only to wait around the house until the school bell has summoned me back without having had a bite to eat.

Then I would sit in the class-room quite unable to put my mind to what the teacher was saying for thinking how hungry I was.

It hurt to see the atmosphere in the other boys' homes, where their mother would be pottering around in the kitchen preparing something for her family to eat. The smell alone would be enough to tell me that they were in for a treat when they all sat down. I would notice too the general tidiness around the place. Clean curtains at the windows, the rooms nicely furnished and everything in place, both looking and smelling clean. These neat and comfortable little homes would be compared with ours in my young mind and I would realise that our mother was different, out of step, casual, indifferent, not a real mother at all.

I was conscious of the lack of harmony in our home and at times felt somewhat ashamed. Yet, it was our home and I also felt a sense of loyalty towards it.

★ ★ ★

Woe is the child torn between varying impulses. He is too young to make a seasoned judgement and he has no experiences to help him towards reasoned conclusions. He is lost and afraid. Bewildered and worried. And of course everything to him is so terribly serious. When those upon whom he depends for guidance are not there to assist him in his search for the truth he can only withdraw into the comparative safety of silence. And this is what I did. I became withdrawn, unsure of myself, lacking confidence, feeling out of tune with the rest of the world.

This feeling, nurtured in childhood, persisted right through life and is very much a part of me yet.

But on the day that we left the bombed-out sweetshop to go to our next house my feelings were completely happy. We were going to have another horse-drawn ride — my second. Not that there was any awareness of this being a less morbid occasion but I have no doubt there was a livelier attitude connected with this move. There was, for example, the excitement in a child's mind of helping to pack up. Our mother had told us we were going to live in another house

19

and this filled us with a sense of curiosity.

'Will it be better than this one, mum?'

'Of course it will, much better,' would naturally have been the answer. What mother would have answered otherwise?

Now my own memory takes over more emphatically. Now I am less dependent upon what I have heard others say on the subject.

The ride on the back of that furniture van, for instance, stands out quite clearly. I was about six and a half now, an age when rides on the backs of furniture removal vans can be fully appreciated. That is why my memory of this one fills me with the thought that there is nothing comparable today.

I feel truly sorry for the modern boy, who can never hope to find himself perched high up on the top of the kitchen table lashed firmly to the side of the van, with a tarpaulin overhead in case it should rain on the way.

The throb of today's car engine is soulless alongside the steady clump, clump, clump of the horses hoofs as he trots rhythmically on his way. And then there were the accompanying sounds too. Like the horses version of the back-firing motor car. Or perhaps a whinny or two. Maybe he would even attend to his toilet needs while still on the run. This would give off a warm, not unpleasant intestinal smell. Oh, it was fascinating. One never knew what to expect next.

Our new 'house' turned out to be a 'Buildings', the old-time counterpart of a modern block of flats, and we were to be housed on the top floor.

It was here on this top floor, fifty feet above the pavement below that I see myself now with my arm through the railings holding a cat suspended that fifty feet above the ground. I can feel the fear vibrating through its body as, afraid to struggle too much in case it breaks my hold and falls, it cries pitifully to be spared. But I had no intention of sparing it. I was filled with an overwhelming desire to let it fall. Why, I don't know. I only know that that cat hadn't a chance of winning me over from my cruel intention that day. No appeal to any part of my nature could have changed my mind. I let go and it fell. As it screamed its way down I ran into our flat in case anyone looked up and saw me. I had done wrong, dreadfully wrong and I knew it. What the compulsion behind it was I will never know now, any more than I will ever know what happened when the poor thing landed after dropping fifty feet, for nothing was ever mentioned in my presence.

Today I cannot pass a cat without stopping to fuss over it. I wonder, am I trying to atone for my evil deed on that balcony that day?

On that same landing from where I sent the cat plunging down we all stood on another occasion watching a Zeppelin caught in the beams of several searchlights.

There it hung awaiting its inevitable end, too big and ponderous to break away from the light's hold, a sitting target, doomed. Anti-aircraft fire was bursting all around it. One could see the flashes as they exploded, some near, some well

21

off the target. It was just a matter of time. A matter of the gunners finding their range.

All of a sudden a huge column of flame shot up from the Zeppelin's middle and a little while later it broke into two, causing two flaming objects to fall slowly through the sky alongside each other. As a spectacle it was simply brilliant. Oohs and ahs came from everyone there. To me it meant we were winning the war right there before my eyes. The might of the British Empire was on display. What a moment for a young boy!

I believe dad must have been home on leave that night, making us all feel a little bit braver for our normal practice during a raid was to take shelter in the cells of a local police-station.

Mother would awaken us with, 'Come on there's a raid on,' and we would hear the cry of the Air Raid Wardens as they went around the streets on their bicycles blowing their whistles and shouting, 'Take cover, take cover.'

The drama of the moment was stark in my little mind as we went trudging through the cold, dark streets en route to our fox holes with the searchlights playing across the skies above and the sounds of enemy aircraft in the air.

Often on arrival at the police-station the children would go straight off to sleep again. But sometimes there was an air of apprehension around the place. The adults were more silent than usual. One could see they were listening to the sounds of the raid outside. These would be heavier than usual. Then we didn't sleep. We knew, instinctively that it would be wisest to stay awake. The self preservation instinct apparently asserts itself quite early in life.

When the raid was over those same wardens would remount their bikes and with whistles once more a-blowing their cry would now be, 'All clear. All clear.' This had a happy ring to it, conveyed, no doubt, by the note of relief in their voices that the wardens were unable to conceal. Even if they wanted to.

Then out into the streets once again to make our way back to our beds, which had grown cold in the meantime.

At those times mum was at her best. Never did I suspect that she was in the least afraid. Always did she give us a sense of there being nothing to worry about. She was the female of the species protecting her brood.

When I think of her now, mustering her three youngsters around her, one of them, my young sister, needing to be carried, when I think how strong must have been the temptation to become flustered or even angry as we delayed her with some of our childish behaviour — like wanting to take a particular toy with us — then I realise that there was another side to her giddy nature.

Those were hard times. Not that the kids really noticed it but the grown-ups must have had the greatest difficulty in finding enough to feed their families with.

★ ★ ★

Rationing was most severe. There comes to mind the occasions when word would be passed around that 'the corner shop has a supply of coal in.' Either Arthur my brother or I would be sent over for our quota. This would be seven pounds. Seven pounds of coal! It used to disappear completely from view in the bottom of the shopping-bag that we had been given to carry it in, and it placed no strain even upon my young muscles to carry it back to the house. Really it seems ludicrous in these days of affluence to speak of buying seven pounds of coal, yet not only did we buy it but we clamoured for it and came home with a feeling of elation — we had received our quota. Some, who came later, would find that the shop was sold out.

It stretches my imagination to its limits to try to imagine what mum did with that miserable ration of coal. How does one get the most out of such a mite? A miner could have carried that amount home in his pocket.

As for the meat ration — it wouldn't have fattened a cat, let alone satisfy the vigorous appetite of a healthy young boy. And talking of cats, they were adequately cared for, for the cat's-meat man came around regularly with horse-meat neatly sliced and skewered on a piece of wood all ready to serve up for pussy's dinner. I suppose she could very well have said had she been able, 'Well it's not we cats who are at war, it's you mugs, you humans.'

On reflection I can see that in giving the children sufficient food for the day the parents must have been very hard put to then find enough left over with which to make themselves a decent meal.

Now came another move and this time we took an upstairs flat in a house in Islington which was to remain our home until our family finally dissolved.

Soon after this dad came home from the war, invalided out of the army with trench fever and shrapnel wounds. Somehow, although he never showed any great feeling for me it was good to have him back. The house took on more the atmosphere of a home with both a mother and a father present. And although he had had two to three years caught up in that holocaust of a war, when men must at times have had experiences that would have left them mentally affected for the rest of their lives, although he was no longer considered fit to serve in any capacity whatsoever, yet to my uncritical eyes he was just the same as when he left. He was my dad. He was the very foundation upon which our whole family rested, or so he seemed to me.

Very soon he took up his role as our father once again and, peculiarly enough, in view of the affliction that most 'old soldiers' seem to have of having to speak at great length of their war experiences at the slightest excuse, he never, to my knowledge, ever spoke of that war again. Maybe that was because he had an even greater conflict closer to hand, for my mother now had formed habits that she found it quite impossible to break. Her love of the 'outside world' now was her master, and I simply cannot remember her on any occasion having an evening at home with her husband and children. As for seeing her sitting there knitting, or reading, or doing anything at all suggestive of domesticity, even a determined effort on my part to evoke such a picture draws only a blank. Mum was, as far as I can remember, always out. And dad was always in.

After the early joy at having my dad back again I very soon realised that my elation was misplaced, for he made it so clear that he had no time for me that eventually I grew to fear him. If I ventured to say something in his presence I was invariably told to, 'Shut up, you,' and that in a day when fathers were never defied. So I shut up, and remained shut up.

Only once can I remember finding myself trapped in the house with him alone and it was torment. I was afraid to speak and for the best part he ignored me completely. Then something happened to displease him — whatever it was it has gone clean from my memory now — and he called me by a name that even in this age of permissiveness I would not dare write. So shocked did I feel at the use of this word, applied as it was to me, that I have never been able to use it since even though I have as reasonably replete a repertoire of obscenities as anyone, having spent years in the army and a spell in the merchant navy. On the odd occasion when the telling of a story has demanded the use of the word it has never failed to cause me extreme discomfort. That day dad did me a grave disfavour. Thereafter I made sure that he and I were never alone in the house together. If I wanted to go in and neither Arthur nor Doona was there I would sit on a step until one of them came along and then we would go in together.

Not that dad could be blamed for being what he was: he only reflected the ignorance of the times. An ignorance that showed itself in many ways. Like the belief that they had in the superiority of the bosses and the inferiority of themselves. It was partly the exploitation of this inbred humility that they went through life with that caused them, as in the case of my dad and me, to look for someone over whom they could exercise some authority. Mum made him feel cheap and small too, so maybe there had to be a stooge somewhere around the place to help him find some small measure of self-respect.

3

The Canal

Near to this 'new' house ran a canal which played an outstanding part in my young life. So many hours did I spend in its presence.

No country boy with river, of whatever beauty, running past his home ever extracted more sheer delight from its waters than did I from my canal.

Here it was that I learned to swim. A section of Regent's canal it was, but there was nothing very regent-like about our portion of it for its waters were stagnant, dirty and smelly. Its bottom was lined with an accumulation of rubbish thrown in that had taken years to acquire. Sometimes an object especially foul would come drifting by at a most leisurely pace, for there was no continuous flow. But no matter how depreciatingly I speak of it now the fact remains that for me, and for many of my young mates, it was little more than a degree or two removed from paradise.

On pushing open a corrugated iron gate and walking down a sloping path to its banks, with its own peculiar, musty smell all around, a sense of real pleasure would sweep right through me. We were there again. We were about to take part in another hour or so of unadulterated enjoyment.

There one could forget everything but the joys of the moment. There we were free to behave just as the fancy took us. We could yell and laugh, run and jump, dive and swim. We were young animals, even to the extent of being completely naked. For we were unbuttoning our clothes from the moment of passing through the corrugated iron gate. And with the shedding of our garments went the shedding of all restriction, all restraint. No boy who lived removed from the vicinity of a canal has ever known the happiness that the many delightful summer hours spent in its waters meant to me. It compensated for all other of life's deficiencies.

There we would cavort endlessly with one idea for amusing ourselves following immediately upon another. What good fortune that that canal should have passed by so close to our street.

At home dad had forbidden me to ever go near it. He didn't say why, that was never his practice. He simply said something like, 'Keep out of that canal or you'll feel my hand around your face.' Now this was the prize understatement of all time, for whenever dad hit me I didn't feel his hand around my face, I rocked and reeled. Dad had enormous strength. A relic from the days when he was in training for his football. He simply couldn't hit lightly, it was beyond his physical powers to merely tap, and so a threat to 'let me have one' was a threat to be treated with the utmost respect. But nothing dad said, or anyone else said could have kept me away from that canal. No cajoling, no bribery, no promise of reward, no plea could have wrung from me an agreement never to go visiting my beloved canal again. It meant too much to me.

Looking back it is a wonder that I didn't do myself irreparable harm there for on allowing our feet to touch the bottom there was every imaginable object lurking in the darkness waiting to leave its permanent mark. I picked up numerous minor cuts, that was inevitable, but never anything serious.

The greatest thrill was to fly down the sloping bank as fast as my legs would carry me and on reaching the canal edge to throw myself out as far as I possibly could. Always with the mad desire to fly further through the air than I had ever done before. Oh, what I would have given not to have landed in the water until I was half-way across. In actual fact I suppose if I managed two or three yards in mid-air that would have been my lot. But I never stopped trying and hoping.

When standing around we made one concession to convention and propriety — we always held both our hands over our little parts, but when the mad rush down the bank was being executed, culminating in the wild plunge in order to gain the maximum momentum we forgot all about convention and, with all sails aloft we went hurtling through the air with hands held straight out before us. Had we but realised it no-one was concerned about our childish nakedness.

There was a bridge over that canal and we always had an audience, so I suppose we felt that this obliged us to do something about our lack of decency.

This canal and the many hours I spent in its murky waters enabled me to one day become the first boy at our school to gain his Hundred Yards Certificate at eight years of age. For this I was stood on the desk at the end of the school hall and given three hearty cheers. A proud moment!

At the time my dad's refusal to allow me to swim in the canal seemed both cruel and heartless. What harm could there possibly be in a small boy diving into those inviting waters on a hot summer's day and having a pleasant bathe? Who was hurt by it? This savoured to me of adulthood exercising its authority for the sheer joy it obtained from doing so. Now I can see dad was perfectly right. Those waters were putrid. Anything could have arisen from swimming in them. Today I wouldn't dip my fingers in. And, in fact, on returning from eleven years spent in Australia I went along to my canal and leaned over the bridge, just as our audience used to do. No children swim there now. All was silent. The flimsy shadows of my little mates were barely discernible as they ran excitedly down that same bank. I saw a piece of pipe protruding from the wall of a warehouse on the other side on which I used to stand and dive into eighteen inches of water.

There were many reminders of the happy times that I spent there but now it is derelict and neglected. No-one today would ever believe that in its day it was the most popular spot in our district. Undistinguished as it now looks it could not even draw the occasional passer-by into looking over its bridge out of mild curiosity. It took me, to whom it had once given so much pleasure, who then only leaned on the bridge in an attempt to recapture the past. Its allure has completely gone.

As I looked at it I didn't know whether to feel glad or sorry that it has sunk into such insignificance. Surely it deserved something better than to be simply ignored. Maybe this is its old-age. Maybe the days when delighted youngsters found such pleasure in partaking of its attractions were its youth, its heyday. After all, everything has a period of growth, an apex and a decline.

I felt, in a way, glad that what we knew was not passed on to others. That made it ours exclusively. That made our memories even more precious. The silence that came back at me as I stood looking at this old friend after nearly fifty years of separation seemed somehow to exemplify the changes that have taken place all round in those forty-odd years. The children are less childlike. It would be beneath their dignity to exhibit their infancy and their poverty as we did by showing ourselves off as we did then. Neither would today's child need to swim in such filth. It has its local baths and it can afford to pay for these things. It would want this year's swimming costume too.

Yet to us it was everything that could be wished for. There was freedom from all supervision. No-one told us not to do this or that. It was our world — a boy's world. There was privacy except for that obtrusive bridge. There was fun, there was laughter and nobody ever complained about the noise we made. What more could a child ask?

So much did it mean to me, such an appeal did it have that I gladly risked a thirteen stone clump from my father's hand rather than give up going there, I was under its spell. To give up was unthinkable.

Yet on entering the house after a swim my father always knew where I has been. This was a puzzle to me and gave him in my eyes some sort of mystical power. How did he know, he'd been in the house all the while that I was there? Yet he spoke with all the certainty in the world in his voice, 'You've been in that canal again.' Not 'Have you been in that canal'?' Oh no, it had to be, 'You've been in . . . ?'

So certain was I that he couldn't really know that I would always deny it. 'I haven't, dad,' I would say, speaking with all the honesty I could muster in my voice. At that his hand would explode around my face. 'Don't lie to me,' he'd say, 'do you think I don't know?'

Well, yes, I did think he didn't know. He was just revelling in the opportunity to give me a hiding. How could he know for sure? He was guessing, and without any real proof he was taking it upon himself to punish me. That's not justice. How it would rankle.

Yet had I but known, when I walked into that house I carried half the canal in with me. I might just as well have had a card hung around my neck saying, 'One small boy, straight out of the canal,' for I must have stunk to high heaven. My hair would have been dank and matted, my eyes all red from being opened under water, my shirt, which I had used to wipe myself on when it came time to go home would have been still wet. Nothing could have been more obvious. Yet I remained completely bewildered as to how my father ever knew.

Either he did possess some magic power, or he was simply guessing.

In any case it wasn't very fair to me.

What boy of today could possibly be so naive?

But nothing whatsoever could have stopped me from being there. Its delights were worth paying any price for. And so dad and I continued to confront each other, while I continued hoping that if I kept on saying 'I haven't, dad,' one day he might believe me.

4

A Citizen of London

London was like a pantomime to me. It was filled with characters of all kinds, all with their own particular brand of appeal.

One could list a whole galaxy of different trades-people, all with something to interest a young boy whose eyes and ears were looking and listening to everything the world had to say. A whole kaleidoscope of life was passing before me there almost every moment of the day and I was its most fascinated observer.

Quite close to our street was a market place, Chapel Street, where once lived Charles Lamb. It must, however, have presented a very different aspect in his day for at the time of which I write it was filled on market days with stalls of all kinds, while the roadway was always littered with waste matter. Often at the end of the day, when the stall-holders had left, I would rummage among the rubbish they had left behind for anything of value. However, a child's idea of value can be so different to that of an adult and many's the time I have been told to, 'Take that rubbish back and put it where you found it.' Once I landed home staggering under the weight of a whole stalk full of bananas. Arthur and Doona were thrilled but mum and dad seemed no more than lukewarm.

35

I can remember they went bad before we could eat them all and then came the problem of how to dispose of fifty or so rotting bananas.

But what a street to explore. I have spent hours captivated by what I was watching only to arrive home an hour or so late for dinner, to be greeted by a clump by my dad. Never could I walk its length without being stopped dead in my tracks by something of interest going on.

There was the stall where they made apple fritters. Here were two steaming vats of boiling fat, and into this fat would be plunged an arrangement of four or five fancy tins on the end of a holder filled with a batter mixture into which was dropped a portion of apple. On making that vital plunge there would be a great sizzling and hissing and the fat would be thrown into a turmoil. All was commotion as a great volume of steam came off, spreading in all directions to fill one's nostrils with the most delectable of aromas. What a spot to fill a little boy with interest. And, incidentally, what a place to stand on a cold winter's day. A little further up the road Sam Marks, the Jew, would be holding forth on what he was going to 'give away' today. No matter what the loss, he wanted only to familiarise the public with this particular brand of chocolate.

'Here, there's one of these half-pound bars of the nicest chocolate you've ever tasted, there's a box of these lovely, mouth-watering marshmallows, and there's a slab of this beautiful Sharpes Creamy Toffee. On top of this there's two delicious whipped-cream walnuts. Never mind about three bob, never mind about two and six, who'll give me one and tuppence?' 'Right, sold to the gentleman at the back there with the saliva dribbling all down his waistcoat.' Then to his assistant, 'Quick, grab his money before he changes his mind. Right, thank you, sir.'

Sam Marks stall used to hold me spellbound. To watch those luscious looking pieces of confectionery as he dropped them one by one into a bag was a child's delight. Not that I had any hope of ever possessing one and tuppence but it was good to be allowed to look on.

There was the stall that sold Sarsaparilla Wine. A fancifully fashioned stall this one, superior, with brass-work around its sides and a canopy overhead. The owner seemed to sense that his stall was a cut above the others for he too took on an air of refinement and never deigned to call out. If you wanted his wine you came over and asked for it. Consequently he never seemed to sell any. But the name intrigued me. So much so the one day I bought a glass. 'With a name like that it must be good.' Tentatively I raised the glass to my lips and tasted — it was awful — undrinkable. When Mr Toffee-nose wasn't looking I put the glass back on his flash stall and walked away. How he ever made a living must forever remain a mystery to me, but I'm glad he was there — he was part of the scene.

But the pie and eel shop. Ah, now that was another thing. That truly belonged. The aroma from there filled that section of the market with the most homely of smells. And the elderly, white-robed, plumpish ladies behind the counter

37

were like everybody's mum (except mine, of course). They simply oozed kindness and jollity 'Yes, luv,' they'd say when your turn came to be served. But it wasn't the words, it was the way they said it. The intonation. And when serving up the pie and mash that you had ordered it came with, 'Here you are luv.'

All this with the sawdust (yes, sawdust) on the floor and the clouds of steam arising from the pans of boiled eels, mashed potatoes, meat pies and fruit pies which gave the shop an atmosphere of warm cosiness of its very own.

Had those plumpish women but realised it they represented a dying race. I have been back and while the shop is still there, serving the same things, yet its atmosphere, along with its plump women has disappeared.

London was my oyster then and I wandered to all its well-known landmarks. And I never went without knowing what I was wanting to see, as a result of having read about it. Frequently Doona would accompany me, for I liked to have someone to whom I could air my knowledge. Looking back it puzzles me that no-one ever questioned our presence, for as a little boy of eight or nine, holding the hand of Doona, a child of four or five, I have wandered through the National Art Gallery, St Paul's Cathedral, The British Museum, The Tower of London and many other such places. All came under our scrutiny, but what we saw in them, how they could ever have interested us I shall never know.

If Doona didn't wish to come along I would

then tell her something about the place to whet her appetite, but usually she was thrilled to be asked along by her older brother and was more than willing. The snag was she was nearly always tired and had to be given a piggy-back home. This was a nuisance. One of our most memorable excursions was the one to the Thames Embankment where we went right down to the last step, lapped by the gently undulating waters of the river and sat down. There we were excluded from every sight and sound except those of the river and the opposite bank. It was a setting perfectly designed for the purpose for which we had chosen it. For we had come back to one of the scenes of the Fire of London. We were there to visualise the events of that great tragedy as the people, with whatever possessions they were able to gather had come down these same steps to go onto the barges waiting there to take them out to the comparative safety of the centre of the river.

'Even then', I told my little audience, 'they were not entirely safe, for sparks would be blown out from the burning buildings and the whole place must have been choking with smoke.'

There was just one other person who was willing to listen while I talked and that was my grandmother, my mother's mother. I see her now as an old woman with rapidly failing eyesight who lived all alone in a miserably small and under-furnished couple of rooms. My mother from time to time took her along with her. Then granny had a bit of company, a drink or two, and a laugh, for to be in mum's company guaranteed laughter.

But to try to fit her into the picture that I am trying to draw is most difficult for she was so unlike my mother. She was a most respectable old lady, clean of habits and speech. Tidy and kindly. I can't imagine my mother having learnt any of her recalcitrant ways from her. If anyone was going to pass anything on to the other it could well have been the other way round, for granny, like so many others, was under the power of mum's personality when they were together.

However, she will remain long in my memory for the reason that she showed a distinct liking for me. It seemed quite clear that I was her favourite. A role so unusual for me to occupy that that alone was sufficient to make me an admirer of hers.

She always spoke kindly to me. Referred to me as her Syddy and generally went out of her way to give me a feeling of being of some importance.

To my eternal satisfaction I can think of no occasion when I was anything but well-behaved and respectful in her presence. So thankful was I for the liking that she showed for me. In return I was eager to please her.

It was a habit of mine, as I have already said, to wander off on jaunts, just caught up in the pleasure of seeing what was around the corner. Often on these jaunts would I find myself somewhere near to granny's place. Then I would decide to look her up. Knowing always that I would be more than welcome, that she would be pleased to see me.

She lived in two tiny rooms above a shop in a busy thoroughfare. To get up to gran's flat one needed to enter a passage alongside the shop and then up two flights of stairs. Never could I proceed beyond the second or third stair without granny had heard me and would call out, 'Here's my boy. Come on up son.' This was music to me, she was glad to see me and made no secret of it, here I would be fussed over. 'Have you had anything to eat, son?' 'Would you like a drink of lemonade?' 'Would you like a toffee?' Granny seemed to have everything. To the last question my answer was an invariable, 'Yes, please.' I loved her toffees.

Then to the chatter and we would talk non-stop, not as grown up to child, but as two people of no age at all, until it was time for me to leave.

Sometimes, at my request, she would bring out the tin box containing the family photographs. This was especially interesting for there would always be a well documented commentary that went with them. One of the phrases that most intrigued me was, 'That's your mother when she was a girl.' So, my mother had once been a girl! This always surprised me. She would have been about seventeen in that photograph but she still looked pretty grown-up to me.

Extraordinarily enough I have no recollection of granny ever dying, but she looked far from imperishable even at the time that I knew her, being small and quite frail. As a clue to where

41

my mother acquired her vivaciousness granny was quite valueless for there was no resemblance between them whatsoever.

That was my grandmother. I'm glad I have mentioned her for she meant so much to me as a boy.

As for other relations, we never saw another one. Dad had brothers and sisters — I had heard talk of them at times and mum too had a brother somewhere, but not one ever called to see us. The off-putting influence could have been our mum. Poor old mum she seems to get the blame for everything. Yet I suppose she would have found it difficult to see how any of our misfortunes could have been thought attributable to her.

So, nothing was passed on to her by her mother, but what of her father? Our grandfather. There was some talk of him having been an unsuccessful inventor. We were told of a scrubbing brush that he had thought up that had soap let into the back that gradually fed out as the brush was used.

He must have died fairly young too, for my mother was still only in her early thirties when I first remember her. So there could have been something unusual about this tenuous father figure. Could he have died of drink? If one has to find a cause for mum's compulsive waywardness then certainly he becomes suspect. Why should he have died so young?

It occurs to me to regret his early demise, for in writing of him I have talked myself into believing that he was the heredity factor behind mum's odd personality. If that is so he most certainly would not have been too stand-offish to call round on us now and then and so we would have had one visiting relative, and perhaps I would even have understood my mother a little better on account of it. However, it was not to be.

My mother's day really began when the pubs opened, for then she would do the rounds of those that she frequented with the object of finding some mug, or mugs, to pay for a drink, to start her day off. Once established, once she had a drink in her hand her exuberance started to exert itself, her day had begin. From then on things, it seemed, just happened naturally and it was a poor day, in her opinion, if she didn't land back home again a little livelier for her trip out.

She never went into a pub until she had first ascertained that there was someone there who would buy her a drink. So, she would half-open the bar door and look all around, trying to not catch the eye of the barman. If there was no mug there she would then gently close the door and away to the next pub. Should she be unlucky enough to catch the barman's eye she would then say, without going in, 'Have you seen my friend Tom (or Fred, or Jack) around today?' This gave her her excuse for looking in. When she saw a likely candidate somewhere in the bar she would boldly march up to him and say, 'Well, fancy seeing you here, I haven't seen you for ages. What are you going to have?'

This never failed to produce the required

answer, 'No, you have one with me.'

From then on all mum's attention was directed towards the business at hand and all else forgotten. Even our dinner.

But to do her full justice, for she was not without her good features, when she did devote herself to a little culinary activity mum was an artist. Her plum puddings were little gems. My mouth waters at the thought of them. Her jam roly-poly will never be repeated. Of that I am certain. Its like went out with the end of the First World War. Yet she never sat down to a decent meal herself. Her favourite was two ounces of gorgonzola cheese and a slice or two of new bread, preferably still warm, soaked in best butter. This last I have bought for her on many occasion. 'Make sure it's new,' would ring in my ears as I went on my way to the baker's.

In those days they would weigh a loaf and if it wasn't an exact two pounds the deficiency would be made up with another piece of bread, or, delight, of delights, a piece of mince straight out of the oven. This I would eat on my way back.

While she was eating her gorgonzola and bread and butter mum would keep up a continuous chatter and the whole room would be alive with her vivacity. She never seemed to lapse into periods of a lower key, for mum's life was lived always at a high pitch. Coming to her cup of tea she would say, 'This stuff's killing me, give me a glass of stout any time.'

This worried me for I believed it to be true,

such is the innocence of a small boy's mind, and I used to timorously suggest that she not drink it. At that she would laugh and chide me, saying, 'I'm not going to die, lovey.'

What education my mother had was virtually worthless. She was at school for a minimum of time. I can remember her once telling me that her mother hated her little girl going off to school and encouraged her to stay home any time she felt like it. Education was not considered so important in those days, at least not for the working classes. That sort of thing was all right for the wealthy, 'them as doesn't have to work.' 'But what's the good of stuffing your head with a lot of knowledge when you've got to go out and earn a living and can't use it?' Their reasoning might not have been without a certain amount of logic, but really, by thinking that way they contributed very largely towards the continuation of their own lowly living standards.

But her lack of education did not mean that my mum was a fool. That is the last term that could be applied to her. She might have had the greatest difficulty in pronouncing any unusual words and her vocabulary might have been confined to the narrowest of limits but she knew how to live. Life was her teacher. She knew how to enjoy life and if her philosophy was simple it was also effective, for living to her was more exciting than it was to the most learned of intellectuals.

She knew what she wanted from life and she had worked out a way of obtaining it.

Her reactions were pure, unreasoned. When angered she fought back. In a temper she was something to be feared and I have seen my father flee the house, bounding down the stairs and out of the front door as fast as he could go. Often I have lain in bed listening to this performance taking place and as dad's last sounds were dying away there would be a crash against the door of something thrown after him. All this accompanied by the most colourful of commentaries on my dad's character that mum's limited vocabulary would allow.

But then mum always knew how to supplement her vocabulary and any deficiency was well compensated by her repeated use of certain spicy adjectives plus the intensity that she was able to put into the key words.

I have seen my poor old worried dad turn quite white and stand silent and shaken as a knife thrown at him by my mother has missed him by a whisker and crashed against the wall. The realisation of what it would have meant if it had hit him has so affected him that he has walked out of the house without saying a word.

With the advent of compulsory schooling and the inevitable improvement in general intelligence, however, my mum's kind died out.

It was easy to see why she and my father were not happy together. Their interests were poles apart. They viewed the world through totally different eyes.

When they were younger if by chance my

dad took her to a theatre, during the interval mum would want to go to the bar for a drink while dad would prefer to sit on and study the programme. As often as not she would be utterly bored with what was going on on stage, and conscious of a deep, demanding thirst. As a result she would quite often remain at the bar for the remainder of the show leaving dad sitting there accompanied by an empty seat. This meant that at the end he would have a half-tipsy, voluble young wife to steer home. Inevitably a row would ensue and in time dad decided he wouldn't take her any more.

In fact it is only at the very beginning of my life that I can remember them going out together at all. And that would only be at holiday times when they would take their young family to the fair at Hampstead Heath. Once they had drifted away from each other they sought their entertainment separately.

The break up of their marriage was inevitable.

5

Street Life

Life was full of excitement for a child in those days. We were children until the day we left school, wearing short pants until the very last day. Then we donned our first pair of trousers and became, overnight, young men. An event that I imagine has caused many an adoring mother to shed a lonely tear, for this symbolised the loss of her little boy. But to the little boys the wearing of their first pair of long trousers was something they awaited towards the end with extreme impatience. We wanted to take on our new status, feeling, I suppose, that we had been children for quite long enough. We longed to cover the scars on our knees. The marks of our childhood.

But until the arrival of that fateful day the world was our playground. The streets were quiet and free from danger. Our street, which was typical of many never saw a motor car pass down it unless the driver had lost his way. So sure were we of having the road all to ourselves that the centre was permanently chalked out for all manner of street games. Both for girls and boys. As were the pavements too.

Our clothes were usually sturdy, designed to stand up to a bit of hard use and there were plenty of us to make up the numbers for whatever we wished to play. Families were larger then. They weren't planned, they just happened.

Most of our games were of a fairly robust character, but occasionally we would include the girls into our play and then we would go in for kissing games, such as Postman's Knock. We had our favourites among the opposite sex too, so it would seem that this man and woman business starts quite early in life.

There was one girl of whom I was really very fond at that time. Her name has disappeared for ever but her face is indelibly imprinted on my mind, thus ensuring that little girl of sixty or more years of childhood, for I shall never see her any way than as she was then. A pretty face it was, with lively, intelligent eyes. For long I have rated myself a fair judge of a pretty face, and, looking back, as we are now, I see that this talent was quite well developed even then. But wouldn't it be true to say that all our talents are with us right from the beginning and that they only mature and develop with the use that we make of them as we go through our life?

I used to try to let this girl see that I liked her by just staring at her. When she looked in my direction I would smile — all tender and full of affection my smile was meant to be, with the message, 'I like you' wrapped up in it. What she saw in it, whether she got the message or not she never did say and one day her family moved. I missed her for quite a long time afterwards.

But kissing girls was never my real idea of fun. All right in small doses, I suppose, but the greatest kicks came from something more manly, like my canal, where a fellow could strip off, or running behind carts — ah, now there was something. Especially if the horse was trotting and one had to run to keep up with it while manoeuvring to jump on the cart.

This was a most popular pastime during my younger years and I have travelled for miles while sitting on the back axle if I didn't wish the driver to see me. But if he seemed a nice, friendly sort of man then I would venture on to the cart itself, all the time keeping a wary eye on him in case he suddenly spun round and lashed out with his whip. Not infrequently he would take no notice of me at all, even though he was obviously aware of my presence. Then I would stretch myself out, surveying the whole of London as it passed before my vision at a steady two to four miles per hour.

At those times I would thumb my nose at any child who yelled out 'Whip behind guvnor,' while still casting an extra glance at guvnor in case he'd had a change of heart.

Surely the sun could not have been shining every time that I stole one of those rides behind a horse and cart, but I can see no other setting as my mind travels back to those days. There am I laid out on the back with a steaming horse jogging merrily along, while a warm sun shines benignly down upon me from a clear, blue sky. I wonder, does my memory play me tricks? Could there have been other days when the weather was not so kind?

Most of our games were seasonal then.

Everybody would be playing them at the same time. Where the signal came from to switch over from one game to another baffles me but it would happen in a flash — tops were out and hoops were in. Away would go our tops and out would come our hoops, and wherever one went the word had 'got around' for hoops would be the fashion down every street.

One can well see how the 'conker season' came about. These were horse-chestnuts that fell from the trees in the parks, and, of course, until they came down from their lofty perches the 'season' could not commence. Then we would put them in a hottish oven to harden them up.

The seriousness with which these games were played sweeps over me as I write. Life held nothing more vital at the time than the possession of a champion conker — a thricer or a fourer.

In between the seasonal games there was always football or cricket, with the lamp-post as a wicket.

Much of the street activity that went to make an average child's life in those days must surely have had some beneficial effect upon his health? Surely the leap-frog and other energetic games that were daily ritual down our street must have been of some good to a growing lad?

Sometimes the playing of our games would lead me to having to climb a lamp-post. And then it was that I would experience my first sexual thrill, for with my legs wrapped tightly around the post the pressure on my genital organs as I slithered up or down, mostly when coming down, I think, would produce a most enthralling sense of excitement. Only a few moments would it last but for that time I was lost in its sheer ecstasy. Sometimes I would try to reproduce this but no matter how often I went up or down it would not come, it would only happen by chance, when least expected.

This was my secret, I never told another boy in case he should be able to share in my discovery. It was mine alone, and whether other boys experienced this affair with a lamp-post or not I have never known to this day, but I rather suspect they have.

Another aspect of street life that helped bring colour and sound to the scene was the array and variety of tradespeople who sold their goods from the roadway. There was the milkman with his hand-cart in the centre of which was a large brass urn. He had his own way of making his presence known. A knock on the door and a call something like a Swiss yodeller and everyone knew who was there. The door would open and there would be the lady of the house, jug in hand. The postman came three times a day and his rat-tat-tat could be heard all down the street. On Sunday we had a man walk down the right-hand pavement (I never saw him take the left-hand side). On his head was a tray covered with a green baize cloth. In his right hand a large hand-bell which swung to the rhythm of his step — a ding as his arm went forward and a dong as it swung back. He was the muffin-man.

The baker came around some time in the

morning and from his hand-barrow he filled
a spacious basket with a well assorted choice
of loaves and then a knock on the door was
followed by his own particular brand of call.
No-one ever attempted to define what it was
he said, it was incomprehensible but it told
all — 'This is the baker'. And every housewife
recognised it. In his basket, to name but some,
there would be a cottage loaf, a long twist, a
long tin, a flat tin, a coburg, a farmhouse. You
paid your money and you took your choice. And
what a dilemma the women must have been
in at times with such a delectable variety of
light-brown, crusty shapes smiling up at them.
Oddly enough, because of their different shapes,
although made from the same batch of dough,
each of these tasted different.

In my infancy two gypsy women used to
regularly walk slowly down the centre of our
street selling bundles or sprigs of lavender. They
sang a song, one in a high pitched voice the
other in a low. The opening lines have remained
with me through the years as has the tune and
the sweet untrained voices of those two gypsy
women with their baskets of lavender swung
over their arms.

'Oh, wont you buy my sweet scented lavender,
There are sixteen sweet branches a penny.'

This simple ditty conveys nothing to the
uninitiated but to me it conjures up a very
pretty little tune and two very mysterious-
looking women. I had been told they were
gypsies and this gave them an indefinable aura
in my eyes.

By the way, their song must have been already quite old when I first heard it for there were not by that time sixteen branches to a penny. More like eight. So, you see, the trend that is with us today of goods being reduced in size for the same price almost day by day was already with us then.

'Rag, bones. Any old rags, bones?' This was another regular. He also took jam jars. And for one jam jar we received one windmill.

Sometimes an itinerant singer would slowly make his way down the centre of the street singing his song, his hand up to his mouth to help direct his voice, his eyes scrutinising every window ready to pounce as soon as a halfpenny, or even a penny, were thrown down into the roadway. Such a love did he have for his music that quite often he would be still singing as he bent to pick up his reward. His acknowledgement was a respectful touch of his cap directed towards the benevolent window.

Coalmen and dustmen, unglamorous as they might seem, always looked like giants to me, with their leather, all-embracing hats with a large flap that hung down their back to take the weight and rub of the dustbin or sack of coal. In those days the dustmen went through the house, into the back garden, took the bin out to their cart, emptied it, brought the bin back to where it had stood and replaced the lid. As I write this now it seems almost incredible that such workmen ever really existed. But they did. For a very poor wage too. Rain or shine. And the coalman, with up to two hundredweight of

54

coal on his back said, 'Where do you want it madam?' and when madam said, 'Upstairs, please', for we said please for most everything in those days, he took it upstairs and followed on her heels to where she wanted it tipped.

If I dare to say that they did these jobs not only properly but cheerily I know that I risk being told that I'm piling it on, but I'd swear it was so.

Into these sights and sounds was I born. They were my world and I thought it had always been and would always be. How wrong I was. But I am truly glad I have known it. It is so nice to look back on.

6

The War Ends

At eight years of age besides becoming the first boy at our school to obtain his Hundred Yards Certificate so young another momentous event occurred. The war ended.

To one of my years there was no realisation that this was about to happen. We had been aware of nothing leading up to it. Our major concern was the playing of our street games and on the morning when it happened there was probably nothing more important in our minds than the scoring of the all-important winning goal. When all of a sudden from around the corner came a taxi. This in itself was odd. Taxis didn't usually come down our street. We couldn't afford them. But there it was, and what's more it had a wildly gesticulating driver leaning out from his seat yelling at us, 'Come on boys,' he called, his eyes aglow, 'jump on, we're going for a ride. The war's over. The war's over.'

We knew this was good news, we had heard our mums say, 'Won't it be wonderful when the war ends,' and even if we hadn't known the look on that taxi driver's face was enough to tell us. He was ecstatic. 'Come on boys, all on board.'

We needed no second bidding, fourteen of us

scrambled on. Some could only remain aboard by leaning out of the window. Three others were seated alongside our host and off we went towards the West End.

All the way there we sang every war song we knew with the driver acting as choir-master. 'When this blooming war is over, Oh how happy we will be' was the favourite.

As we passed on our way some people cheered, others waved, none were sedate. All inhibition was abandoned, this was the day everybody had waited so long for, and some had paid such a heavy price on the way.

There must have been others to whom this day brought sadness — a reminder of someone who would have been so happy to have been there — had he lived. But I was too young to distinguish between unadulterated joy and happiness tinged with sadness. To me the whole world seemed mad with delight and I saw nothing but wild, unchecked excitement.

The West End was filled with revellers when we arrived. Our voices were lost in the singing and shouting, even though we put everything into our efforts.

What a day to remember! What an occasion! The end of the most terrible war of all time. Four long years of continuous suffering and tension. A million of our men had given up their lives. The mutilated were never counted. It had seemed endless and, at times, hopeless. And now it was over. Yesterday we were still at war — today there was peace. What wonder the people were delirious. No longer those dreadful

57

casualty lists to be read in trepidation. There would be no such lists. What relief, what relaxation of strain, what thankfulness must have been felt by all those grown-ups that we saw that day. To us kids it was no more than a free taxi ride — to the adults it was so very much more.

No wonder they were dancing. Strangers were kissing one another, laughter was everywhere. Flags had mysteriously appeared, the roads were practically unnegotiable to traffic. At times we were as securely locked in the crowds swarming all over the roadway as a ship locked in the Arctic ice. But who cared? What mattered anything? All else was as nothing beside the fact that the war was over — we had won the war.

As we looked out from our taxi we saw people who all our lives had acted in dignified fashion behaving just like we kids. Singing, shouting, joining hands and forming themselves into dancing groups. 'Look, there's a man climbing a lamp-post'. This was good. Shop-keepers were giving away things to eat and drink. 'Why couldn't it be like this every day?'

At the end our taxi driver brought us all home again and put us down just where he had picked us up. I hope he found us good company — certainly we lacked nothing in enthusiasm.

It is sad when thinking back that all that exultation and excitement should have been so poorly rewarded. Perhaps it couldn't have been otherwise. I don't know. History goes inexorably on its way paying no regard to justice or what is fair or unfair. Perhaps it has to be so that emotions can be sufficiently disturbed to demand that something be done about it. Perhaps we must have wrong first in order that we might strive after change. Certainly I am old enough to realise that justice does not automatically follow, but that doesn't stop me from looking back to the aftermath of that war and feeling dreadfully sorry for those who were its victims, both at the time of the war and afterwards.

To those people who were singing and dancing that day, with stars in their eyes, nothing else mattered than that the war was over. It would have seemed to them that whatever followed nothing could mar their joy. Now 'the boys' could come home again. Now they could take up things where they left off (as though that is ever possible), now there would be peace, and peace to them meant happiness. They would be able to direct their attention to worth-while things, like bringing up their children, improving their homes, or planning their holidays. Little everyday things that go to making up life in normal times. All the horrors of the last four years were behind, now they could plan.

I suppose those who remembered life as it was before the war believed that it would be just like that all over again. How could they think otherwise, there had never been a war of such dimensions before.

England had been rich before the war. They had little reason to think that she would not be so all over again.

'When this blessed war is over,
Oh, how happy we shall be.'
The words of this popular song of the day seemed so appropriate.

But what disappointment was to follow. What disillusionment. For those same people who now were dancing on the streets were soon to be struggling to make both ends meet. Caught up in an economic crisis that left millions of them unemployed. While even those who were lucky enough to be working were barely able to earn enough to live on.

Soon we were to see disabled soldiers everywhere, beggars, with hat in hand, a card hung upon their chest, 'Four years war service with Royal Artillery. Blown up at Arras,' or 'Blinded at the Somme,' or 'Lost both legs in retreat from Mons.' As I write this it looks mawkish, over-sentimental, but heaven knows it is true. Every boy of that day saw them. Saw them and took them for granted.

In fact we children even enjoyed them, for they brought music and entertainment into the streets.

One could barely pass a public house without seeing a wretch of a man with his foot holding the door open as he blew on a mouth organ or scratched on a violin.

Sometimes they formed themselves into a musical group and wandered slowly along the gutter (as though that was where they belonged) while one of their number stood on the pavement waving a box under the noses of passers-by.

I suppose even that singer who used to stroll

down the centre of our street, humbly touching his cap to an empty window as he stooped to pick up a halfpenny or a penny was one of 'the boys' at the time of the war.

Here there is a danger of allowing my feelings to run away with me. Sentiment is not a popular emotion today and, anyway, this all happened a long time ago.

One aspect associated with these men comes back as I write which seems to exemplify the simplicity of their attitude to life as compared with today. At the end of the war every serving soldier was issued with a certificate that stated that they had served with His Majesty's Forces in the Great War of 1914 – 1918. Today I imagine that at least half of these certificates would be torn up and thrown away, if they were ever accepted. But then, such was the temperament of the average man, these were not only accepted but they were, almost without exception, framed and hung in a prominent position where they were sure to be seen. And they remained there for many years to come. Even after those men had every reason to feel bitter and resentful. They had won this certificate, it was their reward, it spoke of them having done their duty and they could not find it in them to despise it.

I can remember my dad's. It too hung prominently displayed. In the front room it was, the first thing that one noticed on entering that room. And no matter what rearrangement took place a spot always had to be found for its re-hanging. He was proud of it. He couldn't have been more proud if it had been the only one in existence.

Peculiarly enough I was proud of it too. If it had been taken down I'm sure it would have hurt me every bit as much as it would have hurt him.

All this only goes to show that it wouldn't have taken much to have satisfied the people after that war. They had won and were in a mood to be happy. A pat on the head and a reasonable standard of living was all they needed. But this was not forthcoming.

Looking back it would seem that much of the social unrest and industrial strife that has been with us in later years really began in those days after the First World War. The injustice of their treatment finally did strike them and they then felt impelled towards making a stand against it.

Not that they gained much for themselves, but they did start the movement towards the changes that have brought about the vast improvements that we all enjoy today. By the time those changes came about however those 'old soldiers' were almost too old to enjoy them. They were the martyrs, sacrificed that those who followed might benefit.

Many years later with England once more engaged in a life a death struggle with Germany my dad was lying in hospital dying of cancer. My brother and I were paying what we knew would be one of our last visits. Dad asked, concerning the war, 'How are things going?'

'They don't look too good, dad,' we said.

In fact they looked pretty hopeless. It was during the earlier days of the war, when only a fanatical fool would have dared prophesy us winning.

'Don't worry,' said our dad, 'everything will be all right. We'll win in the end. We always do.'

That was it all over again. There it was, the spirit of those First World War men — 'we'll win in the end.'

They had a simple faith and an unconquerable trust in the righteousness of their cause. They deserved a better fate.

Ah, well.

7

Dad's Sporting Influence

Some of my happiest memories as a child come from the days when dad used to take Arthur and I over the local park — with a football.

We both knew our dad had been a professional and were proud of the fact.

With a football at his feet dad became transformed. He became another person. His eyes would light up and we would be treated to a display of ball-control that had us completely nonplussed. No doubt opposed by another professional he had considerable limits, but faced by Arthur and I his skills were boundless. He would twist and turn, swerve and sway, start and stop, look one way and kick another. 'Over there,' he would say and as we went to where he had kicked the ball he put his foot forward and drew the ball back again, leaving us chasing nothing. He would beat us once then come back and beat us again. The ball seemed tied to his feet. He made us look silly and we loved every minute of it. So thrilled were we by our footballing father that we would shriek with laughter.

It gives me pleasure to think of how much he must have enjoyed himself at those times.

Then it would be time for each of the boys to

act as goalkeeper while dad and the other took shots at him.

Dad could as soon kick a ball softly as pat me gently when angry. A ball was made to be belted as hard as one could and that's how dad belted it.

He couldn't help it. The temptation was too great. And so there we would stand with cannon-balls coming at us fit to knock our head off. But what good training.

'Stop it,' dad would yell, and stop it we would if it were humanly possible. Sometimes to stop it would have been positively dangerous. Then we ducked or dodged. 'Don't run away from it, stop it,' we would be told. Other times we would stop it and fall straight to the ground. Oh, how Arthur and I loved those sessions over the park. We had a super dad and wanted all the other boys to see us with him.

As a result of those drives of dad's that sometimes stung our hands for minutes afterwards both Arthur and I became, at different times, the school goalkeeper. He first and I when he left school. Had we had a younger brother I've no doubt he would have taken over from me for those spells over the park with dad left us way ahead of any other boy in the school.

The headmaster thought it was a gift No, sir, it was no gift. It was hard work, much shouting at and stinging fingers, but I'll say this, sir, it might as well have been a gift, it was every bit as happily received.

It's not to say we didn't let goals in in school games but we never found a ball coming at us too hard to stop — never.

Dad was also responsible for Arthur and I taking an interest in another sport. Boxing.

This came about when dad used to go off to Blackfriars Ring on a Sunday morning, not returning until early afternoon. On his return he would simply throw the programme down onto the table without a word, leaving Arthur and I to pounce upon it. Inside there were photographs of boxers in various sparring attitudes. They became my heroes. Fine, well-trained, beautifully muscled men they were, with a look of determination on their faces that I envied. They were my idea of real men.

If dad ever deigned to tell of something special that had happened there that day I would listen agog. I knew that this was for me. 'One day I would go there — I had to.'

Eventually he took to taking Arthur along with him and this only added to my curiosity, for Arthur, childlike, would always give me an account of the day's happenings that was nothing less than spectacular. Once I asked, 'When are you going to take me, dad?' and I was told, 'When you are older.'

I would have liked something more specific than this but didn't pursue the matter.

In the meantime I had started boxing at school and found that on account of my enthusiasm I beat more boys than boys beat me. This was partly due to me having those photographs in mind. They were my ideals, I wanted to be like them, and a look of such determination to aspire after made me a difficult lad to beat.

66

Outside the school I trained and practised too. In the evenings I would retire to our bedroom and fight an imaginary opponent. Heaven only knows what sort of noise was made as I skipped and pranced around the room, lost to realities, always locked in battle with a most difficult 'man' to beat. But beat him I always did.

Never did anyone come into that room and disturb me. This never seemed curious at the time, but it does as I write. Why did no-one ever come in? Could it be that they all knew just what was going on there? Did they deliberately choose not to disturb me. It must have been, for it would have been too much of a coincidence to expect that at no time did anyone wish to use that room while I was there.

Alongside our house lived a milkman, a young man in his teens, George Helens. Now George was a boxing fanatic. He had bought a set of gloves, a punch-ball and all manner of other training equipment and he was forever searching for someone with whom he could spar, with the promise that he would 'take it easy', he 'wouldn't hurt them'. But it was impossible, he was my father with a football, as soon as he saw himself faced with an opponent with boxing gloves on his hands, as soon as he took up his fighting attitude, his promise went clean out of his mind. Consequently he very quickly ran out of 'opponents'. No-one would put them on with George Helens until I came along.

In my young mind, wishing to emulate the men in dad's programmes, I wanted no promise of no rough stuff. I knew it to be a hard game and there seemed only one way to play it — one assumed the look of determination and went in. And so was struck up an arrangement between the milkman, George Helens, and I whereby when he returned from his first round he would call up to our window. I then went down into the garden, over the wall into the garden next door and George and I sparred until the school-bell rang. Then it was a wild dash upstairs a quick wash under the running tap and off to school. Many a time with a bloodied nose or a discoloured eye.

George knocked me out on several occasions, for he was a man while I was still a schoolboy. Then his face would be a picture of contrition and he would swear he would never do it again. But it would continue to happen. He couldn't help himself, as soon as those gloves were tied onto his hands his blood started to speed up through his veins and his excitement dulled his reasoning. I wasn't then a schoolboy standing there before him, I was his opponent, and opponents were made to be beaten.

Poor George Helens, he wanted so much to be gentle but his muscles wouldn't let him.

In those days street fights were more easily come by than they are now. One settled differences that way and through the experience that I gained from sparring with George Helens I cannot remember ever losing one, even though my cause may not always have been the right one. So you see, there is no justice.

Years later with Arthur and I both in our teens we became bosom pals every Sunday and, following in our father's footsteps, used to go regularly to Blackfriars Ring. Arthur's pal wasn't interested in boxing, that's how I came into favour.

Usually we would leave home early and spend an hour or so in Petticoat Lane market before going on to the Ring and here in the market we invariably had a bite to eat in a working-man's coffee shop that would have been old in Victorian times. Our favourite, which we could seldom go past, was raisin batter. This was simply a batter mixture heavily sprinkled with raisins which was baked in a dish well lined with fat. When the batter was ready to serve it was oozing fat. The thought of eating it now would horrify me, but then, then I was young, with a stomach ready to tackle anything, and it used to thrash this fat-oozing concoction with ease.

Having eaten, with a look at each other that spoke of our mutual satisfaction, we would then drift off towards the Ring. This stood on a corner opposite another colourful market place, the Lambeth Cut. The Ring had originally been a chapel, and very well suited to the purpose it must have been, both in size and shape. It was a very small hexagonal building that would have been filled to overflowing with but a handful of a congregation. Any preacher with half a personality should have been able to hold his audience in the palm of his hand for he was practically standing in their midst, on account of its size.

As a boxing arena it was equally ideal for even

at the very back of the hall one was no more than a few yards away from the ring itself.

Every blow could be both seen and heard. Bumps and lumps rising on the boxer's face could be studied at close range. Remarks would pass around among the spectators as these marks appeared. 'Hello, it looks like his left eye is closing.' 'Ay Ay, here comes his ear now.' The crowd was as expert as the men in the ring and heaven help the referee if he gave a bad decision.

Usually we were there well in advance of the start of the show as we had favourite positions and these required a little sacrifice to obtain.

It was then, while sitting in our favourite seats watching the hall fill up that the urge came over me to be one of the participants. We would see the boxers come in, always carrying a little case that contained their gear. As they appeared a buzz would go around the hall, 'That's Dave Crowley.' 'Hello, here's Len Harvey, did you see him the day he beat Jack Hood?'

Sometimes a fighter would look into the crowd in response to a shout and wave to someone. All this fascinated me. I would watch his every movement. Then he would disappear down a passage, away to the dressing rooms, not to be seen again until he climbed into the ring dressed for battle.

What happened during the time that he was out of view? This I found intriguing. I wanted like mad to know what was down that little passage. There was only one way to find out. One day I said to Arthur, 'Some day I am going to go down that passage holding my little bag.' He said nothing but the look that he gave me showed him to be most unconvinced.

My chance came when one Sunday it was announced from the ring that professional competitions were soon to be held open to all and sundry. This was my opportunity. I entered. All I needed was to lay hands upon a little bag and I would make acquaintance of the passage and beyond.

There was about a fortnight to go before I would appear. In this time I spent many hours fighting imaginary opponents in our little room and I ran many miles around the streets at nights. But I had no real training, no tuition. I would have been one of the least learned of all those in the competition. However, there were no thoughts in my mind of achieving anything spectacular. My aim was to familiarise myself with the other part of the Ring — behind the scenes. At the same time I felt that I should not give too bad an account of myself in battle. Remember I was eighteen at this time, the age when my ego was probably at its zenith, when I did not foresee disaster too readily.

The evening came, Arthur had no time to come home to eat, he went there straight from work. He was already seated when I entered with my little bag. As I crossed the hall I looked up to where I knew Arthur would be sitting. Yes, there he was, with a grin spread right across his face. It was all right for him. I waved. Just as I had seen others do in the past. This was my day. Then I turned into the passage — this was it. At the end of the passage I found myself in a room about twenty feet square with a bench all the way around. This was the 'dressing rooms'. Here we all found some part of the bench on which to sit and change into our gear. And to while the time away there was a punch-ball in a corner and some skipping ropes in the centre of the room. Already one pugilistic looking character was on the punch-ball while others were shadow-boxing. It all looked very professional.

I sat there and waited my turn to be called out.

How did I feel? Not terribly nervous. I think I was so thrilled to find myself where I was that I had no thoughts for anything else. There was certainly nothing in my mind about the possibility of being hurt. Here I was, where I had told Arthur I would one day be. I had made it.

Eventually my name was called out along with my opponent's. I didn't hear his. All I heard was, 'Syd Metcalfe. You're on next.'

I can honestly say that even at that moment, which I suppose is the most crucial moment in a boxer's life, I was not scared. Through my mind ran the thought, 'I wish dad was here'.

To think that here was I about to enter the ring at the stadium where dad used so often to go on a Sunday morning leaving me agog with curiosity and speculation. If only he could have come back this night and thrown the programme down onto the table my name would have been on it. Arthur has that programme to this day.

In the ring I sat down in my corner and was

immediately taken over by a second who was as familiar to me as my own reflection. I had seen him nurse one boxer after another — real boxers, well-known characters. And now he had taken charge of me. I looked at his face, now within a few inches of mine and listened to his profound advice. 'Now, take it easy, son. Don't get nervous. Just feel him out at first. I'll tell you what to do after that.' I wondered if there would be any 'after that' from the looks of that chap sitting in the corner opposite me. He looked a lot more eager to win the competition than I was.

The bell sounded and I moved cautiously out to the centre of the ring. Now although I had sparred on innumerable occasions and in all manner of situations; although I had had the odd fight here and there too and at all times seemed to have a good view of my opponent, yet here in this well-furnished ring with the most elaborate lighting shining down upon us my opponent seemed all out of focus. I shot out a tentative left — a feeler — it fell well short. I moved a little closer and tried another left, for distance. Still short. Then my opposite number feeling that it was his turn threw a punch at me. It landed. And this seemed to be the pattern of things throughout that first round.

I came back to my corner with my nose bleeding profusely. Now for the expert advice. The first thing he said was, 'Would you like to turn it in, son?'

It was tempting, but I resisted it. 'No,' said I, with no great force, 'I'll try another round.'

All the while my second was trying to stop my

nose bleeding and at the same time telling me how to avoid those punches that I was finding so inescapable.

The second round was little better than the first. I did find that I was able to land my own punches a little more often, I was focusing better, but I still could not avoid the other fellow's. Oh, well, if he was so keen on winning the competition he could have it. I only wanted to see down that passage, anyway. The referee stopped the 'fight' at the end of the second round. For this I received two shillings and sixpence.

With this two and sixpence Arthur and I had tea and a pie at the coffee-stall outside the Ring. I could see he was enjoying his. He hadn't had dinner on account of having to come straight from work. I was hungry too but my lips were all puffed up and inflexible. I didn't enjoy mine at all. But I can still feel the elation that was mine at this time.

That was both the beginning and the end of my professional boxing career, although more success came my way when later I joined the army.

I remember I had a very sweet girl at that time too. She wouldn't come to see me fight as she hated the idea of seeing me hurt. Her woman's intuition stood her in good stead there. When I saw her the next evening my lips were still protruding and shiny. I insisted that I should not kiss her on saying goodnight. But she was adamant. That must have been the most emotionless kiss she ever experienced.

8

Dad Leaves Home and I Leave School

To go back to when I was about twelve. For some unknown reason my mum took it into her head that she would like to see my dad thrashed and every now and then she brought home one of her male friends to perform this on her behalf.

What sort of weed she made her husband out to be heaven only knows but I feel sure that if most of these contenders for the honour of administering my dad a hiding had only known the truth they would have asked to be excused.

Dad had not been a professional footballer for nothing. He hadn't been a regular attender at Blackfriars Ring without reason. He liked boxing, he knew something about it, he could hold his own. What's more half the characters who mum brought home to do the chastisement were partially drunk. Now this was no state to be in when setting out to thrash my dad.

If they had only asked me, young as I was, I could have told them about the weight of a mere slap from him or the power in his kick.

But no, they went blithely in taking mum's word for it that it would be easy.

Arthur and I would usually be in bed by the time mum with her candidate arrived and we would hear a short exchange of words and then dad saying, 'OK, let's go around the corner for a while.' We always knew what this meant. 'Dad's going to have another fight,' Arthur would say to me.

'Yes, I know.' It was exciting. And there we would lie awaiting the outcome. Never did we have long to wait. In next to no time dad would be coming back into the house, alone. It was all over. The next day we would look to see what signs there were, but dad never looked any different to me. I feel certain one couldn't have said this of the other fellow.

Occasionally feeling a little more elated than usual by the thoroughness of his victory, perhaps, dad would make some remark like, 'Let me know when you are going to bring the next one along and I'll go into training for him.'

Mum's reply was almost invariably 'Clever bastard,' she'd say, at the same time probably thinking she'd do better next time.

This was, of course, more than the average husband would tolerate, yet dad had several fights of this nature.

Eventually he went around the corner to do battle and didn't come back. He'd had enough. Maybe he reasoned that if he waited long enough mum would in the end come up with someone who really could thrash him. Possibly someone a good deal younger than himself. Even the law of averages was against him winning all the time. Anyway, however he felt about it, he finally didn't bother to even pick up his things. He'd left home. And from that time on he disappeared from our life for many years to come.

However, then he still played his part dutifully. He had the old-fashioned belief that having married he then became responsible for the rest of his life for the welfare of his wife and any children that might follow, and for once he found mum in whole-hearted agreement, for this was her belief too. Anyway, regularly each week he now sent her a postal order for a sum of money, being so much for herself and so much for each child. And as each child left school so dad deducted something from his remittance.

Often mum would be short of money and then it was that she became a fervent believer. She would expect God to come to her aid, saying, 'He has never let me down yet.' 'Whenever she was most in need,' she would say, 'He had always turned up trumps.' Although why on earth He should do her any special favours I wouldn't have the faintest idea, for of the Ten Commandments I would say that mum broke eight regularly and the other two at odd intervals.

But there was one temptation that mum resisted to the very end (if it ever came her way) and that was the temptation to look for a job so that she could have a bit of extra money in her purse.

So there we were, the four of us in a most peculiar household, for now mum became more will-o-the wisp than ever.

But now a transitional period was entering into my life for soon I would be leaving school.

This is an event that it seems most children look forward to. Arthur had already left and had been found his bookbinding job. Now he was going out in the evenings with his mate and I even heard talk of girl-friends. His life had begun — I eagerly awaited the beginning of mine.

Like all young animals we look admiringly at our elders and long for the day when we will be such as they. Maybe it is good that we should relish growing up for that enables us to make the change hopefully, without regrets. Were it possible for us to realise that we are really saying goodbye to a large measure of freedom at this time; should we be able to realise that the new phase of life that we are entering into is one filled with responsibilities and inevitable heartbreaks and hardships here and there maybe we would be less ready to cross over when the time came.

But in my mind was nothing but the advantages. I would be free (or so I thought). No more school-bell to goad me into getting a move on if I were running late. No more sitting rigidly in the class-room (for we would be told to 'sit up properly' if we dared to slouch in our seats in those days). No more 'Yes, sir, yes, sir, three bags full, sir' as the teacher asked over and over again, 'Is that clear?'

We resent the authority that adults have over us and we look forward to the day when we might inherit a little of this authority ourselves. It often comes as a great surprise to learn that on leaving school and going out to work we have not suddenly become completely independent of our parents' wishes and so arise the confrontation, the rebellions — we feel we have waited so long for this day and when it doesn't come up to our expectations we are resentful.

But in my case there was no continuation of parental authority. Rather was I too free to make my own way. There was no-one to advise, no-one to guide. No greater experience to call upon. Mum now was so often out that it was almost a surprise on coming home for dinner to find her there.

Come the day when we broke up for the Christmas Holidays. I was thirteen at the time but would not be returning to school as my fourteenth birthday would have come round before school reassembled. So there we were, left school, eligible to wear our first pair of long trousers. My shorts were shed for the last time, my stockings were put into their final resting place and 'a young man' was born.

This 'young man' stepped out of school that day with a great big world to conquer and a whole life-time to do it in. But what a task! Not that he was terribly ambitious, I suppose if he had been asked what he wished to make of himself he would have grandiloquently answered, 'A fine mind in a fine body.' Little enough to ask for, and yet how difficult to achieve.

This then marked the end of my childhood and the beginning of a never-ending phase during which we find ourselves having to make our own decisions instead of mum and dad making them for us. The beginning of a long march towards complete and utter disillusionment. For in many ways, especially for a child, ours was an idealistic age. All our heroes were wholly good and all our villains wholly bad. There was nothing in between. This made it easy to produce a winner. In the end the good always prevailed over bad and the children of the day accepted this as the normal way of life. Our heroines were sweet and uncomplicated and every predicament ended with a satisfactory solution. All endings were happy and many a story concluded with the phrase, 'and they all lived happily ever after.'

Heaven only knows my mother and father did their utmost to demonstrate that this was not always so but I chose to ignore their example.

There were films made specially for children in which we saw bravery and courage and nobleness of character laid on in the heaviest of doses. But we never questioned its authenticity. Somewhere we believed were men like this, and women were wholesome and pure. They fought like wildcats to avoid being kissed by the wrong man and as we watched them in their struggle to preserve their innocence one more illusion was being shaped to add to our already burdensome load. One more to have to rid ourselves of one day.

It was filled with these illusions that I went into the world on that morning that I started work with a firm of electrical engineers. A job that had been found for me by Mr Winston, our teacher-cum-Labour Exchange.

My immediate tasks were to run errands. All day long I would be either taking something or fetching something. Always on my return from one errand there was another all lined up for me. My day was continuous. They never seemed to run out of errands. But in view of the fact that I was their sole means of disposing of anything it is more to be wondered how I proved adequate.

On starting on an errand my route was always planned for me and I would be given the exact bus and tram fares. Had I always followed the prescribed route no doubt my journeys wouldn't have taken so long. As it was the temptation to walk and pocket the money over most of the shorter journeys proved too much and this led to me being asked over and over again, 'Why have you taken so long?' For not only did it take longer by foot but it meant that I was also running into the many distractions that London was so full of in those days.

Looking back there seemed to have been a remarkable number of people making their living by selling in the street and I could never pass them by. Not only were they interesting but often were they quite amusing.

I shall always remember one occasion — a stall-holder was selling something and had gathered a goodly crowd. Now it was up to him to capture first their interest and then their money.

'These,' he said, holding up one of his wares, 'are made in South Africa. You won't buy them anywhere else in this country. I have a friend there who sends them over to me.'

Suddenly a man in the crowd said, 'I've never seen them in South Africa.'

Quite unabashed the cockney said, 'Oh, I see, you are from South Africa, are you, sir?'

'Yes,' said the man in the crowd, 'I've lived there all my life.'

'Oh, do you know Cape Town?'

'Yes, I know it well.'

'I see, then you would know King's Walk.'

'King's Walk?' the man hesitated, 'no I don't.'

'Well,' said the stall-holder, 'they do, you know, they are just like anyone else.'

With that the crowd laughed, the man walked away and the vendor continued with the crowd very much on his side.

It would be nothing for a perfectly respectable looking individual, complete with attaché case, looking for all the world as though he were just off to the office, to suddenly stop, look all around, put his attaché case on the pavement, open up and pull out a pair of lady's stockings. Then the patter would start, 'Now, come on girls, come in a little closer. I've got something here for you.'

Of course the little errand boy would come in a little closer too. What chance did he have?

Imagine being suddenly confronted by a man done up in a straightjacket, manacled, and bound with yards of chain struggling to free himself on the ground in the middle of the road. Try forcing a small boy past that spectacle. Yet this sort of thing came my way all the time I was out. A knot of people would be standing around and over I would go, the firm's errand clean forgotten. The man would be twisting and turning in all directions, the veins on his forehead bulging, his face flushed and grunts and groans to give further atmosphere to the show. This was all deadly serious to the small boy. Finally, with a great heave followed by a huge gasp the man would burst free. Then I would move on. After all the sequel to all this mayhem was the hat being passed around the crowd. That part held no interest for me.

Usually when I took too long over an errand the fault was mine but there were other times when it was due to something outside my control, like whenever I was given a load that was really too heavy for me to carry. Often have I staggered out of a firm with a load over my shoulder that has had me wondering how I am ever going to get back to the 'shop'. Then if there was any question of me being late I felt aggrieved.

I liked the occasions when I was given a barrow with which to fetch or deliver my errand. Then I became one of the traffic, one with the taxis and the horses and carts. It was thrilling being out there in the road. Sometimes when we were held up at a crossing a horse would edge right up behind until his muzzle was right over my shoulder. Always these seemed to be most friendly creatures. Perhaps he saw me as another animal pulling a cart, like himself, for some cruel master. Often I would reach up and pat him and frequently get a handful of saliva in the process.

That barrow could be fun on the flat but on the hills it became near torture. Those cursed hills, I can remember them well, sometimes it required several stops before I could reach the top. My mind goes back to a small boy sitting on the handles of a barrow half way up a hill out of breath and even at times trembling. What was it that caused me to put such effort into trying to force that carrier with its heavy load on, up, up, up that tortuous hill? Why did I not at times go back to the firm and say, 'The barrow is stranded at such and such a spot. I can't push it any further, it is beyond me?' I could even have added, 'I have done my best.' Which would have been perfectly true, for I put everything into keeping those wheels going around, no matter what feeble progress we slowed down to. And all this for twelve shillings and sixpence a week. Plus the pennies I made by not catching a tram or bus here and there.

It was also my job to sweep the workshop up every evening and to fetch the teas and cakes for the men from the coffee shop around the corner. This entailed going to each member of the firm, taking his mug and writing down his order. The whole, some twenty or so mugs, were then put into a wooden drawer and away I went, whatever the weather. On my return I would take each man his order, and if I dared to make a mistake I was a bloody little fool. No allowance was ever made for the fact that it wasn't always easy to remember to which man each mug belonged. If the coffee shop hadn't the particular cake or filling for a sandwich that was

84

ordered I was expected to make a snap decision and order something else. But if this cut across the taste of the man who I was acting for I was made to feel through my stupidity I had wasted his hard earned money.

But they were a good bunch of fellows and my recollection of them sees them as mostly in good humour, endlessly working, chained to their machine or bench. At dinner time, from twelve till one, they would all take up the same thing each day to while the hour away. Some would take out the morning paper, one had always a cheap book with him. A couple would regularly discuss the races. Every day from twelve to one, non-stop, they had but one subject and for the whole year that I was there they were never stuck for something to say. And it would seem that the horses of those days were every bit as unpredictable as they are now for I can distinctly remember that the phrase 'If only' kept cropping up.

But it was clear too that they received their reward for the money lost in the enjoyment that they derived from these hour long discussions every day. One wonders would they have suddenly become silent, conversationless had they been forbidden to talk on that subject any more. For if they knew of other things they kept their knowledge a dark secret. Certainly they were not given to talking about women. Even their jokes had to concern a horse or a jockey.

There was one retired sailor who gave me to understand that he had been all around the world several times. He was my favourite and

I was alongside him with questions concerning life in other countries at every opportunity. He told me that the most interesting country and the prettiest, in his opinion, was Japan — 'especially when the cherry trees are in blossom.'

I could never understand why he had chosen to live in England in retirement from the navy when he had seen the wonders of other countries of the world.

'After all, England was so ordinary.' His answer was that 'there is no place like it.' Yet I remained certain that there must be somewhere far more exciting than the life that I was seeing all around me.

He gave me the itch to see more. If there was no place like England I was not prepared to take his word for it. This I would prefer to judge for myself.

At the end of a year I handed in my notice. In true boy-like fashion I boldly told the manager that the two shillings and sixpence rise that he had given me to last me through the next year was not enough.

'It's the firm's practice, Sydney,' he said, 'to give rises only once a year, and the first rise is always two and sixpence. Then you are taken inside to learn the trade. Don't be foolish now. Think about it. The big money will come later on.'

Think about it. What did I want to think about it for? I knew what I was doing. I was fifteen now. I could earn more than that.

'No thanks, I'm not interested, I'm giving my notice in. I'll be leaving next week.'

And so I left.

Whether this can be regarded as unwise, or foolish it is impossible to say now. Certainly I never did learn a trade, but who's to say that as a tradesman life would have been more interesting, or more worthwhile? Or more anything for that matter? That which makes us tick is not dependant upon what trade we learn. Becoming an electrical engineer would have done nothing for my character. Why, I might even have ended up one of that party discussing the day's racing every lunchtime.

Other jobs followed in rapid succession and the ability to stay long in one place just as rapidly diminished.

Then came the day when working as a storeman at a warehouse not too far from where we lived I came home for a midday meal. A lad now of sixteen. On arriving at the top of our street there ahead of me was what looked like a whole pile of furniture heaped up in the roadway, just off the pavement. From where I was it could have been right outside our house.

My heart leapt into my mouth. 'Could this be ours?''Could this mean we had been turned out?'

Well did I know that if anyone was going to have their furniture tossed out into the street it was more likely to be our family than any other.

'Should I turn back and walk off?'

To go on could prove most embarrassing. As I approached it it became recognisable. Yes, it was ours all right. Nobody else would have owned such a heap of rubbish. And lying as it was, unstacked, just a conglomeration of bits and pieces with table legs stuck awkwardly into the air, mattress protruding through a gap between the wardrobe and a chest of drawers. Other oddments of our home flung carelessly onto the heap to rest shamefully awry as they exposed their unpainted parts.

The whole scene was a shambles. One which no doubt the neighbours were enjoying as they peered from behind a gap in the curtains. They wouldn't have dared to take up too bold a vantage point, too openly exposing themselves, in case my mother was there and yelled out, 'That's right, black your nose you nosey sod.'

This was the first time I had ever seen a household turned out into the street. The first time, and it had to be us. This was our final degradation.

However, although while walking towards this ungainly heap I was feeling terribly ashamed, yet by the time I arrived alongside it and recognised some of the objects that were peculiarly ours, as there are in all households, I became angry. Look, there was Doona's doll thrown down as though it had no value. Arthur's suit was lying there under a heap of other things. Hey, that's not going to do that any good. What's Arthur going to say? And there's my Fifth Form at St Dominics. Damn it, what right had anyone to tip our things out like this? These were ours and I didn't care what anybody else thought about them. My blood was up. Someone had to defend

88

the family and I was the sole representative present.

Bounding up the stairs in a temper I flung myself into the front room. There on their knees on the floor were two men taking up the lino. On the stove was a pot with something still cooking inside it. No-one else was there. Mum must have left on their arrival. 'Hey, what's going on here?' I demanded, with all the authority of a voice not yet broken, as though I didn't already know.

The two men stopped what they were doing and one pointed to the door.

'It's up there, sonny,' he said.

I looked at the door and saw that there was a notice pinned to it. Walking across I stood looking at it, but to this day I've no idea what it said. I was too upset to read it. In any case it didn't take a genius to realise that this was a Notice to Quit. So we had had our home taken away from us, we were turned out.

All the fight went out of me.

'Do you mind if I take a few things?' I asked.

'No, take what you like, son.' They appeared sorry for me.

I gathered together mum's Marriage Lines and the Birth Certificates of we three children and left. As I walked down the stairs, out of the door and away from the street I was walking away from life as I knew it. I was saying goodbye to the last vestiges of home life. What lay ahead wasn't yet important. I was conscious only of what lay behind.

That night when I came out of the warehouse

Arthur met me and said, 'Mum was waiting for me outside the firm. She has found a furnished room for you and me. She's taking Doona with her.' Then he added, 'What a bloody mess!'

'Yes,' said I. There didn't seem need for much else. Arthur's remark just about summed up everything. 'What a bloody mess!'

Looking back it is clear that my mother must have been receiving notices regarding her non-payment of the rent. She must have received warnings that if she didn't pay such and such would happen. She must have received a final notice that even told her that this eviction was about to take place. Yet such was her nature, such was her complacency when she chose to ignore that which displeased her that not by the slightest sign were any of us aware that all was not perfectly well. Never did I see a frown, a look of concern, never a tut, tut, nothing, nothing that gave me the remotest hint that mum wasn't perfectly content. As no doubt she was. For the important things in mum's life happened not in the house but outside, and if her outside life was going well nothing else mattered.

Well, now we were thrown out of the house. Now she wouldn't have to bother about coming home to cook the dinner, for from now on my mother became no more than an occasional acquaintance.

In fact within a very short space of time she disappeared altogether and to this day no one of us has known what were the circumstances that caused her to go.

We assume that she is dead. She didn't take

90

sufficient care of her health to have lived to a good old age. But how long she lived, what were the events of her later life, where she moved to — all these questions will now remain unanswered.

Doona, my sister, was the last to see her and on account of holding her in some affection she it was who made some effort to find out just what had happened to mum. But although Doona visited every known one of mum's usual pubs, although she met and spoke to dozens of friends and acquaintances of hers who would have been most interested to know where she was, yet no one could offer the remotest clue. No-one had seen her. No-one knew how she had come to leave. She had disappeared in unaccountable fashion.

The more one thinks of it the more extraordinary it seems, for mum's way of life was dependent upon her having a large circle of friends. Within this circle she moved, at ease, at home, sure of the helping hand that she so often needed. It is unbelievable that mum would have willingly walked away from this atmosphere, that was very largely of her own making, to start life all over again in a strange district. Yet walk away from it she apparently did, for one day she stopped making her usual round and she has never been seen since.

Mum, you were a strange person. I never did understand you — now, of course, I never will. And where did you go to when you walked away from your friends? . . . silence.

9

Growing Up

Our new home turned out to be a small over-crowded front room with a large double bed, a settee, a gas-ring standing in the fireplace, a washbowl and jug on a stand and table and chairs all struggling to fit conveniently into insufficient space.

As we stood there looking around there was no sense of loss, no regrets concerning what happened. If this was to be our new abode, oh, well, at least it was clean.

Arthur and I fitted ourselves into what space was left and lived there for the next nine months.

Here I was desperately poor. My wages were sixteen shillings per week. By today's standards everything was ridiculously cheap but, even so, after paying eight shillings towards the rent what was left over was woefully inadequate to buy all that was needed.

Those were hard times and I was also dreadfully lonely as Arthur was now a 'lad about town'. He was eighteen and he and his mate used to regularly spend every evening trying to pick up girls who would prove not to be too sparing with their favours. This left me very much alone.

Occasionally Arthur's pal would call round

for him and then they would discuss the results of 'last night's' escapade. For they apparently would separate when the time came to make their individual efforts to persuade the girl to take part in their idea of a good way of ending the evening. And it wasn't until Arthur and his friend met again the next evening that they found out how they had each fared.

The conversation used to be hilarious. They were two teenagers, out to enjoy themselves and as they laughed and joked about their exploits with the girls so would I laugh too. They seemed to me to be living life as it was meant to be lived, at that age, at any rate. Perhaps my turn would come later. I envied them.

If the girl had let them they poked fun at how worried she was afterwards. If she didn't let them they still poked fun — at the panic she exhibited as she fought to save her honour. Whatever had happened they always found it amusing. Then out they would go to see what they could manage tonight. As they went so the life went out of the room and I would be left to pass the evening away the best way I could.

Often at those times I have gone to bed to put an end to the day. Thankfully I never had any trouble falling asleep. At sixteen one doesn't toss and turn in bed.

Somehow I hadn't yet got around to thinking about girls. My interests were mostly in sport. Each night I would exercise and my imaginary sparring partners found me just as hard a man to beat in that little room as they had in our previous home.

Girls would come later. Plenty of time for them. I couldn't afford to take one out anyway. What would I look like out with a girl with the soles of my shoes worn right through? No, this was no time to be thinking of girls.

Yet without looking for it it was here in this isolated little room that sex did put in an appearance. It came searching me out.

Brief and casual though it was, it was here one Sunday afternoon that it glanced in and attempted to introduce itself.

It came about this way. Behind our room was a flat which was occupied by a couple who I suppose were in their early thirties. The wife was a blonde who might or might not have been good-looking in her younger days. I couldn't express an opinion on this for as I saw her she was just a woman, a grown-up. Her looks meant nothing to me, any more than did the fact that she was a woman. Certainly there was no question of fancying her. Any mention of this would have left me bewildered. How could one fancy a woman so much older than oneself and so very ordinary? I believe that if I had thought further on the subject I might even have considered that sex could surely no longer interest her.

From time to time she would speak to my brother or I in the passage and she had even stood at the door of our room and chatted awhile, but no more.

On the Sunday afternoon when I was nearly introduced to a new aspect of life I was sitting in my little room alone. Arthur was, as usual, out with his mate. From what I could gather from remarks he let drop their hopes were running high that day. They had met two girls the previous evening and something the girls had said had caused them to think that they were in for an interesting afternoon and evening. As they left, taking their laughter with them, little did I know that my afternoon held some promise too.

Back to my little room. As I sat there a knock came at the door. Just a gentle tap, suggestive of it being the lady in the back flat, I opened the door.

'Hello, Sydney,' she said, 'Are you all alone there?'

'Yes,' said I, completely unconcerned.

'What have you had for dinner?' she asked.

Hm, this seemed an opportunity to cash in on a little womanly sympathy.

'Oh, I couldn't be bothered to cook anything. I've just had a cup of tea and a piece of toast.'

'Oh, you poor thing, that's not enough for a growing lad. Wait there I'll get you a dinner. I've just had mine, there's lots left over.'

With that she went back to the flat and I retired into my room thinking this is good, I'm going to have a nice dinner.

Nothing else crossed my mind. Why should it, hadn't she just said, 'I'll get you a nice dinner?'

But as soon as she returned it was patently clear that she now had other ideas than just catering to my hunger. For she had powdered her face, rouged her mouth, touched up her eyes and soaked herself in scent. This was not the innocuous, motherly creature who a short while before had shown such gentle concern for my not having had enough to eat. This was a female on the prowl. She had not only prepared my dinner, she had prepared herself as well. I was going to be offered both, on a plate. Dinner first, madam afterwards.

And her whole manner had changed. There was now a part being played. She was girlish, turning on the charm. 'Here you are, you poor dear,' she cooed, 'we can't have the little man going hungry, can we?'

This was embarrassing. She was in the room now and laying out the table for me. The atmosphere was filled with the overdose of scent with which she had swamped herself.

Actually this over-use of make-up showed poor psychology on her part. It made her even less appealing to a young fellow. No amount of disguise could have deluded me into seeing her as other than a grown woman. And the attempt to make herself physically attractive to me, coupled with the skittish behaviour only served to make me realise how ignorant I was of these matters.

An older man would have known exactly how to behave — he would have met the situation before. To me it was all so new.

Had she remained motherly and played me along gently there might have been a chance of me responding. As it was she became a tart in my eyes, acting quite unlike her age. And

96

I was filled with the realisation that she was so experienced in this field. It was all a little frightening. She went the wrong way about it, she should not have made her aspirations so clear with such startling rapidity.

So there we were, with dinner now fully laid out and her inviting me to, 'Eat this, Syd, you'll feel better after.'

This I doubted very much. In fact I had a strong suspicion that I'd most likely feel worse for it was after eating 'this' that the curtain would be going up and we would be expected to play our two parts in another of life's constant dramas.

As I sat there eating she sat there encouraging me, commenting on each mouthful, remarking on my appearance, I was a big lad for my age. How blue my eyes were. How sorry she always felt for me being so alone in the room. Did I like girls? Ah, this was coming more to the point.

To all of these questions and others I tried to pretend that I was quite unaware of them having any significance. I tried to pretend that I was not able to read the message that she was wishing to convey . . . that she was ready to be made love to. As far as I was concerned she would have to be much more blatant than that. And much more blatant she was for with the last mouthful demolished she then said, 'Let's leave the dishes and come and sit over here, dear.'

Over here was alongside her on the settee. This was the moment I had dreaded for I was so afraid of whatever it was that was about to

97

happen that no other feeling had the remotest chance of asserting itself. However, afraid as I was of what this was all leading up to I was equally afraid of offending her, and so I sat down alongside her on the settee. She took hold of my hand and said, 'Kiss me.' And so I kissed her. Or rather I made as though to kiss her but it was not me kissing her it was her kissing me, for when I was ready to withdraw my mouth she wouldn't let me. This was a new type of kiss — there was an urgency about it. It was more than affectionate, it had a touch of desperation about it. We continued to kiss and I felt myself caught up in this struggle to make each kiss more exciting than the last. It was almost as though we were locked in battle, each trying to destroy the other.

We were caught up in the flood that would allow neither of us to turn back. Suddenly there was a knock at the street door. 'Keep quiet' she said. We both sat still and silent. Then came another knock, a little louder, and a man's voice called through the letter box, 'Are you there Annie?' It was her husband. Immediately she jumped up ran to the door and I heard a short exchange of words. Then she came back, gathered up the dirty crockery and left without a glance in my direction. I gathered from her manner that she was distinctly angry. Me, I felt intensely relieved. The atmosphere a moment before had been quite stifling. Now I could breathe. In a few moments I dressed and went out. Outside everything seemed so fresh and clean.

What on earth her husband must have thought when she opened the door to him that afternoon made up like a cheap prostitute I will never know. He must have suspected, unless he was even more naive than me. Maybe he had struck a similar situation before, for she was certainly one to seize upon her opportunities.

However, this must have pulled her up with a jerk, for from then on she was propriety itself. She even gave me the occasional dinner, but never again stayed to watch me eat it.

I have written of this in semi-jocular fashion but recently a hypnotherapist friend of mine read it. His work, of course, involves the use of psychotherapy. He saw nothing the least bit funny in the reading of it. His reaction was one of sympathy for the lady. 'Poor thing,' he said, 'how embarrassing and humiliating for her. And the fact that it never happened again suggests that she must have been overcome on that one occasion.'

Yes, simply relating the facts is not really 'telling the truth' as we would have once thought, is it? The truth goes much deeper than that.

I wish Annie had been able to explain herself to me afterwards. Maybe then I could have treated the whole affair in a fashion much fairer to her.

A whole year was to go by before I would be given a further chance to open my account. And the circumstances couldn't have been more different, for this time I was the older of the two, I felt on top of the situation, while she, a girl of fifteen, was hesitant, afraid, yet at the same time eager to go ahead and take the plunge. In fact she it was who set the ball a -rolling.

I must have been about eighteen at the time for my sister had now broken away from her mother and was working. From time to time I would meet her by arrangement and always she had a young friend with her. Arthur and I had now moved to another bed-sitter, where the landlady was ultra-respectable. A fervent believer who would try to make the occasional conversion. My brother and I had both been sounded out but I think she had come to regard us as not very good material.

What I particularly remember her for was the fact that she made all her own bread. Delicious stuff it was. She would make a batch of white and a batch of wholemeal. We always knew when it was in the oven for the whole house would be permeated by the most appetising aroma. To make this even more enjoyable we both knew that as soon as they were taken out of the oven one would be brought up to us. Sometimes even one of each, one white and one brown. Both still steaming. Hot and tempting, with a layer of flour sprinkled over the top.

Dear Mrs. Barrett, she was quite elderly and she told us she had made her own bread all through her married life. But even this, delicious as it was, had not managed to keep her husband's affections. He liked her bread, of course, but wasn't prepared to pay too high a price for it, for he, it seemed had even given up talking to her.

The thing to do when her bread first arrived was to cut a chunky piece off and plaster it with butter. This would immediately soak right into the hot, spongy slice and one would then be faced with five or ten minutes of sheer enjoyment.

It was here, surrounded by religious fervour and punctilious housekeeping that my initiation into the realms of eroticism took place. In other words, that I made love for the first time.

Although earning more money now — I was a baker's roundsman — I was still outrageously poor. And so was still confined more to the room itself than if I could have afforded to go out more often.

Two knocks on the door-knocker to those who were familiar with our ways was the signal for us to answer the door. One knock was for Mrs. Barrett. So when the knocker struck twice this evening I opened up. There, to my surprise, standing looking at me with a look that told all, was my sister's young friend.

'Can I come in?' she asked, timidly.

'Yes, come in,' said I, liking the look of concern in her eyes. 'Come in. Take your coat off. Sit down. Would you like a cup of tea?' I couldn't do enough for her. This was a most unexpected, a most welcome opportunity. 'Do you take sugar, Lucille?'

Yes, Lucille took sugar. She, it appeared, was as eager to please me as I was to please her.

But we were new to each other. This was our first time alone in each other's company. This was the first time we had been able to contemplate being able to do more than just talk to one another.

We talked generalities as we sat drinking our tea but there was a tension in the air. Nothing that we said really interested either of us. Our minds were racing ahead and it was only a matter of making a move in that direction and then everything would just naturally follow.

I would like to think that that evening Lucille was as much a novice as was I. That would account for the hesitation on both our parts. It would also account for the timidity and the nervousness. There was a certain apprehension as well as expectation. We were both about to enter into an unknown realm. A realm that we had heard speak of only in hushed whispers. And never having been there before we were both a little afraid, or, let us say, we were both lacking in confidence.

Yet, over our cup of tea, it was clear that we were equally as eager to go on into this new experience. We were on the brink and there was no turning back. It was a one-way-street, we could only go forward.

After about half an hour of useless chatter (yet perhaps it helped us to feel a little more settled) I took her in my arms and kissed her. It was heavenly. She was so warm and soft, and willing. This was something I had never known before. Her very compliance filled me with longing.

We laid down on the bed and I can remember we had not another thing to say to one another. Our idle chatter had ended. Now we were indulging in what she had really come round for, what I had had in mind when I said, 'Yes, come in.' Now we were not a boy and a girl, we were one tempestuous emotion that was just bursting to destroy itself.

That evening our inexperience showed itself clearly. We were too hurried, too eager. And we were devoid of all technique. Just a couple of kids taking a plunge into adulthood.

I believe we were both terribly disappointed afterwards. It had all been so hurried — we had rushed impulsively towards finality and we were left with a feeling more of shame than satisfaction.

Not much was said. Somehow neither of us wished to stay any longer in that room. The scene of our initiation. Our misdemeanour as we saw it. We left and I saw her to the bus.

It seems sad looking back that there was no affection between Lucille and me. It was like a matter-of-fact arrangement. There was never any talk of fondness. We behaved as though we recognised that there wasn't, and wasn't likely to be, anything more than the desire to enjoy each other from time to time. For from then on Lucille took to calling round whenever she was in the mood and always we simply made love and then parted. A strange affair, but we accepted it as having some value for it went on for quite some time.

We acquired a technique of a kind and we learned to proceed more unhurriedly but we never recaptured the wonder that was ours on that first evening. We had lost our shyness and it was past finding again.

I never knew when she would call. It was a case of waiting for those two knocks on the street door. For a while they were quite frequent. Then they started to spread out, and eventually I found myself waiting, and hoping, but they had finished. Lucille must have got herself a real boyfriend. I hope so. And I hope that he was good to her, for she had a very loving nature. One that would lead her into a lot of trouble if luck wasn't on her side.

I rather suspect that she was the type to run into trouble, but at least, Lucille, as far as I am concerned I have never forgotten you. You were my first 'love'. It was with you that I was overwhelmed with wonder and longing. Somehow no other was ever quite the same.

10

A Bike And A Horse

About this time I acquired a bike from somewhere. Not the kind that we jocularly called the 'sit up and beg type', but a real roadracer. Drop handlebars and all. And this became my introduction to the wonderful countryside of England. An introduction to a world of which until then I was only remotely aware. I was a city lad and to me London represented the hub of the universe. What happened outside its boundaries did not concern me.

But now, with my bike, I was able to leave the sights and sounds of the metropolis behind and enter into another world — a world of near silence, of smells and scenes both fresh and beautiful. Where I was surrounded by cold buildings I was now hemmed in by trees. Where I could never see beyond a few yards I now had vistas stretching way out to the horizon. Where my immediate neighbours had been people I was now rubbing shoulders with sheep and cows.

For now every weekend and holiday found me out on the open road, alone, heading for somewhere, usually on the south coast.

This was a delightful period in which to be cycling, for the roads were completely uncongested. I would hear a car coming from as far back as a quarter of a mile. Slowly it would overtake me and as slowly pass and move away into the distance.

Really, there was not the slightest danger of being run down. In fact on looking back I cannot recall even being involved in a situation of any kind with a car. My worst accident happened very early one Sunday morning when I had set out for a trip to Brighton. Being situated in North London, as I was, this meant going right across London from north to south before coming to the country roads. My idea was to rise about five o'clock and be on the road before the day's traffic was about. Also it meant a few good hours to spend enjoying the seaside at Brighton before having to start back again.

So there was I, with the streets practically empty, head down, going a steady fifteen miles per hour. While still in London, in the early morning light, I had turned into a street and ahead of me was a milkman with his horse and cart. The man had left his van and with a carrier full of bottles was going from house to house. The horse was standing almost in the middle of the road awaiting his master's call to move forward. These horses could almost put the bottles on the doorstep, they were so well trained. I can remember now that to pass him it meant swinging out right onto the right-hand side of the road. I decided to pass him fairly close. It was my fault — I should have known better, for just as I was about to go by, Neddy, hearing this sound alongside him looked around to see what was the cause of it and I went smack right into his head. He reared into the air, I fell to the ground and the bike went skidding along ending up several yards away.

Fortunately it needed no more than a few adjustments. There was no serious damage, so, with apologies all round I patted the horse to show him that there was no ill feeling and was able to proceed on to Brighton. That is the worst thing that happened to me in years of cycling.

On the roads they were calm, sedate, peaceful days. There were still small country farmhouses where one could sit in the garden laid out in front of the house for the serving of teas and cakes. Where the only noises were those of the birds whistling in the trees.

One could sit there watching the occasional passer-by in a silence that could actually be heard. So attuned were my ears to the din of the London traffic that they were startled into being acutely aware of this great difference.

There was something about the beauty and the serenity of it all that affected one. I used to feel as though it took all my cares away. To sit in that setting worried would have been incongruous. There was such harmony that it would have been irreligious to introduce an inharmonious note.

Always the lady who served me my tea and cakes was as one with the scenery — soft-spoken and gentle.

Then, having eaten, it would be out through the wicker gate and onto the open road again, refreshed and happy.

Sometimes I have come to the top of a rise and

107

there before me has stretched a vast, panoramic picture of countryside that has compelled me to dismount and stand in admiration. I would be the only visible human being. This that I was seeing was all mine, there was not even need to share it. What wonder then that I was proud of my country when its beauty could take my breath away.

Then there were the times when I would sleep out under a blanket that was always carried rolled up on the back of the bike. To be awakened in the morning by the persistent chatter of the birds. They could see the dawn, for which they had been impatiently waiting and now they hadn't a moment to spare, they wanted the whole world to awaken with them and to this end they were playing their part. Not that I minded; what finer reveille could one be roused by?

There would quite often be a damp mist in the air filled with the aroma of mother nature. The earth, the trees, the grass, all blended together to make a smell sweeter than any artificially produced. It was heavenly to just lie there listening to the sounds of fellow creatures, also just awakening. Perhaps a cock would crow in the distance, or a dog would bark, or a crow would caw. To think that they and I were all one.

Eventually, unable to withstand the taunting cries of these other early risers I would reluctantly throw off the blanket, which would then be rolled and stowed, and set off in search of a stream where I could wash and somewhere where I could have my breakfast. That air would have me starving.

Often these mornings were quite chilly and it would require a mile or two of brisk cycling before I warmed up. If by chance a farmer should come by we would always exchange greetings, for that was the way of life in these parts. All of which went towards making me feel very happy.

Up and down the hills of Devon and Cornwall my bike has carried me, into what I consider some of the loveliest of English scenery, past thatched-roof cottages, past village ponds, along narrow lanes so covered with the intertwining leaves of trees on each side that I could barely see the sky above, past fields of corn, past grazing cattle who have barely rated me a glance. These are the pictures that flood into my mind as I write. Pictures that leave me with some of my most satisfying memories.

A few years back I ventured to re-live those days. It was while staying with Arthur and his wife in their house in North London. Not far from their house ran the Cambridge Road which was a direct run to Cambridge, some thirty or thirty-five miles away. One day the thought occurred to me that I would love to find myself on the open road once again. Maybe I could even recover that sense of escape from modern life and know once again the quiet peace of the country.

It seemed prudent not to mention my intentions to Arthur and his wife, for I was turned fifty at the time. I felt quite sure that

109

I could manage the sixty or seventy miles there and back if I took it steadily but I didn't want Arthur's 'Bloody fool!' ringing in my ears as I set off. So it was unbeknown to anyone that I mounted the bike and pedalled away.

The thought of what lay ahead filled me with elation. I was that young fellow all over again. Scenes of those earlier days all came back. At the moment it was not possible to let my mind drift off too much for I was still on the London streets and it needed all my time and attention to keep from being run down. But soon, soon we would be out in the country and then I would be able to relax, to take things easily and enjoy what there was around me. This was going to be just like old times, with the occasional country pub passing slowly by. Perhaps I could even pop into one on the way and have a quiet pint of beer. So ran my thoughts. I felt happy.

Then the main road was reached. I turned into it and set off for the long ride to Cambridge. But no sooner was I on this road than I was looking for a way of getting off it again. It was terrifying. Thirty or forty years had gone by since the days when I used to hear the birds singing as I went quietly on my way. Now one heard nothing but he continuous sound of speeding traffic. Where once I had heard a car coming from as far as a quarter of a mile behind and would listen to it coming closer and closer, now I didn't know it was there until it went past me within a few inches at a speed that left me quite frightened. There was the feeling that had that been a few inches closer I would have been gone. There was no warning, only at the last moment, when it was right upon me was I aware of its presence. And then if anything was going to happen it would have been too late to avoid it. Even the large lorries, of which there were many, were able to hold their own with regards to speed, and the continuity of the traffic was unbelievable. For the brief period that I was on this virtual race-track I was in danger of death at any moment. Clearly no cyclist had any right to be there except at peril of his life.

At the very first opportunity I turned off and headed back home. My search for the past had ended. Like all pasts it had gone.

This must mean then that no young fellow of today has those experiences that were so dear to me at the time, and since, of going out into beauty and solitude and leaving all one's cares behind. Well, if that no longer exists I count myself all the more fortunate that it lasted long enough for me to know it.

Among the many jobs that came my way during my growing up period was one in which I drove a horse and cart around London delivering bread and rolls to cafes and restaurants. This job, although only one of many, comes in for special mention because of my horse. She must be found a place in this story for she was a character. She had been christened Chiquita by her previous driver, who was an elderly Italian. 'If you are not sure which turning you take, Chiquita she take you. She know the round better than me,' he had said. How right he was. She not only knew the round but she took a really intelligent interest in all that was going on concerning the job. Her mind was on all that was happening all the time and she needed no notice of when to stop and start. These, and many other things, she did of her own accord.

If I took too long over a delivery — perhaps I would be chatting to a customer — she would neigh, advising me that time was getting on and that there was still plenty to be done.

Quite often she has saved me at those times from someone who wanted to talk and who had an unbreakable hold upon me. Then upon hearing Chiquita's neigh I would say, 'Oops, I must be off, the horse is getting restless.' And on reaching the cart I would say, 'Thanks Chiquita.' Her reaction was usually to look at me in a manner that I'd swear said, 'About time too.'

When the old Italian had passed the job over he had also given me a list of those customers who didn't check their bill. They were always charged a little bit more and the extra pocketed. He had also made it quite clear that it would be most unwise to attempt anything with those not on the list. But, of course, after a while I felt I knew better than he did. For example there was the old chap with the cafe on the corner of Market Street. Surely he was an easy touch. Why, he never counted his change. And look at the unintelligent look on his face. If ever I knew a fool I knew one here. And so I took him off the list of 'untouchables' and added him to the list that the old Italian had given me. The first Friday after that when I presented him with his bill I added an extra shilling and he paid like a lamb. Not a murmur, not a moment's demur. He was easy. I knew he would be. So that was another shilling I could add to the regular supply of extras.

But on the Monday when I went to deliver his order his whole manner had changed. Somehow he didn't look such a fool this morning. He was angry.

'You charged me a shilling too much last Friday,' he said. 'Now I wouldn't do that if I were you. The last chap tried it once. But only once. I would have thought he'd have told you.'

From then on I stuck strictly to Tony's list. He knew what he was doing when he made it out. If I could only have asked Chiquita I'm sure she would have put me right.

Every Saturday morning there was one cafe that was shut and as this was the only reason for going down that particular street it meant that on Saturday we could pass the top of that street without turning into it. But here I found the limit to Chiquita's remarkable good sense. She would not recognise that there were days when the routine could be broken. To her doing the round meant going halfway down the street, stopping outside a certain cafe and then coming all the way back again.

At first I used to insist upon her going past the top of the street — no point to going down there unnecessarily — but the distress that I caused her was so intense that in the end I took to going down as far as the cafe, getting off the van with my basket over my arm, waiting a while out of her view, then climbing back onto the van. This left her completely deceived and entirely satisfied.

Now this might seem a ridiculous procedure to have gone through, and I agree it certainly sounds that way, but to have seen Chiquita's frantic efforts to tell me that I had made a mistake when I insisted on her passing the top of the street would have convinced anyone that the other way was far preferable, and much kinder.

First of all we approached the top of the street she would start to turn, left it was. Then I would pull on the right-hand rein (quite hard, for she was already trying to fight the pull of the rein), at the same time saying, 'No, not this morning, Chiquita, we don't go down there this morning, come on, old girl.' But no, we do go down there, we always go down there. There's a cafe down there that we must serve. By now she had almost stopped, still trying to turn. I would still be urging her forward. Then she would stop completely, right in the middle of the top of the street, and look right round at me. Honestly, the look on her face, the struggle that she was having to tell me that I was making a mistake was quite disturbing. It was wrong to hurt her so — this meant so much to her.

Finally I would force her past but even then she would be trying to turn back.

What else could I do but to go through the other rigmarole and pretend? She so wanted to do the job properly, and that from no more than

114

a mere sense of what is right and what is wrong. Good old Chiquita!

When we came to the end of the round she would be so tired that she could hardly pull herself along. She had done a good day's work and I used to feel sorry for her. But, along with the 'a woman's work is never done' act this was a gag, for, with the last customer served she suddenly found new reserves of energy. And what reserves! She became all at once super-charged, barely allowing me time to get back onto the cart. Her 'feet' were going up and down, just itching to get away to a flying start. I could barely control her. Could hardly keep her down to a respectable pace. In fact I couldn't. We became a spectacle as she went tearing through the streets heading for home. There to 'undress', to indulge in a manger full of feed, a bucket of water, and to relax.

When we were stopped by a policeman at a crossing she would be all the time edging forward, impatient for the signal that would allow her to be on her way again. My remonstrations were useless, she had done a good job and now she was going to enjoy a good rest. A splendid example to some of the constantly complaining workers of today who only seem to recognise the second part of this maxim.

Some Sundays I would go out of my way to pay her a visit. Certainly if I happened to be nearby her stable I would never dream of passing without looking in. Then she would be demonstrating the art of complete relaxation.

She seemed to spend the entire day in bed. Lying comfortable and apparently quite happy on her bed of straw.

I would sit down with her and scratch behind her ear. This she loved and showed her enjoyment by the look on her face.

Quite frequently when I was leaving she would neigh and I would take this to mean that she had been pleased to see me. In any case, whether I had interpreted that neigh correctly or not her whole manner suggested that she was glad that I had called, and this was sufficient compensation for having gone out of my way.

On icy days it was not at all uncommon to see a fallen horse with men struggling to remove the harness and unhitch the cart to help the horse find its feet again. This always had me thankful that it was not me. And although we had some pretty near misses — Chiquita has gone right down onto her belly when her feet have gone from beneath her — yet never did she fail to right herself almost immediately. At those times I would beg her, 'Up Chiquita, up girl, don't fall.' And up she would get. I have seen every muscle in her splendid body heave and strain to prevent herself from losing control. That was Chiquita, a fine intelligent animal. I loved her, and I'd swear she loved me too.

11

On Wishing To Travel

That old sailor at the electrical engineers had implanted in me a desire to see as much of the rest of the world as possible. It was all right for him to say that England was as good a place as any, and better than most. He had seen so much else. When he spoke of Japan as being the prettiest country he had visited, 'especially when the cherry trees are in blossom,' he painted for me a picture of a country of exquisite charm. One that I would very much like to see for myself.

In any case I was a curious lad and in reading of other places I had realised that the world was a fascinating place, made up of a mixture of peoples all with customs and habits passed on by their forebears, each one different to the others. Each offering something of interest to the newcomer. This was my world, I reasoned. Every bit as much my world as was England my country. A citizen of England but a member of a world-wide community. And just as I longed to see what was around the corner so did I yearn to know what was over the hill, across the ocean. This was everyone's right.

With this in mind by the time I was twenty I had made several essays to leave the country in one way or another.

My first attempt came when I was sixteen. There was a constant advertisement in the daily papers asking young lads to emigrate to Canada under a particular Scheme. The basis of this was that boys from England would be placed with farmers in Canada who would agree to pay a certain sum of money and guaranteeing the lad a home and work for at least two years. During those two years the boy's pay would be banked for him and at the end of that time the contract was void. The farmer could then discharge the boy or the lad could leave.

Pictures were painted of the vast open-air life. The prairies, the plains. Endless vistas of grain waving in the wind as far as the eye could see. A man could feel at one with nature there — no hemmed in feeling, such as one might have in my home town, London.

I wrote in. This appealed to me. The very name, Canada, had a magic ring to it. In return in our letter-box one day was a largish envelope addressed to Master Syd Metcalfe. One of my very first postal communications. Inside was a wealth of information on the 'Scheme' showing youngsters what sort of life was on offer to them. As with all holiday brochures the weather in all the pictures was perfect. One saw photographs of young fellows already out there, standing bronzed and smiling alongside a tractor with cloudless sky above. This looked the life. Also in the envelope was a questionnaire to be filled in by Master Syd Metcalfe. One glance was enough to show that as far as mentality was concerned they were prepared to accept any but a perfect idiot. There was also a form to be filled in by the doctor and this too made no very great demands. I read it all, excitedly. It was all so easy, there was nothing to stop me.

The next day this same envelope was on its way back to the offices of the organisers (I think it was the Canadian Pacific Shipping Co. in Trafalgar Square) with questionnaire and medical form completed.

For the next few days my world was filled with fixing fences, harvesting grain, driving a tractor and various other jobs that I knew to be part of farm life. All being done by a smiling lad under a cloudless sky, sun-tanned and happy.

Then came my next envelope. Not so big this one. Inside it told me that I was accepted. All that was now necessary was to have one of my parents, or guardian, sign the enclosed form and to bring this with me along with five pounds 'landing money' when reporting to the office ready to leave en route for Canada in two weeks time. I was given a date.

'All that was now necessary' the letter had said — they might just as well have been asking me to bring a piece of rock from the moon, for I had virtually no parents and I didn't have enough money to live on, let alone five pounds left over for 'landing money'. I wrote telling them of this and was asked to call at their office. This I did and was shown into the room of my correspondent.

'Sit down, son,' said he, 'I liked the sound of your letter, I thought I'd like to see you. Now you say you have an older brother.'

119

'Yes, sir.'

'Well, he can sign as your guardian. That's that fixed. Now about the money, you say here that you haven't a hope of finding five pounds.'

'No, sir. That's right.'

'Well, supposing I offer to lend you the money, out of my own pocket. Would you promise to pay me back?'

'Oh, yes, sir.'

'Yes, I believe you would. But I wouldn't want you to send me a little bit here and there. I would want you to save up and when you have the five pounds to send it over in a lump sum. Would you do that?'

'Yes, sir, I promise.' I would have promised him the Northwest corner of Canada had he asked for it. The lovely man had just made it possible for me to see my first country outside England. I would have promised him anything.

It was with feet barely touching the ground that I went home. As I looked around me it was with the realisation that many of these things I was seeing for the last time. Very soon I would be a citizen of Canada. It sounded good to me.

Now, Arthur knew all about this venture. I had kept him in touch with all that had happened. His attitude towards the whole thing seemed to be one of casual indifference. 'If that was what I wanted.'

But when he found himself confronted with the form to sign as my guardian he was a picture of confusion and indecision.

120

'Supposing you don't like it there, Syd,' he intimated.

'Well, I'll save up to come back. But I'll like it, I'm sure I'll like it.'

'I don't know, I don't fancy the idea of signing this. It makes me feel as though I'm sending you away. It's such a long way. I wouldn't mind if we could still see each other from time to time.'

He didn't want to sign. The responsibility was too much for him. This was perfectly plain.

'Does it mean so much to you?' he asked. 'There'll be other opportunities, perhaps even where you won't have to feel so cut off.'

'No, Art, it doesn't mean all that much.'

That was the end. I wrote to the kind man in Trafalgar Square, thanked him for his offer and told him that I was relinquishing the idea. It's very probable that I even used such an expression for I was very fond of big words as a boy, they gave me the opportunity to let people see how clever I was.

That is as near as I ever came to Canada. Extraordinarily enough I came about as close as that a second time, much later in life. It was some time after the Second War, I was a man in my forties and a cook in the Merchant Navy.

On seeking a ship I was told that there was one wanting a cook in Surrey Docks. Her crew were home on leave and they needed a cook for the few who were remaining on board. Her next voyage was to be to — Canada — and if the cook chose not to rejoin her I could sail with her. 'So,' thought I, as I made my way to Surrey Docks,

'I might get there after all, all these years later.' But no. It was not to be. The cook did choose to rejoin her and she sailed without me.

There was no disappointment this second time. There would be other ships, as there were, but the first time it was a great blow to me. The opportunity to travel had knocked at my door and I had not opened it. At that age set-backs are so serious. 'I'll never get the opportunity again, I'll never see other countries now,' I thought.

With the passing of the years Arthur would occasionally ask me whether I regretted him not signing that form and always I said 'No'.

Such is the capriciousness of life, I have travelled quite extensively since. Almost certainly much more so than had I been based on a farm somewhere in Ontario, Canada.

While still in my early teens I one day wrote to a shipping company asking them if there was any way that I could be taken onto one of their ships.

Yes, there was. I was to write to the Gravesend Sea School, where, if I were accepted they would train me for a position as an officer of some sort for that particular company. This was great news. Even Arthur couldn't very much mind me becoming a seaman. So off went my letter, replete with big words to let them see what a bright lad they were getting. A few days passed, then back came the officious looking large well-filled envelope, post-marked Gravesend.

Conditions of entry were laid out — a boy would be trained in various capacities for a role with one or other of the shipping companies. Length of training depended upon what branch of service he was selected for. The School would, at the end of his training, hold themselves responsible for finding him his first position. After that he would be free to find his own engagements. Always this first assignment that the School found for the youngster was a contract entered into by both parties, the shipping company and the School on the boy's behalf, which committed them both to a period of engagement. By this arrangement the School was able to recover some part of the costs of training.

None of this interested me much. 'Let's get on with whether I could join or not.' Yes, there was the form to be filled in by a doctor and the usual questionnaire. A brief glance was enough to tell me I would have no trouble there.

So once again a large envelope filled with answered questions and a young man's hopes was placed carefully into the local pillar box, and once again the young man settled back to await his fate. This time, however, instead of my head being filled with visions of waving corn it was as a young naval officer that I saw myself. Not that I wanted to raise my hopes unwarrantedly but these pictures would keep coming into my mind.

The letter box was watched assiduously until one day it came. Another official-looking letter from Gravesend. Inside it said that I was accepted for training as a naval officer in the Merchant Navy and I was to report to the School

123

with 'the following items of kit'. These were such as, two towels, two shirts, white, short sleeves, two pairs pyjamas, one pair plimsoll shoes, and on and on it went. The further I read the more dismayed I became. My wardrobe didn't contain one solitary item that was requested, and to buy them would have cost the whole of five pounds. This was distressing. I was accepted, surely they wouldn't refuse to admit me on such a flimsy pretext as having insufficient of the required clothing? I wrote explaining my position. 'A young lad, all alone, no parents, not earning much money, unable to save anything out of my wages, could they possibly advance me the money for the gear and stop it from my future earnings?'

Then I waited. I felt hopeful. It seemed a reasonable enough request. The reply was 'No'. They had never done this before and it was not the policy of the School to set a precedent on my account. They advised me to seek some other way of raising the money. And they wished me luck.

However, this I was unable to do and it was as a very disappointed lad that I finally had to accept that I was not going to be trained for a life at sea by the Gravesend Sea School.

There was the time when an advertisement told me that a boy from fifteen to seventeen could be recruited into the Royal Air Force to be trained in any one of a wide range of the most attractive trades. There were electricians, radio mechanics, aeroplane fitters, motor mechanics all waiting to be filled by youngsters such as me. At least that is what the advertisement said. And what is more, when these youngsters such as me were trained into these worthwhile positions they could then be posted abroad to names such as Egypt, Hong Kong, India, etc.

This had me thinking. I liked the sound of it. But I didn't very much like the idea of having to sign on for a certain term of service. Suppose it didn't suit me. One couldn't just walk out as they could with a job. However, there seemed no other way in which I could be taken to Egypt, Hong Kong, India, etc. and so I applied. This time the application was made in person. I presented myself at the RAF Recruiting Offices in Whitehall.

It was with a certain amount of apprehension that I entered this imposing building. With a feeling that I was about to be sacrificed. Already the very tone of the place seemed to sap me of some of my independence. It was with great care that I trod the corridors, making sure not to make too much noise. In writing this it occurs to me what a vast difference there is between the child of today and the child that I was. Children today are filled with confidence, sure of themselves. Then every adult was my superior and I readily recognised this. They all had the authority to admonish me for doing anything that they considered to be wrong. They were the judges of how I should behave. 'Don't do that you young rascal,' I would be told at times and, generally, the young rascal stopped doing 'that'.

We treated everyone with a certain amount of

125

deference. And let a person speak with accents that suggested a superior education and we became immediately humble and respectful. More than that, whenever I encountered anyone who I recognised to be speaking grammatically correct and in cultured tones I was always struck stutteringly dumb, if that is at all possible. They took away the last vestiges of the already minute amount of confidence that I was blessed, or cursed, with. Cultured tones overawed me. And let me know, by chance or design that the person confronting me was a Public School man and I straight away saw him as a man of extreme intelligence and myself as an utter fool. I became acutely and embarrassingly aware of my own speech shortcomings and only spoke when I had to. I knew my English to be bad but was unable to correct it. It was for that reason that if I were conversing in a bus or a waiting room, or any public place where I could be overheard I always spoke in whispers.

A man's worth and quality in my young days were measured by the amount of plum in mouth he could produce.

So there was I in this awesome building a bundle of humility surrounded by swarms of educated sounding officials. Actually I was not kept in suspense for long for the officer who interviewed me very soon found that my schooling was inadequate to fit me for the role of trainee for the positions that they were advertising. So Egypt, Hong Kong and India were struck off the list of places I was hoping to see. That day I felt that if I couldn't join a branch of the Services there seemed very little hope of my ever leaving the country. Until then I had considered that the Services were always open to me, if only as a last resort.

Just one more attempt left me more depressed than ever. This was when I failed to enlist into the Royal Navy. This time my rejection was on account of having two front teeth that needed drilling and filling. It sounds incredible to me now that an otherwise perfectly healthy young fellow who had cycled all over the south of England and who regularly thrashed imaginary sparring partners as fast as they climbed into the ring could be considered as unfit for His Majesty's Navy on account of a spot of decay affecting two front teeth. 'What if I had the teeth attended to?' I asked.

'No use, son,' I was told, 'if I pass you the doctor will only turn you down when he sees you. Sorry.'

Sorry! He wasn't half as sorry as I was. This seemed the last straw. I could have done anything the navy had asked of me. I knew that. There was nothing that they could have required of me that would have been hindered by me having two well-fitting false front teeth. But no, it had to be 'Sorry, sonny.' The whole world seemed to be against me.

As I came away from that office I had the dreadful feeling that the rest of my life was going to be played out there where I had been born. I would never see outside my own country.

There was only the army left, but, ugh.

So it was back again to civilian life, back to

the hum-drum, the tedium, the routine.

Perhaps it would be as well to explain here to the puzzled young man of today who has no idea what conditions of the past were like that that elusive five pounds which I found it so hard to obtain was probably the equivalent to a hundred pounds today. As for taking a second job, working overtime or any of the other means that would come so readily to him these days if he wished to supplement his pay, in those days no matter how willing or eager one was to earn a little bit of extra cash the jobs were just not on offer. An advertised vacancy brought such a host of applicants that the road outside the firm sometimes became impassable.

I mention this in case the younger readers wonder why I hadn't the initiative to go out and earn that five pounds one way or another. The older reader will already have understood. Work was just not available. One counted himself lucky to be in a job of any kind at all, however poorly paid they were.

So with my failure to enlist into the Royal Navy went my last hope of travel abroad. I settled down to make the most of what was left.

12

On Being Out Of Work

After a succession of jobs our speck of humanity eventually found himself out of work. The unemployment situation in Britain had been steadily deteriorating over the years and now it had caught up with our young hero. Although a more un-hero-like character it would be hard to find. For at this stage of his development, about nineteen or twenty years of age, a fully formed person, whose present characteristics would form the basis of his character for the rest of his life, he was very seriously lacking in confidence and determination.

There was an expression that was being very widely used at the time that has since become standard psychological terminology, 'inferiority complex'. We applied it to all and sundry. It covered all forms of timidity in our wide, indiscriminate use, but I think that it fits the young man that was now me more aptly than any other.

Everyone somehow appeared superior to me in my eyes. In the company of others I always felt the odd man out. All present seemed to be suited to the occasion, in their right place, but me. This feeling has never left me. With varying degrees of force it recurs over and over again. That is why I avoid company, and when I cannot avoid it I stay only until I can conveniently slip away. Only alone, or with someone with whom I have become completely familiar is the character that is the inner me happy and at ease.

It is easy to equate this attitude with that of the little boy who fully realised that he was by far the least popular in the family. It was no more than a carry-over. It was the family setting repeating itself in all other walks of life. The reproachful 'Keep quiet you,' was still hanging over my head conditioning my every reaction. In company, as when as a child seated around the family table, I have the feeling of not belonging. And no amount of reasoning can alter this. I can tell myself that I am as good as the next man but that doesn't affect my feeling of inferiority.

Hence the urge to show others, by performance, that I am as good as they are. That little boy was not allowed to make assertions — he could not tell those other members of the family that he was every as important as they were. The only option left to him was to let them see by that which he was able to do — sort of slyly bring to their notice his capabilities by doing something unannounced that would cause them to realise that he wasn't without a certain amount of prowess, and thereby bring some credit upon himself. And life has proceeded that way. Always has there been as part of my nature a reluctance to take part in anything until I had achieved some degree of skill at it. This also ensured me not tackling anything of which I was unsure. An attitude that engendered a reluctance to accept a job that had any responsibility associated with it. A certain method of ensuring that one will remain a nobody, a nonentity.

And so the speck of humanity that was I at the beginning has neither grown nor diminished. It has remained a small spark of life struggling to give off a little light. Restricted by all the stultifying influences of birth, environmental factors within the family and the cramping effect of the caste-ridden society into which he had to live out his youth.

This led to me being always careful to keep to places and situations where I would not feel out of my element, where I could not be embarrassed.

If I were wanting to eat while out, for example, I would choose a 'working man's coffee shop' rather than a respectable looking cafe or restaurant. In the coffee shop I would know what to expect. If I ordered a meal it would arrive all on the one plate, just as it would have done at home, just as I was used to. And the person who brought it would be some ordinary looking individual, one of my own kind.

In fancy cafe or restaurant I was not sure what I was going to find. A meal might be served in a fashion to which I was not accustomed. I might have to wonder how to use the utensils, or whether to tip the waitress, and if so how much? No, let's have no wondering whether we are doing the right thing or not, let's go to that 'working man's' on the corner, I like it there.

To be out of work at those times could have

131

done nothing good for our confidence either, for we then became one of a huge mass of useless, unwanted, dispirited men who knew that once they had achieved this position they had little hope of ever working again in the foreseeable future. By the time I joined their ranks there were already men who had been out of work for some years. The effect of this pitiable situation could be plainly seen in their faces. Their whole manner suggested their fatalistic acceptance of the uselessness of it all. They were like a machine that had broken down and was now becoming rusty. They were caught up in conditions that inevitably resulted in a steady moral decline. It took an immensely strong and stable character to keep a hold upon himself and retain any degree of hope. For the most part they saw the futility of it all and just gave up. They stopped hoping. When they were married men with children and could see that they were not bringing enough money into the family to provide for all that was needed, when they could see their wife struggling to put a meal onto the table when it came time to eat, and when they could see their children shabbily clothed and were totally unable to anything to help, how must they have felt? If a man, or a woman, lost hope, became bitter and sunk their principles — if, in fact, they did anything that society did not approve of because they could not stand seeing what they came home to every day, who could blame them? Whole ethnic groups have become near extinct because their way of life has been taken away from them and replaced by

132

nothing worthwhile. How descriptive that would be of what had happened to the unemployed.

In my case, I was single. I was young. The future never seems quite so hopeless to the young. Besides which, being hard-up was not a new thing to me. I had never had much money anyway.

For a while being out of work even had its compensations. In the summer, when the weather was fine it enabled many of us to spend so much time over the local open-air swimming baths. Some of us became almost unrecognisable owing to the magnificent suntan we were sporting. As well search the streets for a nugget of gold as look for a job.

It was at these local baths that I met the husband of Nellie. He was of no account and wouldn't have figured in my story had he not married Nellie. And neither would she had she not lost interest in him and been eager for attention from other quarters.

His name was Bob and we struck up a conversation one day whilst soaking in the sun's rays as we lay alongside each other, our bodies nearly touching, on the lawns surrounding the bath. These lawns were filled to the point where one had to search to find a spot where they could lie down. They were filled to overflowing with unemployed bodies. We became the 'idle poor'. There was indeed nothing better for us to do. To look for a job would have been laughable, and so, having signed on at the Labour Exchange, where we reported with towel and swimming costume under our arm we then headed, all

133

haste, to the baths to pass away much of the rest of the day.

Bob had asked me if I would like to come to his place for a bite to eat and to meet the wife. He was on perfectly safe ground with the offer of a bite to eat but the invitation to meet the wife was both unwise and foolhardy.

She was working, it seemed, and so he was able to put on a bit more of a show with regards to laying the table for a meal than was the average unemployed person. We were both eating (the baths used to put an edge on our appetites of razor sharpness) when she arrived. Immediately the room was filled with tension. Her whole manner suggested that she was keenly interested and I have no doubt my manner conveyed a similar impression for I found her most attractive. She was passing pretty, with a plump but shapely figure that filled one with covetous thoughts. But her most striking feature was her beautiful blue eyes. They held me captivated.

My popping around for a bite became extended to chatting throughout the entire evening. I didn't want to leave. I didn't want to part from her. And no-one encouraged me to go either. Once or twice, when I thought I might be overstaying my welcome, it was made quite clear that in fact they were finding the evening very enjoyable. And so I stayed.

Later on Nellie suggested that Bob pop along to the corner for a bottle of milk and the door had hardly closed behind him than we were in each other's arms. Her kisses were as soft and

134

warm as I would have expected them to be. She was made to love and it seemed that her husband had been neglecting her lately. She didn't tell me this that first evening, that came out later, but she did tell me all I wanted to know, even in the short time that it took Bob to buy the milk and return to the house. In that short while we had made enough fuss of one another to both know that this was but the start of something. No more than an introduction to other things.

I would venture to say that I walked home from that house that night in love. She swore thereafter that she felt the same way from the moment she entered the room and saw me sitting there. By the time Bob came back our plans were already laid for our next meeting — tomorrow night, after she had had dinner, we were to meet at a particular corner.

If I should have felt any conscience pangs at the time I didn't. All my emotions were concerned with my feelings for this lovely, warm-blooded, lively creature who had dropped straight out of heaven right into my arms. Rather than conscience stricken I felt extremely lucky.

We met the next evening and that was the first of many more meetings to come. Both found the other to be what they had hoped and our relationship was immediately one of complete mutual understanding and admiration. Nellie was tremendously sentimental, with an over-abundance of affection. Today we would refer to her as sexy. I like the old-fashioned terms of reference best. She was very loving and, of course, this suited me fine. We met at every conceivable opportunity and inevitably we were found out.

Bob came to realise that the little woman wasn't around the house as much as she used to be and he took to following her. This led him straight to me. But he didn't show himself on that occasion. The first we knew about it was when he told Nellie that he had shadowed her and that he now knew how she was spending her evenings and who with. Nellie didn't deny anything. In fact, she told me later, she felt glad that he knew. Now she could tell him everything. Now our love could come out into the sunlight and show itself for the fine, clean, upright thing that it was, rather than having to hide itself in corners and only come out after dark. She told Bob that she loved me and that she was sure that I loved her too. His reaction was to tell her that in that case she had better 'clear off and live with me'. I hadn't realised he could be so independent. He invited her to ask me around to their place so that we could discuss some settlement of the matter.

And it was then that I realised that my love had very strict limitations. It was not prepared to take unto itself a 'wife', no matter how blue were her eyes. Falling in love had been very exciting and it had helped me to make the past months most satisfying but to take on the responsibility of a life-long relationship, especially when I was already out of work had no appeal whatsoever.

We had our discussion, during which I was made to feel very silly. Bob had the whip-hand and he used it to full advantage.

'I told you he wouldn't want you if he had to keep you,' he said to her, sneeringly.

'If I weren't out of work, it would be a different thing,' I said, but I don't think my voice carried much conviction. Certainly it didn't convince me, for I knew that I didn't want her as a full-time partner. And had I but realised it I was behaving as I would behave ever after, for this has been the basis of all my relationships with women every since. Deeply emotional but not very long-lasting.

And so we parted. But Nellie and I would still meet at times. We could no longer boast of our love but we still enjoyed each other's company.

It was Nellie who first wakened me to the realisation that in most women there is an earthy honesty, verging near to crudity at times which one seldom meets in a man. A woman will often discuss matters that to me are embarrassing in a fashion that shows her to be much more basic than a man, much less tempered by the demands of society, more natural.

I am thinking of the time when Nellie eventually told me she no longer wished to see me. This was some years after we had first met. Her relationship with her husband had remained unsatisfactory. In fact Nellie would have found it difficult to settle down contentedly with any one man. Now she was telling me that she thought it best we part.

'I think it would be best if we don't see each other any more, dear,' she had said. 'I've been meaning to tell you this for some time, I've been seeing another chap. That's why sometimes I've said I couldn't get out.'

'Are you in love with this other fellow?' I asked. Thinking that with her professed great regard for me this other character, whoever he was, must have swept her off her feet.

'No,' she answered, 'It's not that. I'm not particularly fond of him even, but he is bigger built than you are. And you know how important that is to me.'

Now this is something that I could never imagine a man saying to a woman. Yet since then, from time to time, women have made, not the same remark, but others of a like kind that have shown that the veneer that we call refinement is more thinly spread over a woman than a man.

It has struck me too through life that if one or the other is going to leave the toilet door open while they are inside it is more likely to be the female of the species than the male. The male is more readily made to feel ill at ease. Once during my years in the army we had to use a rough and ready toilet in which we were all exposed to one another. All of us hated it and cut down our visits to an absolute minimum. We would sit facing or alongside one another trying to be casual but feeling utterly uncomfortable and foolish. Had we been women I feel certain that we would have used the occasion to discuss current affairs, like the new fashion in footwear or the merits or demerits of our respective hairdressers. But of one thing I'm certain, we would have refused to feel silly.

I feel equally certain that women are less squeamish than men. If by chance all nursing positions had suddenly to be filled by men I'm sure there would be far fewer applicants, for the very reason that men would find some of the hospital sights more distressing.

It was during my unemployed period that Arthur, who was occasionally laid off from work for a week or two, but for the most part continued working, became twenty-one and decided to have a party to celebrate. We were still at Mrs Barrett's little back room, so we could be sure of good bread for the occasion.

Doona was to come along and, to provide a second girl to balance with the two boys, she was to bring the daughter of the landlady at the house where she was staying.

So provisions were laid in and both Arthur and I set about arranging a good meal, with plenty to drink, and nuts, fruits and sweets to help pass the time afterwards.

The gramophone was placed in position and our stock of records was dusted off with 'Carolina Moon' placed on top.

Then the girls arrived.

'This is Emmie,' said Doona, and we both found ourselves gazing into the rich, brown eyes of one of the most beautiful faces we had ever seen. She was lovely, with a smile that made everyone feel happy and an abundance of long, wavy, dark hair. She was a dream.

'Hello, Emmie, come in,' we both hurried to say, each putting on his best girl-captivating manner. 'Come in.' And that night our little room came alive.

Arthur has since told me that some time during the night he vowed the 'dream' would be his girl. Well, he wasn't going to have things all his own way for someone else had made that same vow too. One of us had to miss, of course. We could both have missed, but today Emmie is Arthur's wife.

She had the choice of the two of us. I think she chose right.

In any case I didn't lose her, for I have had the pleasure of her presence right though the years.

Much of my life has been spent out of England but it has always been Emmie who has kept me up to date with family news. And when I have returned to England it has always been, almost without exception, to Arthur and Emmie that I have gone to stay. And there I have always had all the comforts of a well-kept home. It is then that I learn of the meaning of the expression 'home made', for her cakes have me making a glutton of myself.

I might say here that even my dad had cause to feel thankful that Emmie became one of the family for when we eventually caught up with him again he had many a hearty meal at Arthur's and Emmie's and demolished many a bread-pudding (a favourite of his) made specially for him.

13

I Join The Army

Summer passed into winter with me still out of work. Nellie wore her fur coat and the open-air baths closed down. To help pass the time away now that it was no longer possible to lie around sunbathing I took to spending quite frequent afternoons at the pictures. Afternoon matinees were as cheap as threepence or fourpence. These sessions might be considered a waste of money in view of the fact that I had so little even for necessities but at least it took my mind off all other things. Even a touch of hunger could be forgotten in the engrossment of a good film.

The unemployed figures were now rising all the time and life became quite boring with the prospects of ever working again becoming fainter and fainter. To make matters worse my clothes were beginning to look shabby and there was no way in which I could replace them.

My twenty-first birthday was not far off — there was to be no party for this one — and there seemed little option but to try to enrol into the army. Experience had told me not to be too enthusiastic about being accepted, they were being a bit choosy on account of having such a constant stream of applicants. I reasoned that if I joined for the lowest term possible I could then leave with a very fair chance that the economic situation 'outside' would have improved and jobs be more easy to find. It was to be a stop-gap. Somewhere to tide me over until things improved. I didn't really want to join, any more than did the average fellow in that constant stream of applicants, but it offered 'work', a wage and a restoration of some part of our dignity. To be a soldier was perhaps only one degree on the social scale above that of being an out of work, but at least it was above.

So came the day when I was to offer myself to the army. Once again I presented myself to Whitehall. Yes, they were quite interested.

'Take a seat over there along with the others,' I was told.

There they were, a whole cluster of them, all young fellows around my own age, all joining the army against their wishes for the same reason, they were fed up with hanging around doing nothing.

Questions were asked — nationality of father? Nationality of mother? Had I ever tried to join the Forces before? and eventually I found myself before the doctor. His whole manner suggested that he was finding all this tedious. One healthy fellow after another to examine, it was like stamping a whole pile of envelopes, a kid could have done it, routine stuff. It offered him no challenge whatsoever. Then all of a sudden his eyes lit up. He was gazing into my mouth.

'Say ah,' he said.

I said 'Ah'.

'Again.'

I said it again, 'Ah'.

'And again.'

Once more, 'Ah,' I was becoming quite accomplished, I'd swear this was a far nicer one than the first. But it was not the quality of the tone that captured his professional interest, he was watching my tonsils swing backwards and forwards as I uttered my monosyllabic sound.

'Hmm, do you get many sore throats?' he asked.

'No, sir, not a lot.' What's he getting at? I wondered.

'Your tonsils are very enlarged,' he muttered, more to himself than to me. 'Right, put your clothes on and wait outside.'

This looked ominous. Don't say I was to be rejected from the army. Anyone can join the army. I looked around me and there were chaps there who I could have wiped the floor with (the ability to fight was my measuring stick at that time. If I could beat another fellow in a fight then I was the better man), but the army apparently did not see it that way. They gave points according to the size of one's tonsils, and on that score I was adjudged the loser. I was told that they could not take me.

'What if I have my tonsils out?' I asked.

'Yes, you can do that. Have them out and come back again.'

'But I meant have them out in the Army.'

No, this could not be done, I would have to arrange to have them out outside and come back and try again.

So once again I walked away from Whitehall

wondering just what sort of jinx was hanging over me.

But this time they had offered me a loop-hole. 'Have them out and come back,' he had said. OK I'll do that.

Within a week the Royal Free Hospital in Grays Inn Road had taken me in. They had listened to my story about wishing to join the army and had sympathised.

Unfortunately during the operation I swallowed my tongue and in pulling it back a certain amount of irritation had taken place and the tongue became ulcerated. In addition I had lost my voice. For a week I lay there somewhat sick and unable to make other than animal noises. Then quickly started to recover.

It was Christmas time and out of the windows the snow could be seen on the roofs of some of the hospital buildings. It looked mighty cold, but inside all was cosy and warm.

As my vigour came back so did my impatience to be on with my mission. Let's get out of here and into the army. I had a fear that they might fill up and have no need for another such as me. When I asked if I could be discharged the reply was that they would gladly do so on condition that I go straight home to bed and stay there for a week with someone taking care of me. This I promised to do, but I would have promised anything, I was so eager to get back to Whitehall before the army became overflowing. I felt one hundred per cent fit, what was the point to hanging around?

So I was discharged.

Two days later I was in Whitehall again. Snow was still lying all round. It was freezing.

This time the doctor remarked on how sore my throat was but passed me. It was a pity he did. In actual fact I was a far fitter person when I had applied the first time, with the enlarged tonsils. I can see now that it was most unwise of him not to have sent me back home the second time to wait until the throat had recovered more from the effects of the operation. As it was I was passed as fit and sent to Catterick Camp in the heart of the Yorkshire moors.

Catterick Camp is the depot for the Royal Corps of Signals, where I was being sent for training as a wireless operator. We had settled on this when the Recruiting Sergeant had asked, 'What regiment do you want to join?' Now, I had always known that no form of infantry would be in my line. Going over the top with bayonets poised ready for insertion into the first enemy belly that came along was not my idea of sensible behaviour. Also I was not particularly keen on the infantryman's type of uniform. It was not glamorous enough for me. My favourite was the one with the riding breeches. That, I felt, showed off my figure to its best advantage. I put this preference to the sergeant.

'What regiments are there that wear riding breeches?' I asked.

'Well, we have the Royal Artillery and the Royal Corps of Signals.'

The Royal Artillery, I knew something about them. They were the ones that had horses. Someone had once told me never to join a

145

regiment that had horses. It means your work is never done. Seven days a week the horse always has to be attended to.

'I'll join the Royal Corps of Signals,' I said.

And so I was signed on for eight years with the colours and four with the reserves.

On arriving at Catterick Camp I thought I had never known anything so cold. Where the snow had been inches thick in London here it was over a foot in places. As for barrack life to which I was now subjected: there was nothing that one could even mildly regard as comfortable. Our huts were like great big barns. Barren of any adornment, they were guaranteed to depress the spirits of the most optimistic of men.

However we eventually became accustomed to them. In fact, when later we all got to know each other, our room was often a hive of activity and laughter.

The training that followed our arrival irked me beyond measure and I hardly did a thing without complaining to my mates that it was utterly stupid. Yet there were signs that all this stupidity finally had a beneficial effect. For one thing I'm certain I still, quite unintentionally, hold myself in soldierly fashion. Whether this is commendable or not is a matter of opinion but certainly it looks good to me to see an elderly man holding himself erect. It does something for one's agility too, I find.

But far from deriving any benefit in the early days after my arrival on the Yorkshire Moors, the intensely cold weather coming on top of my recent operation nearly killed me. Within a few days I was lying seriously ill in hospital. My throat, which was not yet fully healed was an easy prey to the first germ seeking a comfortable breeding ground.

Immediately my head hit the hospital pillow I fell into a heavy delirium. It was diphtheria and my temperature was sky high.

The Medical Officer realised at once that my condition was desperate and the Camp authorities sent for Arthur. He was asked to come up as soon as possible and be prepared to stay. On arrival he was told he could put up at the large army canteen run by NAAFI, and to look in and see me any time he wished.

So, in my great eagerness to leave the Royal Free Hospital and make sure of a place in the Army I very nearly enrolled for a place on high, if that is where I am destined for.

After six weeks my youth and my condition saw me through. I was released from hospital and took my place back with my new squad.

Then began a friendship which was the kind that comes but once in a lifetime, if ever.

His name was Jack Higgins.

Why on earth I took to him, or he to me I shall never know. We had absolutely nothing in common. He was a more serious young fellow than me. Had been an amateur radio operator. Hence his reason for joining the Signals. Sport didn't interest him — it seldom does the studious type. But away from his hobbies he liked girls.

His home was in Hartlepool and our homes were as far apart as were our natures. At that time I was not at all serious and would break my neck if it would raise a laugh. I was fond of all sport and was not particularly interested in dames. They interfered with one's interest in more manly activities.

But that first night when I joined the squad the others all knew each other, the squad having been formed while I was in hospital and Jack, wanting to help me feel at home had sat on my bed and chatted to me. We talked all the evening and that was it. That was the beginning of a friendship of great depth that lasted for the whole of the eight years that I was to serve.

From that evening on we had a complete understanding. Every night we would sit on one or the other's bed and chat. These talks were most enjoyable because we were so at ease in each other's company. There was really little opportunity to go out at that stage for our programme was so full. A recruit in training was kept busy for every minute of the day and right on through his 'off' time. There really was no 'off' time — I suppose by that I mean the time when our squad NCO wasn't lording it over us with his big, raucous, ignorant witticisms. Corporal Dendy was ours, and he never stopped telling us what a heap of rubbish we were. So that when we came back to the barrack room, even though we had so much to do in preparation for tomorrow's events, the mere fact that no-one was there picking us to pieces in the most impolite fashion meant that it felt like time off.

So Jack and I would be polishing the studs

on the bottoms of our boots while seated on the bed, but at the same time keeping up an endless conversation.

Then sometime during the evening we would down tools and hie ourselves off to the NAAFI for a cup of tea, a cake and to carry on our conversation in more congenial surroundings.

Not that we had to be always talking. Ours became the perfect relationship where a silence was no longer embarrassing.

After our period of training on the barrack square, where Corporal Dendy must have felt something like Hitler at the fall of France, we were given two weeks leave. This we spent at Jack's home in Hartlepool.

Here I was introduced to his parents, two quite elderly people. It seems they married late in life and Jack was their last child. That meant that Jack had always had an old mother and father. It was for this reason that he had not interested himself in sport. His dad had never played with him and had stopped him from using such things as skates or riding a bike. Too dangerous, he thought. How different to my dad who used to kick a football at me that would have killed me had it hit me. And what an illustration this is to fathers of the effect they have upon the character of their young sons.

On arrival at Hartlepool Jack had a girl all teed up for me. And he had given the matter some careful thought. He told me later that she was quite well-known in the district as the girl who was raped as a child and had been acutely interested in boys ever since. He had thought

149

that this aspect of her character might help to make my leave particularly interesting. He was right. Before he told me this I had thought that his choice of a girlfriend who had turned out to be such damned good company had been pure chance. I was thinking how lucky I was. Instead of which it was all praise to Jack.

Hartlepool being a coastal town with a promenade this girl, whose name I have forgotten (it was never very important, anyway) and I used to finish off every evening out with a session in one of the of the shelters along the prom.

It was good to be free of Corporal Dendy's big mouth for a fortnight. I found the change of company most exhilarating.

With our holiday over it was back to the barracks. But this time we were no longer rookies. Now we were to report to the centre where we would be taught our trade.

Before we left Big Mouth gave us a talk that changed our whole opinion of him. He told us that we were one of the finest squads that he had ever had the pleasure of training. 'But you wouldn't have been if I'd treated you with kid gloves,' he said. 'Didn't it give you a thrill,' he asked, 'realising you were moving around the square like a well-oiled machine?' Yes, I must admit it did.

'And,' he continued, 'when I stood you at ease on the square and then proceeded to 'dress you down' it was so that you could have a good long rest. The square is overlooked by the colonel's window and if he had seen you just standing there with me doing nothing he would have wanted to know why I wasn't working you harder. Anyway, goodbye and good luck in your army career.'

After that we all clubbed together and bought him an end of training present. You see, he wasn't a loud-mouthed, ignoramus, after all. He was something of a psychologist.

As embryo radio operators Jack stood out. He already had some speed at Morse and some understanding of the principles of radio. The rest of us were complete beginners.

Life in this part of the camp became slightly more refined. The 'rooms' had a little more comfort, the NCOs looked at us and spoke to us as though we might even understand what they were saying. No-one pretended now that we were a heap of rubbish and the feeling of worthlessness that Corporal Dendy had so skilfully instilled into us began slowly to evaporate until signs of an intense regard for ourselves began once again to reappear. We felt more like human beings and the evenings were no longer spent with us busily engaged in useless occupations like polishing the backs of our cap badges. We could go out in the evenings, in civilian clothes if we wished.

By now Jack and I were inseparable. We became known as 'The Twins' and I can remember I actually missed him if he weren't there. This is a relationship, perfectly decent, akin to the love of a man for a woman. There is in it an affinity that makes one almost a part of the other. Certainly there is a mental need of one for the other. And the happiness

151

and contentment that the lover finds in the presence of his loved one is also experienced in the relationship of perfect friendship. Likewise the sense of loss when the loved one is not there is also felt. If one carried this comparison further I suppose it is a form of love.

Let us forget for a moment today's obsession with everything having a sexual basis, for this oneness that Jack and I felt in each other's company had nothing to do with sex. And I'm equally sure that the early, young love that most of us have experienced at some time or another for a girl also has no foundation in sex. Can't you remember loving a girl beyond that? Can't you remember ever loving a girl so much that the thought of having intercourse with her would be tantamount to defiling her? I can. She seemed too fine to engage in such a crude practice. She was above that. That was love without a sex basis. And what is more, when sex enters into a relationship of that kind it often tends to destroy it. The very purity that had you worshipping her is no longer there — she has become human, and from my experience there is nothing more fatal to love than the realisation that the loved one is but another human being after all.

So, there was Jack and I, in perfect harmony. And we remained that way right through the years.

Back in Catterick Camp winter passed to summer and with it was created memories of sitting outside an old country pub drinking a glass of good Yorkshire ale with the quiet of the moors all around. This pub was not far from the camp, a mile or so down a remote country road. A favourite walk of Jack's and mine. We liked the ale at the end of it too.

Eventually we both passed out as wireless operators and time for posting to other pastures arrived. Being unable to stand the strain of wondering whether we would be fortunate enough to be posted to the same place the Sergeant Major was approached and asked if it would be possible to send us both the same unit, 'Sir'.

Gruffly, not wishing to appear too kindly he said that that might be possible, but he wasn't promising anything. Profuse 'Thank you, Sirs,' from Jack and I and we withdrew hopefully.

When the postings were made known we were both down to go to Aldershot. Some say 'Good old Sergeant Major'.

Looking back to the time spent at Aldershot, seeing mostly only the happy times that we had there, this seems a period of my life when things were at their best. We started to play games that we had previously considered beyond us. Beyond our means, at any rate. Tennis became a great favourite of ours and Jack and I spent many a pleasant couple of hours after duty on the tennis courts. Speaking of sport reminds me to mention that at Catterick Camp anyone interested in boxing was encouraged to take part in weekly tournaments that were run in the ring which was housed in a shed-like affair that was known as 'The Blood Tub'. Everything had a name suited to it in the army. There was, for example, the fatigue that was allocated each morning to a number of we trainees which we designated 'the big dig'. This was an area that was being dug up to provide a sports ground. Each day a civilian landscape gardener was given a group of forty or fifty 'soldiers' and with this crude labour force, digging at his command, he eventually produced a first-class sports arena. I was back there after the evacuation of Dunkirk and anyone who did not know would never have believed that such a fine stadium was created in such an irregular manner.

But the Blood Tub: of course my name went forward, and in fact it appeared quite regularly. This compensated me for my failure at Blackfriars Ring, as my opponents were not nearly so skilled nor so keen as was the chap who bloodied my nose and finished me off in two rounds. In fact I acquired quite a reputation at Catterick and can only remember losing once. That was to an NCO who had been welterweight champion of the Army in India.

Then came something which had it not been for Jack's ingenuity and quickness of thought might have made our friendship a little less close. I was sent on a cookery course and on its completion was put in the cookhouse. At first this seriously affected our movements for it meant that our hours of duty were quite different. We couldn't have this, but what to do about it?

Then one day on parade Jack along with half-a-dozen others was detailed to report to the cookhouse for 'spud bashing'. But instead of leaving with the others when they had finished he pretended that he had been sent over on a permanent basis. I immediately claimed him as my assistant and from then on our time on and off duty was the same.

This led to us being free of all parades and working only one full day out of three, and on the other two we finished at midday. We bought a racing bike each and became a common sight on the country roads around Aldershot, dressed in plus fours, cycling side by side en route for some nearby country town. When we discovered Guildford and its lovely river we took to cycling that far only, garaging our bikes and spending the rest of the afternoon in a punt on the river. In time we developed such proficiency with the paddles that with one reaching over the side, the other at the back, both paddling like mad we actually had that cumbersome craft moving at quite a speed.

Then followed a most idyllic period, we picked up two of the local girls. They were friends, quite young, mine was eighteen, she said, while Jack's was only seventeen. By now I was twenty-three. Now our routine was slightly altered, as is often the case when a girl comes on the scene. Now we arranged to be at a certain spot on the river with our punt at a particular time. At the appointed time the girls would appear, having been home from work and met somewhere. Then they would come on board and off we would 'sail' for a laugh, and later, a cuddle. This was indeed a most happy chapter in my life.

My girl's name was Ethel (I'm surprised I remember it after all these years) but I

155

preferred to call her Chink. This on account of her oriental-shaped eyes. Lovely eyes they were. Brown, and bright.

Chink and I become quite fond of one another and there was even talk, in time, of marriage. After all, I was twenty-three, quite old enough to be considering taking a wife, while Chink was eighteen — she wouldn't be the youngest girl ever to marry.

Jack's affair with his play-mate was on a more temporary basis. They were neither of them very serious. They seemed to be doing a lot of laughing there in the back of the punt. Often Chink and I would yell out, 'Why don't you shut up, you two'. They were ruining our atmosphere. Some time during the evening, having moored the punt we used to erect a canvas covering that created a box-like arrangement, and inside this we were completely shut off from the rest of the world.

One day Chink said to me, 'My mother wants me to bring you home. She would like to see you, Syd.'

And so a day was chosen. I was to come home to tea. I liked this. So her mum wanted to see me. Chinkie must have told her how serious we were and mum wanted to see who this potential son-in-law was. Yes, it was a good sign.

It was a little apprehensively that I arrived at the house, dressed in my very best. The bike had been discarded for the occasion and I had come by bus. I didn't want mum to see me all wind-blown. Her first impression could be most important.

156

But whatever timidity I had felt concerning Mrs Chink was unfounded and soon forgotten, for she was a smiling, friendly, most homely person. I liked her a lot, and, whoopee, she liked me too. This wasn't being conceited, she as good as said so. We got along beautifully together. It was easy to make her laugh and her homemade cakes were delicious.

Sometime during the evening it occurred to me to think that if Chink was going to grow up into this sort of woman then that would do me very nicely. Everything was working out perfectly.

Then came the bombshell. Mrs Chink said to me, 'I would like to have a little talk to you in the other room.'

'This is it,' I thought, 'she is going to ask me to be good to her little girl after we are married. She is going to give me her consent.'

'Syd,' she said, after we had sat ourselves down in two armchairs facing each other, 'has Ethel told you how old she is?'

This didn't bother me, there seemed no cause for concern. 'Yes, I know how old she is, she's eighteen,' I replied.

'Well, she's not,' said her mum. 'She tells everyone that. I know she looks quite grown up but in fact she is only fifteen. Now I want you to promise you won't tell her I've told you this. She'd be terribly annoyed if she knew.'

This was an awful blow. In a flash my whole world had changed. From having a girlfriend of whom I was very, very fond I had become a man taking out a child. I had lost her. As distinctly

157

as if she had left me, or had even died. The girl that I was courting up till then no longer existed. In her place was this little girl, just left school, masquerading in a grown-up's clothing who didn't interest me in the least.

For the sake of not letting her suspect that her mother had told me I had to continue seeing her for a while, but she no longer even looked the same to me. She looked a kid, and when I kissed her I was most careful to make it a meaningless kiss, unprovoking, such as one might throw disdainfully in their sister's direction occasionally.

She, of course, realised that a cooling off had taken place and in next to no time had taxed me with the half question, half statement, 'My mum has told you how old I am, hasn't she?'

I denied it but she knew. Apparently this had been going on for some time.

It was no strain for Jack to part from his girl, so we left them and concentrated on trying to get a little more speed from the punt. Occasionally we saw them and we'd wave, or we'd talk, but it had gone. A couple of words, a simple revelation had destroyed what up till then had appeared to be a feeling of some depth.

It was whilst I was at Aldershot that a letter arrived one day from Arthur telling me that he and Emmie were going to be married. They had weathered some of the storms that they had run into during the courting period and they now could see blue skies ahead.

In some of the storms I had been asked to help in some small way to bring them through to clearer weather. There was, for example, the time when I was on leave and Arthur told me that he and Emmie had quarrelled and parted. He was still at Mrs. Barrett's, but was finding life very lonely now.

He had no intention of openly asking Emmie to come back to him, but he made it quite clear that he would like nothing better than just that. We both knew that if it were left to her to make the first move we would wait for ever. She had no need to feel lonely or neglected. With her beauty she had only to put her head out of the door and she had drawn attention upon herself. Once or twice in those days I had taken Emmie out for the evening (I don't know where Arthur was at those times) and even though she was in the company of a young man (me) it was extraordinary the number of glances that would settle upon her. It used to make me feel quite proud. 'They think this beauty is my girl,' I would think to myself.

So, unless Arthur did something about it he was quite likely to lose this most popular creature. She had a personality as pleasing as her face and Arthur was taking an awful chance leaving her temporarily exposed to temptation.

He wondered if I would care to drop her a line and tell her I was home on leave. Perhaps she would like to see me, he thought. In which case maybe I could let her know how much he was missing her.

He couldn't bring himself to ask her back but he said that he didn't care how much I suggested that he was sorry for what had happened.

159

I wrote. In those days phones were not as frequent as today. So we had to wait for her reply. Emmie being Emmie, a letter came back saying how nice for me to be home on leave and of course she would be pleased to see me. Up till now there had been no mention of Arthur.

And so I went off to meet her at her flat.

Arthur watched me go and wished me luck. Actually he was wishing luck upon himself for I had nothing to gain by spending an evening in conversation with Emmie. I was simply an emissary. My instructions were to make her feel sorry for Arthur in his loneliness and to make it quite clear to her that if she would have him he would be back like a shot.

Arthur's concern showed on his face as I moved off.

Emmie welcomed me in her usual fashion. She was always one to greet all and sundry with a kiss. A very nice habit, I must say, and one which I enjoyed and took advantage of repeatedly.

That night we talked right through the evening and when I left my mission had been most satisfactorily accomplished. I was to tell Arthur that she would be happy to see him the next evening.

Poor old Art, he had sat around all the evening wondering when on earth I was going to return and put him out of his misery. When I told him of my success he had no need to tell me what this meant to him. His face was a study.

So, now they were to be married, and 'could

160

I manage a day's leave for the occasion to act as best man?'

Yes, of course. This could be done. It was fitting that I should be best man. Not only because I was Arthur's brother but also because we were all three such good friends.

So the wedding took place, I handed over the ring and they were declared man and wife.

They set up home in a little flat and from then on this was to be my new home whenever I was on leave.

14

Jack Goes To India and I Follow Later

Once a year it was customary for postings overseas to appear on the notice board. At this time everyone would cluster around anxious to see if their name was listed and if so to which country they were being sent.

Those were the days when 'the sun never set on the British Empire.' One could have been sent to Aden, to Egypt, or to Hong Kong, or Cyprus. There was Mauritius, there was Palestine and there was the Persian Gulf. Then, the biggest list of names by far, there were those down for posting to India, the Jewel of the empire. We all knew of these places and we had all met at some time an 'old sweat' who had returned from one or the other of these many outposts. We all had our fancy too, with the North-west Frontier of India being everyone's last choice. Here we knew there was quite a bit of skirmishing going on much of the time. We knew it to be an isolated region, hot, barren and unfriendly.

So, when one day postings abroad appeared there was the usual scramble towards the notice board, with Jack and I well to the fore.

First of all Jack's name appeared. There he was on the long list of names for India — the North-west Frontier. We read on and came to

Signalman Metcalfe, S — India — the North-west Frontier. So, there it was, we were both posted, to the 'farthest flung outpost of the British Empire'.

We moved slowly away, sunk in thought. 'What do you think?' asked Jack.

'I'm not all that keen,' said I, 'but at least we are down to go to the same place.'

We agreed that the main thing was that we should stay together. But did we want to go anywhere, even together? Weren't we doing quite all right here where we were?

On this we both agreed. Life at Aldershot with our two afternoons off out of three, with our cycling trips to nearby towns, occasionally picking up a 'bit of skirt' to help make life more interesting was not too bad. There was no occasional 'bit of skirt' on the North-west Frontier. We both knew that, and that helped sway us in making our decision. We decided we would both think up some excuse whereby we could ask to be taken off the draft on compassionate grounds. Jack had a ready-made reason — his old parents. Should he be sent abroad for the usual five years span the chances of him seeing either of his parents again would be slim indeed.

OK, that was Jack's excuse, but what about me? Mine took a little more thinking up. Then it came to me. Doona. My little parentless sister. She would be all alone in this great big world with only a married brother left who barely earned enough to keep his home going. I had been contributing towards her upkeep I would say. Yes, that would be my reason for not wishing to go abroad. I couldn't leave my poor unprotected sister all on her own. Actually Doona was now in 'service' with a well-to-do family as a cook. She was quite well looked after and had never had to ask me for a penny.

So our two applications were written out and handed in to the Company Office. We both thought Jack would be safe for exemption, but whether my case would fool them or not was another matter. We continued to watch the notice board. That was where we would be notified.

Remember it had to be both or none. We would rather both go than one go and one stay. Then one day our wait was ended — there on the board was the result of recent applications for exemption from drafting overseas. Mine was granted, Jack's was rejected. He was to go and I was to stay. We had made a complete mess of the whole thing. This was serious. Unless we could think up something our friendship was going to be torn apart.

But what to do? I could hardly tell them that I had changed my mind. However, after much discussion Jack assured me that when the time came for leaving he would be in hospital.

'There's nothing much we can do now,' said he, 'but just before we are due to move off I'll make myself ill, even if I have to poison myself.'

'Don't do anything silly, Jack,' I urged him. 'What do you intend doing?'

'I'll give myself the flu. Don't worry I'll think

164

of something, but I'm certainly not going.'

And so we settled back, both feeling reasonably reassured.

Then a week before the boat was to leave Jack started his 'get unfit' campaign.

It was mid-winter and the nights were frosty and cold.

The first night of his campaign he rose from his bed at one o'clock in the morning, went into the wash-house in his pyjamas and bare feet, soaked his head in icy cold water and stood on the freezing cold stone floor with his teeth chattering until it became almost unbearable. Then with his whole body shivering he clambered back into bed. He told me the next day that lying there all a-tremble he felt as though he would never be warm again. Sleep was impossible and when the morning came round it was all he could do to struggle out of bed. But there was no sign of a cold. Not the slightest thing was amiss. He was terribly tired from loss of sleep, but nothing else. Not a sneeze, no cause to have to blow his nose. Nothing. His ordeal had left him exactly as he was before, perfectly fit.

So, the next night called for sterner measures.

This night he rose once again after making sure everyone was asleep, went once more to the wash-house. There he soaked his shirt and pyjamas in the icy cold water, he let the tap run over his mop of dark hair, then a miserable, bedraggled wretch he went outside and stood in the bitterly cold wind and shivered. He went back to bed quite certain he had a fever. He felt

165

dreadfully ill. So much so that he was afraid that he had gone too far and that instead of making sure that we would not be parted he had now made that parting even more permanent.

However, when he awoke the next morning, wondering whether he would be able even to stand up he found that during his night's sleep he had fully recuperated and not a thing was wrong.

He made one more attempt to catch a draft-dodging cold and then realised that now, instead of this behaviour having a weakening effect, it was actually toughening him up. His system had become used to it and was probably now even deriving benefit from it. So he stopped his nightly excursions and took to begging me to give his ankle a not too hard yet not too light tap with a meat cleaver. We could do this one evening in the cookhouse. We had the key, no-one would see us. Jack was perfectly serious. He really did want me to so injure his ankle that he would be unable to walk for a while. But I couldn't accept the responsibility of having to so gauge my blow that he wouldn't be crippled for life.

The next day was Draft Day and when they formed up ready for departure there, in the ranks, with equipment hanging all over his torso was Signalman Jack Higgins, my mate.

The order came to mount the lorries that were standing by and in next to no time they had moved off. As they drove away I stood in the middle of the road waving while Jack leaned out of the back of the truck waving back. He looked a very sad lad. I felt dreadful.

When there was no longer any point to standing there I went back to the barrack room, and broke into tears.

There was not another soul there, thank heavens. I feel quite sure that had there been I would have managed to restrain myself. But at the same time it was good that I should have had the opportunity to give way to my feelings, for I felt so miserable.

After that nothing seemed quite the same. I continued to cycle around the countryside, but no longer was there anyone alongside me to laugh and joke with.

Life takes on another meaning when one looks for something to do alone where once they had done everything with a partner.

The punt no longer interested me — who ever sees a lone punter? Games of tennis came less readily my way. Our evening chats as we sat on each other's bed had gone. And, most important, nothing that I did seemed the same. In a whole barrack room full of young fellows of my own age I was lonely.

But every week without fail a letter arrived from the North-west Frontier telling me of all that he was doing. And every week regularly I sat down and replied. Photos came through the post showing Jack in uniforms and surrounds that made him look quite glamorous. He was so tanned and somehow looked so much more adult.

Of course we discussed the possibility of my coming the next year if it could be arranged.

Jack was reluctant to say anything that might influence me one way or the other. He told me of life there exactly as it was, the good and the bad, and left the final decision to me. 'Of course, he would always say, 'I want you to come, Syd, but I would hate to urge you to come out here just for my sake only to find that you detest it.'

But I knew that as soon as next year's drafting came around I would be on it if I could only be given a promise that I would be sent to Jack's station. With this in mind as the season drew near I approached the office and asked whether this could be arranged. They were only too ready to agree. Here was a soldier actually asking to be sent to the Frontier. 'Yes, yes, that could be arranged. Was there any particular part to which I wished to be sent?'

Yes, it had to be Waziristan, and this was immediately granted.

So, come the next year, there once again was my name on the notice board on the long list. There was no excuse to be thought up as to why I shouldn't go. I couldn't get there soon enough.

When the lorry moved off on the first stage of the journey there were no tearful farewells this time. This was adventure. Off to the Afghanistan border, via Gibraltar, Malta, Suez Canal, Aden, Karachi. What names! What a thrill!

We had been issued with our tropical kit before leaving Aldershot and we felt like the Foreign Legion with our topees so placed that everyone could see them.

Our boat sailed from Southampton. There she was patiently waiting us as we disgorged from the train, eager eyed and more than a little excited. All white she was. And how right that she should be so dazzlingly painted, for this was a bright occasion.

Up the gang-plank we trailed our assortment of kit, to be given at the top a card telling us the number of our deck and mess table.

On arrival there we found ourselves at a long table stretching from the bulkhead towards the centre of the ship. On each side of this table was a long form. Above our heads were racks fixed in every inch of space. The early arrivals had filled them with their kit and it looked to us new-comers as though it would be quite impossible to fit in any extra. But ours had to go in somewhere and in it went, with more to follow as other arrivals followed us.

There were twenty men to our table and this space alongside and above was to be our home for the next three weeks. To give some idea how cramped we were, when we were seated on the forms at meal times our backs were touching the backs of the table next to us.

We were down in the bowels of the ship and lights had to be kept going all day otherwise we would have been in darkness. Looking around it gave the appearance of one vast dining room, capable of holding some several hundred men.

Trite as it might sound it was impossible not to be reminded of the slave ships of olden days, there were so many of us in so confined a space. Some likened our conditions to those of cattle being transported by sea. The difference was, largely, that we sat down to our meals.

These were served in bulk. The man at the end of the table would take our dishes to the 'servery' where he would have ladled into them whatever was on the menu. When he came back he was then faced with the problem of dividing it into twenty helpings. This, naturally, led to quite a bit of argument, all to add to the lowness of the life we were now being compelled to live.

Before the ship had even left Southampton the deck had become dank and smelly from the breath and body odour of all the men milling around, jostling one another in their efforts to find some place where they could stow their kit.

One could hear from all over the remark, 'How are we expected to fit into here, there's no room?'

That's right, there was no room. Yet fit in we somehow did and we stayed fitted into insufficient space for the whole of the voyage.

A feeling of disappointment was in the air. The bewilderment that we all felt regarding the inadequacy of space that we had been allocated had us all wondering how on earth we were going to manage to all live together under such conditions for the next three weeks. It was like being told by a hotel proprietor that the only space that he had left was the cellar, in which there were already six others living.

But at night it became far worse. For then we had to draw a hammock from the store and whereas in theory we were expected to sling these

170

from some part of the ceiling in actual fact it became a case of first in first served, for no more than a half could be slung, then the rest had to find somewhere on the floor on which to lay out their hammock. Then the floor space became full and for the last there was nothing left but the table tops and the forms. Every inch of space was taken up and at night when asleep or simply lying there listening to the chorus of deep breathing and the medley of snores it was like a scene from a Dickens workhouse. Heaven help us if there had been a fire break out aboard. The escape ways would have been jammed to suffocation.

Sometime during the night everyone would feel the need to go to the toilet and then it was a case of picking a way across the huddled bodies, at the same time ducking beneath the swaying hammocks. The place then stank. The air was foul. No wonder that many of us, young and virile as we were, contracted bad chests on the way. It was like living in a poisoned atmosphere. An analysis of what we were taking into our lungs would have frightened us.

And the noise. It was eerie, for above the sounds from the half drugged men came the continuous creak of the ship as she rolled from one side to the other. On and on it went right through the night. Sometimes she would take a bigger roll than usual and then one wondered if she would manage to right herself.

The first day out from Southampton the sea was a little rough. This meant that at least three quarters of the men were sick. And so sick were

171

many that they could not reach a convenient disposal site. And so the corridors and all the decks became slippery with pools of vomit. This with the stench that it all created made the ship hideous. There was nowhere where one could go to get away from all this distasteful squalor. When one found themselves forced by nature's demands to enter a toilet it was to find that it had become blocked up and that the floors were overrun with all kinds of effluence. And all this would be continuously on the move, rolling backwards and forwards in time with the ship's motion. (Ship's motion here seems most appropriate.)

Later on, when the seas calmed down and we became used to our new cramped way of life things seemed somewhat rosier. It really is extraordinary what one will eventually become used to and accept as normal. I suppose the most brilliant example of that in recent times is the conditions in the trenches that men of the First World War learned to live under and in time to treat as every day circumstances.

On the fine days, which now followed one on top of the other, we would all make for the open deck and lie down, drinking in the warm sunshine at a time of the year when we had known nothing else but mist, damp and cold. For it was winter time back in England.

On one occasion we passed quite close to a troopship on her way back to Blighty. Immediately there was a concerted rush to the side of the ship to watch her go by and we were treated to the derisive cry from the troops on her, the 'old sweats'. 'You're going the wrong way.' We had no reply to this. Maybe our turn would come later. We would keep this cry in reserve for another day.

She looked lovely as she passed so smoothly on her way, a shapely form in white — yes, there was a blue line which ran right around those troopships — with the green sea and the blue sky for a back-drop.

She looked lovely, but we knew that down below those soldiers, as with us, were packed together like animals.

We could have been given a bit more room in which to stretch out if the officers, no matter how lowly their rank, down to the merest sub-lieutenant, were not all installed in cabins, with other space-taking facilities available to them that made the difference between their living conditions and ours almost unbelievable.

The army in those days encouraged this disproportionate distinction between the officers and the men. It was a psychological move designed to make us feel completely inferior. That was one of the ways in which they could ensure the officer always receiving absolute obedience. To some extent this worked too, for an officer was so far removed from us, both physically and socially that he assumed in our eyes a distinction and a dignity far above his worth. His fine uniform plus his manner of speech left us so deluded that obedience just naturally followed. Most times, at any rate. Never, for example, did I hear anyone on the boat complain about the vast disparity that there was between the treatment that they were receiving and our treatment.

Each week we lined up and received a portion of our pay and practically the whole of this was passed over to some member or other of the ship's crew. For they, quite illegally, yet without them having to make too great an effort to conceal their activities, all ran some form of gambling game or other. Crown and Anchor was a favourite. But there was a variety. If we weren't tempted by one then they had another with a member of the crew urging us to have a go at 'this one'. They set up all alongside each other in some corner of a lower deck and there was always a crowd of suckers around them. Some took longer to lose their money than others.

The crews of those troopships — especially those carrying troops going 'the wrong way' must have made a fortune. It is my belief now that the money they made would have been pooled and shared out including all the other members. What a good wicket they were on.

As we came to the various places of interest on the way so we were treated to all the thrills of seeing life as it is lived elsewhere. Gibraltar came first and here we disembarked some of our 'passengers' and took on others. I can remember thinking as The Rock was looming up far ahead how familiar it was. How like its pictures. There are many places in the world that we have never seen and are unlikely to ever see with which we are utterly familiar. Gibraltar was one of them. I knew it as I would an old friend.

We were not allowed ashore but vendors came

174

aboard and set out their wares on the open decks. And here, as with everywhere else en route, we were robbed of whatever the crew had left us to spend. For most of us found when we moved off again that we had paid twice or even thrice what was normally charged for the odds and ends that we had bought. The native knew these raw Englishmen on their way out east and he knew how to handle them. We were easy pickings.

Our next port of call was Malta. Here we went into Valetta Harbour and once again stalls were set up on the decks.

The navy was there at the time and two destroyers steamed past and out to the open sea under our admiring eyes.

We took on stores there, then on our way again.

At Port Said we were allowed ashore. This was the only time we were able to leave the ship. And even here it had to be under the surveillance of the authorities. We were formed up on the dockside and marched through the streets of the town. Like a dog on a leash we were taken for a walk. Also like the dog on the leash, we went where our master took us. And when he said, 'come on, boy, back home now,' we marched back, up the gang-plank and down to our one square foot per man below decks.

Restricted as our movements were it was still good to stretch our young legs. We had been cooped up for about ten days at this stage, and we were to remain so until we reached Karachi, some ten or eleven days later.

During our march around Port Said the feature that captured my imagination most was the brightly coloured homes of what appeared to be the wealthier residents. They were greens and oranges, pale blues and pinks. Such audaciousness was unknown to me. This was my first time out of England and all I had known up till now was the dull, dark brick houses of London. And whatever colour they had set out with most of them were now reduced to a sameness by years of accumulated grime.

This that we were seeing at Port Said seemed almost unreal. Whoever heard of anyone living in a green or a pink house? But it was attractive. Made all the more so by the sunshine reflecting from their bright clean walls.

Along the Suez Canal we saw the occasional Arab pass by mounted on his camel and the odd village drifted slowly past. We were all eyes. This was real picture book stuff.

Aden came next. But once again we were only able to gaze ashore from the deck of our ship. Then it was off across the Indian Ocean for Karachi.

At Karachi everyone disembarked. We were in India. Our home for the next five years. We looked around us like children at a fair.

In next to no time a crowd had gathered around, some wanting to read our hand, others wishing to sell us silks, another wanting to cut our corns. There were barbers ready to shave us right there where we stood, there were fruit wallahs. In fact there was every degree of service imaginable. The lure of the East was all around us. Tea was being sold — sickly sweet tea that tasted most unlike anything we had ever drunk before.

Nearly all of these noisy gesticulating characters with their strange way of speaking English were touching their foreheads to us and addressing us as Sahib. This was good. After just being transported in something little more elegant than a prison ship; after being treated as though we were without entitlement to any form of respect whatsoever we were now being confronted by these people touching their foreheads to us as a mark of respect and calling us Sahib.

Clearly they saw us as being above them. This was something entirely new to us. Something we were quite unprepared for. We were flattered. We were overcome. At last we had found someone beneath us. Someone to whom we now gave the orders. And in many cases it didn't take too long to adjust to this new situation and take advantage of it.

And so we all became Pukka Sahibs and no longer wondered at the oddity of someone touching their forehead to us. It became our due and we disdainfully gave a dignified slight nod of the head in recognition.

I did it. We all did it. I became elevated. One of a higher order. And this too has left its mark upon my susceptible character.

15

Some Snipers I Have Known

During the voyage over Jack had become promoted to Lance Corporal and in those days this raised him way above the ordinary soldier. So it was with some surprise, tinged with a little disappointment that on our meeting I found him to be wearing a stripe upon each of his shirt-sleeves. I knew that this would make it a little more difficult for us to maintain our close friendship, for the authorities would discourage any close ties between NCOs and the men.

However this did nothing to detract from the pleasure that we both felt from being together again, and on that first night we were most reluctant to break off our conversation and retire to our beds.

But, of course, there were no more excursions out into the countryside. Now we were in what was known as a perimeter camp. Situated in the heart of a huge plain with heavy, grim-looking hills fringing the whole of one side. It was these hills, or rather a passage through them that was the cause of our being there. The passage led through to Afghanistan territory and we were there to guard this entry into India from any unwanted incursion.

Yet our troubles were caused, not from possible invaders, but from the very people whose land we were there to protect, the local population.

This was Waziristan, part of the North-west Territory, inhabited by various Pathan tribes whose loyalty was reserved almost entirely for the tribe to which they belonged. They distrusted one another but were ever ready to unite against the British and Indian troops who had established themselves in their land. They took every opportunity of making our life unpleasant. They fired upon us when we were out on column, they tore up the roads that we built and the only co-operation they ever gave us was given when they considered it would be of distinct advantage to themselves.

We were advised never to stray beyond the barbed wire entanglements surrounding the camp and it was recognised that to be caught outside after dark, when the camp gates were shut and the guards highly alerted would be tantamount to committing suicide.

So here Jack and I renewed our friendship. Here in this small encampment stuck out right in the middle of a vast barren plain.

Games became very much a part of our way of life to help pass the time away. Anyone not playing some game or other would have found their days terribly long and boring. It was here that while playing hockey one day against an infantry team we came under sniper fire. A tribesman had managed to conceal himself behind a slight ridge and the game had been in progress for half an hour when suddenly from close by came the crack of a rifle shot.

179

We were all familiar with this sound and the game came to an immediate halt as we looked around to see from where it had come. Then came a second shot and one of the players fell. This was enough. Every man dropped to the ground. There was not a trace of shelter where we could make ourselves less of a target. All we could do was to press our bodies as close to the ground as possible, while the sniper continued to take pot-shots at our brightly coloured jerseys. These stood out horribly against the light fawn of the hockey pitch (few sports grounds had a grass covering. Grass didn't grow very readily in the mineral-starved, clay-like substance of the soil, baked hard by the hot sun.)

Some years later I was to assume a similar posture when stranded on the beaches of Dunkirk.

But at the moment I am pressed hard against the surface of the hockey pitch just outside the barbed wire of our camp at Wana in Waziristan. My thoughts, quite simply were, 'You're under fire, Syd, and you're not frightened. Good.' I had always wondered what my reaction would be.

But how long I would have remained undeterred I shall never know for all of a sudden the camp guards picked up our sniper's position and opened up a continuous machine gun barrage. Under cover of this barrage we leapt to our feet and ran like startled deer for the camp gate. A whole cluster of us went though the gate together. Two remained lying on the hockey pitch. They had to be carried in and their funeral took place that same evening.

Once a month we went out on 'column'. We vacated the camp, leaving a token defence force behind, and we followed a six or seven days route that took in all the villages in that locality. The next month we went off in another direction.

During the whole of the march over some of the most difficult terrain we would be harassed and resisted most of the way.

Every hill that could harbour a sniper who could hinder our progress had to be held as the column passed by. Here it was that I, and other signallers, came into the picture. A patrol of infantrymen would be sent up to hold the hilltop and I would accompany them. These hill climbs were tough, for the temperature would often be well over a hundred degrees and we would be loaded down with equipment. In addition to the regalia strewn around my body (water bottle, filled; bandoleer heavy with bullets; haversack; rifle slung over shoulder) I would have also a signalling flag and a heliograph. This is a piece of signalling equipment that operates with mirrors reflecting the sun's rays. All this when climbing a steep, stony hill, with a possibility of being sniped at the same time made for really hard work.

Once established on the top I would then signal to the column that all was clear for them to continue.

The column passing through a native village.

A column casualty.

Another casualty.

A holt for refreshments.

The column would be followed at some quarter mile distance by a small body of troops known as the Rear Party. When this body arrived alongside our position there would be more signalling and we would be 'called in'. Then it was a mad scramble to reach the bottom and race across the open country to the comparative safety of the Rear Party.

This descent would be accomplished in a fraction of the time that it had taken us to reach the top, for we would slither and slide down in most undignified fashion. We had but one thought in mind, 'Let's get out of here.'
It was hot, hard work, and dangerous too. But, God, were we fit. Sometimes on returning to camp from a column we would turn out next day for a game of hockey or football. We all agreed then that we were tireless. We could feel the strength in our bodies throughout the

whole of the game. Our breathing would be effortless, so little did the game take out of us by comparison with the efforts of the six days of marching, running and hill climbing that we had just returned from.

Sometimes when the scenery or the occasion was specially spectacular it would occur to me that this person taking part in it was me — the lad who had wanted so much to travel, yet had once thought it was all so hopeless.

During our columns when we came to a halt at the end of the day's marching no matter how tired we were we would immediately start digging a hole in which to sleep in safety that night. Anyone who couldn't be bothered to dig couldn't be bothered whether they saw the dawn next day or not, for some time during the night bullets would come thudding into the camp from the ever-present nearby hills.

We signals had to dig a larger hole in which could be set up the radio station. Around this hole would be built up two or three layers of sandbags, to protect the operator who would be sitting up during his hours of duty. Then finally would be erected a tent to help subdue the lighting that the operator needed.

Once when it was my turn to take over from the previous operator, as I sat down I realised that the sandbags had not been built up high enough. My head as I sat at the set was above the top row. This didn't suit me and so I set about raising the 'wall' until I was fully protected. Then, some time during the night the expected happened. From the nearby hills came the crack of rifle fire. They were sniping upon the camp. The trace of light that crept through our tent would now become a beacon. I would be a target. All of a sudden there was a short, sharp whine and one smacked straight into the sandbag right alongside my head. In my cautiousness I had saved my life. For quite a while afterwards I felt really shaky. One doesn't virtually die every day of their lives.

Although our object during those marches was to show the local inhabitants that we were still there, yet never once did I see them take cognisance of the fact. As we passed by a village the only eyes that we saw gazing upon us were those of the village dogs. Miserable, mangy, angry looking things they were with their ribs plainly on display through their thin layer of flesh. They would stand sullenly a little way off growling in the depths of their throat as we went quietly by. But as for inhabitants they had shut themselves up in their mud huts and would not emerge again until we were well past. Some of the menfolk, no doubt, were following us in the hills, awaiting their opportunity to open fire upon us.

The women folk were under lock and key.

For four years Jack and I did these columns together and I rather feel that some of the hardship we encountered on those occasions went some way towards giving our friendship a little more depth, for at the end of a long hot day's march our faces would be covered with the fine dust that was raised by hundreds of marching feet and had settled upon our sweating faces. A man's tiredness showed clearly in his eyes.

Yet, no matter how tired we felt Jack and I would never retire to our respective holes without a last cigarette and a discussion on the events of the day.

Then it would be, 'Goodnight, Jack.'

'Goodnight, Syd.'

And within five minutes we both would be sound asleep, exhausted.

For the whole of the time that we were out on column our uniform never came off our back, and on our return to camp some days later our first night between sheets, in a real bed, with all our clothes off was a luxury that we never failed to talk about. Another luxury was our first shower after being for days covered in a layer of near mud, and that first night in the canteen with all the grime washed off, a clean uniform on and our hair nicely brushed we were so different to how we had been for the past few days as to be almost unrecognisable.

Those were days of close comradeship. Life held dangers that we were not only sharing but were all helping one another to overcome. This made us inter-dependent and so created a tie between us all. Not that we recognised this, but viewed from this distance it is clear that the unity that there was had some basis in the life we were living. For one thing our portion of the camp when we were not out on column was so small that it meant we were living on top of each other all the time. We worked together during the day and then in the evenings, when off duty, in the cosy little canteen that was our 'club house', on looking around there were the same old faces all over again. We did everything together. We knew everyone's jokes, we knew one another's little quirks and often laughed at a quip not because it was so humorous but because it was so characteristic of the quipper.

There were no women in our life. I wouldn't say it was 'a man's world', for a man needs a woman in his life, and it was for that reason that just here and there a certain relationship did arise. We had one Corporal Foster who was nicknamed Flossie. Flossie Foster. He carried his eccentricity in his manner of walking. Certainly his walk was not the type that would have been encouraged on the barrack square during his early training. Corporal Dendy would have had something to say about it had he been training him.

There was another pair who we regarded as husband and wife and it was accepted that their relationship be given the special treatment that one normally gives to a married couple. No-one ever interfered in their affairs. If they were seated together in the canteen we left them to themselves. They didn't want other company, they were content to be alone with one another.

Repugnant as it may seem to some, yet when couples such as these eventually became separated they were to be pitied. I saw this very couple that I speak of parted, and the misery that the one felt who was left behind was quite equal to that of a man losing a wife he loved. He was inconsolable and used to sit at the same table that he always occupied with his 'wife', refusing to talk to anyone.

Eventually he 'remarried' and seemed to be happy again.

During those years on the Frontier my age advanced from twenty-four to twenty-nine. The boy had been left well behind. Arthur and Emmie were becoming an old married couple but were still without the start of a family, while Doona had married a fellow I had never seen and had settled down to married life in a flat, still in Kentish Town, a suburb in North London.

It seems that Doona had finished her working life as a barmaid and it was behind the bar that her future husband had met her. He was a regular customer at her pub and she noticed that whenever he wanted his glass refilled he always held back until he could be sure of being served by her. Eventually he became sufficiently emboldened to ask her out on her day off and so the courtship proceeded with Doona keeping his glass filled every evening during her working nights and holding on to his arm during her evening off.

This all came to me by letter while I was still serving on the North-west Frontier of India.

From time to time Jack and I would discuss the possibility of what we would do when our eight years with the colours were finished. We knew we would be asked did we wish to re-sign for the next four years. If not we would be discharged from the army to take our place once again in civvy street.

Outside the situation had improved. There were not so many unemployed as when I joined and the prospects of obtaining a job were reasonably bright.

By the time we were giving the matter serious consideration Jack had become a full corporal. This made it all the more difficult for him to consider leaving. He was well and truly installed on the promotion ladder and the army was now offering him a worthwhile career.

My mind was made up at all times. Providing jobs were more readily obtainable outside I would leave. The life did not appeal to me. I had seen other parts of the world. I had been involved in situations on the Frontier that would be considered most unusual by my listeners, should I be able to hold anyone's ear. I was a man of the world, in a modest sort of way.

It was in this unconcerned fashion, towards the end of our eight years spell that Jack and I went on leave down to Karachi.

For two days and nights we travelled in the same train, giving largesse out at each station to the swarms of beggars who would gather outside our carriage window pleading for alms. A few small pieces of money brought profuse forehead touching and muttered blessings upon our heads, giving Jack and I a feeling of great importance.

In Karachi we settled down to three weeks of making the most of our holiday.

This was a large fairly modern city with activity all around. A city full of colour and

190

interest. Having spent our entire time among the barren hills of the Frontier where the local populace completely ignored us this new atmosphere where we couldn't move without being besieged by hordes of beggars was most fascinating. We spent half our time telling these hangers-on to jao (go away).

We felt like men of some worth, ordering the ordinary folk to be on their way.

Life on holiday at Karachi became luxurious. We were staying at a holiday camp where a 'boy' was allocated to us to wait upon all our needs. He woke us first thing in the morning with a cup of tea, which he handed discreetly to us through our mosquito nets. Then he laid out our clothing for the day. He polished our shoes, washed and pressed our uniforms, made our beds and ran our errands. All this and much more for one rupee (1/6) a week.

Had we so wished we could have been shaved while still asleep in bed before rising. The barber who was urging us to accept his services guaranteed that the whole performance could be completed without us knowing a thing about it. We would awaken fully shaven. This was nothing new to us, we had seen others take advantage of this offer, but we preferred to shave ourselves. There was always a limit to the fussing that I felt entitled to accept. This limit I found to be still with me at later times. In Durban, for example, I could never allow one of those Zulus to pull me around in one of their gaily covered hand-carts. Neither could I ever, at any time, put my foot upon a stand while a boot-black

191

then proceeded to polish my shoes. The very stance that one takes up at such times, standing there looking down upon the man bending over one's foot seems so haughty in my eyes that I don't feel justified in taking part in it.

But it was difficult not to feel superior whilst on leave in Karachi. No-one ever addressed us as less than Sahib. Sometimes it became Sahib-ji. This was an even more exalted form of address. The beggars were continuously informing us, 'You rich man, me poor man.' Or, 'You big man, me small man.' This was flattering stuff, yet at the same time not without a trace of truth in it. For by comparison we were indeed rich, we were indeed big. They, poor beggars, would have made anyone seem rich and big. Their poverty had to be seen to be realised. And it was an unusual one who wasn't deformed in some way or another.

Yet, no matter how sympathetic one might have felt it became most inexpedient to give them anything. This we learned only through experience, for at first, being on leave and having a few annas to give away, we started to throw coins to all who asked for them. In a flash we were surrounded. We couldn't move. And the chanting of pitiful cries for 'Buksheesh Sahib,' added to the ghastly sights that were thrust under our eyes made our charity most inconvenient.

We decided that we would not give again until the end of our leave, when we could spend the last evening playing Father Xmas.

On coming out of a restaurant on our

first evening there, feeling most pleased with ourselves — we had eaten well and were now smoking the cigarettes that we had lit up before leaving, we were confronted by a little boy who asked, 'Sahibs, you come see my sister?'

I doubt very much whether she was his sister. I couldn't see a trace of family likeness. But I must say she was a very nice girl. Jack liked one of her friends too. She seemed to have several friends and Jack had a fairly wide choice.

Thereafter we didn't need the little boy to guide us to his 'sister's' house. We had it well implanted in our minds.

That holiday had everything. The camp was right on the beach, where the sands were truly delightful. There were several very good tennis courts and, it being India, we didn't even have to bend down to pick up the balls. These were thrown to us by a boy at each end who never seemed to stop running. The sea was always gloriously warm and we were free to swim and sunbathe to our hearts' content.

Sometimes we would hire a sailing boat which would take us out into the harbour where the owner would then drop a huge stone over the side on the end of a rope and hand a fishing line to Jack and I.

At nights we always dressed in our fanciest gear and finished the evening with a fine meal complete with wine. Nothing was really expensive as wages were so pitiably low. As a result we could afford to live up to a standard we had previously only dreamed of.

Then, of course, there was, quite frequently,

the little boy's 'sister' and her friends. They never seemed to have retired for the night.

I suppose that coming, as we did, from five years cut off from all the luxuries of life this all seemed doubly exciting to us. Even the small things, like going into a hairdresser's for a haircut where when he had finished the cutting he bathed my hot face in lovely-smelling, refreshing Eau de Cologne and gently patted my face dry with a soft towel. Only a little thing, as I say, but it has outlasted many a bigger one in my memory. I came out of that shop feeling so different to when I went in and smelling something like the little boy's 'sister'.

We were coming to the end of our eight years 'colour service'. We both knew that soon we would be on the boat again, this time going 'the right way', unless we decided to sign on. So we frequented the bazaars where there were the most outrageous bargains to be had compared to prices back home. Table cloths, bed covers, carpets, material for curtains, all with the most colourful patterns, were to be had for a song. So we stocked up.

Towards the end of three of the happiest, most carefree weeks of my life a cable was received from 'Wana Camp, Waziristan, N.W.F.P. Please ascertain whether either or both of the following wish to re-engage for a further four years colour service. Corporal John Nicholson Higgins, 2321591, Signalman Sydney James Metcalfe, 2321289.'

This was passed on to us with the instruction

that we had until late afternoon to hand in our reply.

The holiday was over. The gaiety had gone out of our mood.

We talked the matter over at great length, going into various aspects, at times, over and over again. The question was would Jack leave with me or would he stay on? My decision was made.

'Jack,' I said, 'I only came into the army because I couldn't get work. Now things are better outside I've no wish to stay on. I'm for leaving and taking a chance.'

It was not an easy matter for Jack to settle. He was doing well in the army. He was on reasonable pay, had some authority and further promotion was automatic. Also he had no wish to go back to West Hartlepool. It had become too small for him. His father was still there but his mother had died while he was away.

'If I leave and come back to London with you where will I live?' he asked.

'We'd have to take a furnished flat,' I answered.

'Supposing we can't get work?'

Jack was hedging. Underneath I think that he knew very well that he'd be staying. He just didn't like saying so.

Then he pulled himself together, 'I think I'll have to stay, Syd. I can't throw up the safety that I have here for the uncertainty that I would be going to outside.'

'You'd be a fool to leave,' said I, 'if I had your rank I wouldn't consider it. I'm only sorry I can't stay on with you, but I must go. Soldiering's not for me.'

So our decision was made, Jack would stay, I would go.

The message was sent back to this effect.

Back in Wana Camp Paddy Burke was on duty at the radio station. He was a friend of ours. He knew the extent of our friendship. As he took the message down he was confident that it would be either two yes's or two no's. When the message came through Corporal Higgins to re-sign, Sgmn Metcalfe to leave, he couldn't believe it. He refused to give receipt for it thinking that the whole thing was a mistake and insisted on the text being repeated. And so it was transmitted all over again. Still a yes and a no. This time Paddy accepted it but still insisted there was some mistake. It would all be straightened out on our return from leave, he thought.

This he told us when we met back in Wana.

But there it was, this was to be the end of eight years of friendship, during which I can, honestly, not remember Jack and I having one worthwhile disagreement.

There were no tears this time. We were mature men now and had had some of the rough edges knocked off us. Instead we shook hands, wished each other all the luck in the world and I moved off, on my way back to England.

We never met again. A few letters were exchanged before the war broke out, then they stopped and I have never heard of or from him since.

Sometimes I wonder if there is any way in which I could find out his present whereabouts. We should have so much to tell each other.

So, once again on board the troopship I looked around for somewhere to stow my kit as I arrived at the mess deck that was printed on the card that I had been given at the top of the gang plank.

But this time there was no disillusionment. We were a tougher breed than when we came out, and, crude as were our living conditions on the boat, we had known worse. Much worse. Besides which, we were going home. Going the 'right way'.

16

We Find Dad Only To Lose Him Again

My return to England was greeted with the greatest enthusiasm on the part of my handful of relations.

It was agreed that I would stay with Doona as Arthur and Emmie had moved to a new flat and they hadn't spare bedroom.

So I arrived at Kentish Town on Xmas Eve, the one suntanned man in London sporting its winter pallor.

Doona introduced me to Mick, her husband, my brother-in-law, and I was then shown my bedroom. In this was blazing the biggest fire I have ever seen confined to a domestic grate. The room was stifling.

'What's the idea of the furnace?' I asked Doona.

'We thought you'd be frozen here after all those years under the hot sun,' was her answer.

'Well, it was hot there, Doo,' I said, 'but even at its worst it was nothing compared to this. Coo, let that fire burn right down, lovey.'

I couldn't possibly have slept in the hot-house conditions that Doona had created for me.

Then my bags were opened and the oddments that Jack and I had stocked up with at the bazaars in Karachi were laid out and fussed over. They looked so exciting in their new setting.

They were exotic with their high colouring and their gaudy patterns. It was like planting one of those pink houses that I had seen at Port Said down in the middle of a London street. They stood out.

While I was away in India Arthur had run into our dad and I lost no time calling round on him. He was now a lonely, old man, although he put on a brave face, joked, and generally behaved as though he hadn't a care in the world.

In actual fact he was quite hard up and a glance around his room was enough to tell just how straitened were his circumstances. He had only the one room, which would have cost no more than a few shillings, and this was more than half-filled by one piece of furniture, his bed. Over at the window was his table and on this were a few scraps left over from his last 'meal'. His milk was condensed (it was probably cheaper that way) and it would seem that his main sustenance came from bread, for there was the remains of a loaf on a board on a corner of the table and the many crumbs littering the spot where he had eaten showed that he had had quite a few slices.

But his poverty didn't deprive him of his cigarettes, for dad was an inveterate smoker. Once when he was younger, when a certain brand was offering quite good presents for enormous quantities of coupons given away in their packets dad very nearly smoked himself to death. He had wanted the radio set which was one of the presents and to obtain it at a normal rate of smoking would have meant a wait of several years. Dad set out to achieve this in one year and he did, but the colour of his fingers — a rich nicotine brown — and the irritating phlegm-laden cough that he ended up with suggested that it just wasn't worth it.

However dad wasn't one to reason things out this way. He had reached his target and he now owned a radio set that he insisted had cost him nothing. He was happy.

That same radio was in this miserable room in which he now lived, and it is my belief that it gave him pleasure even to look at it.

But I felt dreadfully sorry for him. He looked so much older. So much thinner and so much less prosperous.

On the death of his father he, being the eldest son, had inherited the building business, but by this time, on account of his father not being able to supervise matters towards the end of his life, it was not a very profitable proposition, and with the business came a lot of bad debts. Not being given to applying himself too heartily to anything that called for hard work dad had not put as much energy into reviving it as he should.

Dad was a man who needed lots of encouragement. Left to his own devices he tended to be a drifter. He had need of a wife who would have shared his work with him, to have pretended an interest even when she hadn't really felt it. He wanted praise, and, heaven knows, he got so little of this. As it was there was no incentive for him to throw himself into making what he could of a flagging business. What did it matter? Who was there to see and appreciate anything that he did? There was no-one. He had only himself to answer to and he could easily fool himself.

Anyway, whatever the reason, whether it could have been avoided under other circumstances or not he became a bankrupt and being unable to meet his commitments had had to serve a spell in the debtor's prison at Wormwood Scrubs. When he came out he had to start all over again. But he was now without ambition. His youth had gone, as had his concern for the future, and, being a weak man, he had made no very great effort to re-establish himself. And so he had drifted along doing the odd job here and there but with long (and growing longer all the time) spells when he was doing nothing, when he had only his unemployment money to live on. In those days one didn't live very lavishly on their unemployment money.

This then was dad's circumstances when I met him again.

I had last seen him when I was thirteen. Then he was a vigorous, dominating figure. I saw him as a man of great strength. A sportsman, who thrashed all who mum brought to our house to be the first to win the honour of bringing him to his knees. I was afraid of him.

Now sixteen or seventeen years had gone by. Sixteen or seventeen vital years and now my dad along with his loss of vitality had become a more docile character. Now he was nothing to be afraid of. In fact I saw quite a lot of him and he and I became really good friends, buddies.

Any lack of regard for me that he might have felt in those earlier years had now gone. Now he seemed to hold me in some affection. I once asked him why he hadn't liked me as a boy and he swore that I was mistaken. I knew I wasn't. He knew I wasn't. He had made it quite clear at the time, but he preferred to deny it. I didn't pursue the matter. All that mattered by then was that we were very good friends now.

We spoke of my mum now and then and dad told me that she had led him a dance from the day he married her. He couldn't trust her right from the start. She was too fond of a good time and had really made no very great attempt to be a happily married woman, even in those earliest days. He said it wasn't very long before she was going out on her own too much. But the war had really proven the greatest factor in the destruction of their marriage. For after that he had no control over her movements whatsoever.

We continued to meet quite frequently and we saw many a football match together. He obviously enjoyed my company and once when I met him in the company of another man he remarked to his friend, 'Now just listen, it'll be dad this and dad that.' I was a man by this time and hadn't realised that I was using the expression so much. He made me aware of it after that. Maybe I was subconsiously trying to make up for all the years when he didn't want to hear from me.

At the football matches dad became the expert. Here he knew exactly what was happening and his comments and observations used to make the game doubly interesting for me. But, heavens, what partisanship, when he was watching the Orient, the team he had played for as a young man, he was blinded to half that was happening. And the result of the game had a tremendous affect upon his mood for the next few hours. When his team won dad was real good company.

No matter how short of money dad was he was irresistibly drawn to a game of any importance. He loved his football and got much happiness from it.

From then on we never lost touch with dad again and in addition to getting his 'children' back again he found that in his absence there had been an addition to his family, for Emmie became a devotee of his. She loved my dad, and he loved her. She loved him for his old-fashioned courtliness. While he loved her for the attention she paid to his comforts. Whenever he called on Arthur and Emmie he was always fed to the point of bursting, often with his favourite dishes, and he was always sent home with tit-bits to see him over the next few days. And, more important, he was made to feel he was somebody. His opinion was courted and his jokes were applauded. For when dad was happy and wanted to please he had quite a repertoire of humorous stories, which he would often embellish with a little soft-shoe-shuffle.

Then one day dad was taken ill and had to go into hospital. We visited him there and he told us that he had abdominal pains which were caused by the piece of shrapnel that he had picked up in the war. They were going to operate, he said, to take it out.

They operated and eventually dad came out of the hospital with a tube protruding from his side which assisted in draining his bladder. Back in his little room he used to have a nurse call regularly to attend to him. Still we had no suspicion regarding his illness, and believed, as did dad, that there was nothing to worry about, that it was simply a matter of finding that piece of metal that was proving so elusive and then all would be right.

But as the months went by and dad became slowly worse: as we could see that whatever it was that was wrong with him it seemed to be sapping his life away, we began to wonder whether there wasn't perhaps something more seriously wrong than what he had told us. He went back into hospital for a longer spell this time and when we visited him he now looked really ill.

In our discussions we all agreed that dad looked like a man who was slowly dying. His weight had gone from some thirteen stone to more like nine. His skin was deathly white and he was without all energy. He just lay there, a very sick man.

Always his remarks concerned what he would do when he came out. I'm certain he never realised that his appearance had taken on such a dramatic change. In his mind once they found that offending object he would quickly recover.

Then we were told, 'Your dad has cancer of

the bladder. He knows nothing about it and I think it would be better not to tell him.'

I couldn't have agreed more. He was like a child in his innocence. He never suspected. His faith in all that he was told by the doctors was absolute. It never occurred to him to doubt them.

The war was on now and both Doona and Emmie were pregnant. We all hoped that dad would live long enough to see his grandchildren. But it was clear that the end was not too far away now for dad had even taken on the colour of a dying man. We even took to saying that it would be a blessing when he went.

Yet right to the end he had maintained his old-time sense of values, like when he had asked how the war was going. Really, at that stage it seemed that only a miracle could save Britain from defeat. The Germans were carrying all before them. We were being forced to evacuate one position after another. I was quite sure in my mind that the end of the war could not be far off. Yet dad refused to see it this way. He had said as he lay there with life ebbing from his body, 'We always beat the Germans in the end.' There was no logic in his thinking but there was something else. There was a faith, an unquenchable belief in Britain's infallibility. We would win because we were who we were. He would be quite prepared to credit them with being a difficult nation to beat. But that was all. The result was without doubt.

Throughout the whole of dad's life Britain had been a powerful nation, a world power, a proud nation. Dad had heard and sung 'Sons of the Sea,' and 'Land of Hope and Glory' from being a little boy and these songs typified for him the impregnability, the indestructibility that was his country. It was outside his credibility that Britain could ever be anything else than supreme. She would win this war and carry on as she was before, an influence in every corner of the world, both respected and feared. He died thinking that way. He also died without seeing his first grandchild.

When that day came we all knew that the end was near. We had been waiting for the news for days. He was hardly alive anyway. Yet, when the news came through I was filled with sorrow. For nine months he had lain there without a hope of surviving. Each day we had found him a little bit weaker, a little bit thinner. He finished up a useless heap of skin and bone. Nobody told him that he had cancer and he retained that simple faith that was so much part of the society to which he belonged right to the end.

I was at my brother's place at the time. He was at work but his wife was home. The phone rang and she answered it. Then she turned to me and said, 'Syd, your father died a few moments ago.' A great sadness overwhelmed me. I felt dreadful. Not that he wasn't happier now. It was a relief, the end of his suffering, but over me swept the realisation of the futility of it all. The uselessness, the utter senselessness.

'Why, why,' I thought, 'had he come on earth to live the miserable life that he had, only to end up taking nine long months to slowly and painfully die?' What sort of a life was that? The gift of life indeed!

I could see him as a comparatively young man quarrelling with a wife it was impossible to handle. I could see him at home, alone, with his bag of sweets wondering what to do with himself. In my mind's eye he went once again around the corner to do battle with a new contender. I could see his War Certificate hanging on the wall, and I saw him as he was at the end, impoverished and struggling to make both ends meet.

Not only was his domestic life unhappy but he also lived at a time when the working classes were treated as little better than animals. And yet, for all the unfairness of it, they were prepared to consider themselves as less worthy than the upper classes. They were prepared to say 'sir' on every called for, and sometimes uncalled for, occasion. They were prepared to humble themselves for fear of losing their job and in the face of it all they had a loyalty and a love of their country that was touching in its earnestness.

I saw my dad again coming home on leave from the front. He didn't come home to a loving wife — they quarrelled then as they always did. I wonder, could he have possibly been glad to go back again?

For the whole week that he lay in the small chapel that the undertaker had at the back of the shop I went each evening and stood looking at that pitiable corpse that had once been so big and powerful. I went along each evening so that he could see that at least he had created some respect and regard during his life, small as it was. I wanted him to feel that he had not been forgotten, insignificant though he had been made to feel at times during his lifetime.

As I stood there we would be over the park with him shooting a football at me. God, how he could kick. If it had hit me it would have knocked me straight to the ground. It was a matter of stop it or get well out of its way.

Why he hadn't liked me as a child I never did find out. I have a theory now that we never do like our children to resemble us too closely, especially if they remind us of our faults. And I was my dad all over again — including the trend towards moroseness. He wouldn't have been one to analyse his feelings, any more than he would have made any great effort to control them — he disliked me and so he acted accordingly.

However, now he was dead and all I could see was what a miserably sad life he had lived and how unfortunate he had been in all respects. Married wrongly, estranged from his family, caught up in that dreadful war, and finally, with barely enough money to feed himself with in later years, had died of that scourge of a disease, cancer.

We couldn't afford to give him an elaborate funeral and he was buried in a communal grave, along with four or five others, and today we can't even find the plot to put a flower or two on it.

If it were possible to offer my dad the chance of another life on this earth I feel certain he'd turn it down. 'No thanks,' he'd say, 'once was quite enough for me.'

17

The Second World War

That day, when I arrived back from India, being Xmas Eve we were all invited round to the party being held at Emmie's parents' home. Here I was introduced to Phyllis. The introduction was made as though we had met quite by accident, 'Oh, you two have never met have you?' But I'm sure on reflection that she had been planted there specially for me. If this were so the plot was a complete success, for from that moment she became my girl. Actually they could have planted my granny there — I was a sucker for the first girl I saw. I had lost all sense of discrimination through being cut off from all womenfolk, and every girl I saw looked beautiful.

I was twenty-nine now, while she was twenty-seven. Both very eligible, age-wise for the marriage stakes, and Phyllis made this fact a constant theme for conversation.

Once we were invited to visit a newly-wed friend of hers and the subject of why Phyl and I didn't become engaged couldn't be kept down. It kept cropping up. Apparently these newly-weds were so enraptured of each other that they just couldn't understand why anyone ever wanted to remain single. At this point war clouds were in the air. Neville Chamberlain had been to Munich and returned with a promise of 'peace in our time'. But there were many among us who doubted the wisdom of this belief. The newly-weds remarked on the possibility of a further outbreak of war crisis and advised us to get married and 'have a bit of happiness before it is too late.' They seemed to think there was no happiness to be had outside of marriage. This of course gave Phyllis cause to raise the subject again and all the way home the question of when we were going to marry became hotly discussed.

At first the idea struck me as reasonably attractive, both Arthur and Doona seemed to have settled down to married life happily enough, and all Phyllis's friends, who had now become my friends, were married. There seemed little point to not taking the plunge myself.

The only snag was I was not in love, and as time went by I was less overcome by the mere thought of having a girl on my arm. I became more critical, but felt quite unable to withdraw from the situation.

How many couples marry in this fashion? They have been going together so long, and have become so used to one another, plus the fact that they recognise that it is expected of them. There is also the thought of how much it would hurt the other one to tell them that they no longer wish to marry them. It seems so much easier to go ahead and marry. So it is, of course. Much easier. But how wrong and foolish to have taken the easier course simply because it was less involved.

Phyl and I were in this situation. She, I'm sure was wanting to marry simply to be married. She was not in love with me but she was prepared to forget that small matter for the satisfaction that would be hers from being able to call herself Mrs. That to her represented some degree of promotion from the lowly rank of Miss.

So the drift was on towards the eventual last lap down the aisle to the altar.

We were just going aimlessly towards this and with no special enthusiasm on the part of either of us.

When it had been Chink, before I had learned of her extreme youth, with whom I had been discussing the question of marrying it had been a different thing. Then I had urged matters along. But this was so loveless, and yet at the same time so inevitable.

Doona would ask me what were my intentions, and I would say, 'Oh, I don't know, Doo, I suppose we'll be getting married before long.'

To this Doona would then always reply that there was no need for hurry. To give myself plenty of time. 'Have a look around. Why marry the first girl I met on arriving back in England?'

This, of course, made good sense but it didn't change the course of events.

Then more war rumblings filled the morning papers. Hitler looked like invading Poland. Should he do so it was almost certain that England would declare war on Germany. In that event the Reserves would be called up and that would include me.

This gave me cause to think. I would be one of the first to enter into a new war. I would be in it right from the start. By now we all knew of the power of the German army and air force. In my mind, looking back to the course of the first World War, when a man who was 'Over there' at the very beginning had little chance of still being there at the end, I felt sure that the soldiers who started off the next war would all be wiped out long before it was finished. And I would be one of the first in.

So, when the Reserves were called up and told to report to their depots I felt that I had virtually come to the end of my life.

This recall to the army had come about within nine months of my leaving.

Phyllis and I talked over what was going to happen to us. She thought it wisest to marry straight away. 'I would then have a wife and a home to come on leave to.'

This was my opening. I suddenly became all considerate and insisted that it would be quite wrong of me to marry with so much uncertainty in our minds as to whether I would even live long enough to ever take a leave. I was adamant. It would be unfair of me, I wouldn't consider it. And so the matter remained. Nothing could persuade me, I was like an accused man with no defence suddenly finding an alibi become available to him.

And so it was back to Catterick. Back to where I had nearly died of diphtheria, to where I had almost literally frozen at times. The place was beginning to haunt me. From Catterick it was but a matter of days before being attached to a unit that took on several lorry-loads of equipment and was soon at sea, on the way to France. It was with no feeling of 'let's get at them' that I disembarked — I had read too many books on the First World War.

We landed at Dunkirk and immediately ran straight into an air raid right there on the dockside. Two of our small number were killed and one lorry-load of equipment was lost. 'God,' I thought, 'is this what we can expect from now on?'

But this was to be the last raid I was to take part in, for the next day we passed through Arras, and here I was reminded once again of my dad. Much of the action that he had taken part in had centred around this town. He had picked up his piece of shrapnel in this area. Now here was I, my father all over again. In the same uniform, in the same spot, twenty-odd years later. How much would our lives follow the same course?

Soon after leaving Arras behind we turned into a quiet country road and wondered what we were heading for. It was little more than a country lane. Clearly we were nearing some stopping point. Then we turned into the drive of a chateau, through the large iron gates, up the drive and into the courtyard alongside the house. As we dismounted and looked around us we were most impressed. If this large mansion-type house was to be our new home we'd be doing all right.

But no. We were ushered into the stables

where there was a great heap of straw in the corner, told to fill the palliasses that were alongside and make ourselves at home as this was to be our new abode for heaven knows how long.

We were accompanied by two Post Office technicians whose job it was to supervise the installation of our equipment (which we now learned was to be a high-speed radio station), and to instruct us in the use of it. After that we would be in the sole charge of our captain, a genial soul, who had had some rank with the G.P.O. outside and was an officer in the Territorial Army. A week-end soldier, kindly and not at all authoritarian.

That evening four of us who had become friends took a stroll to see what was the lay of the land. There was Jim, Ginger, Norman and myself. Only one of us, I feel, merits any special mention. That was Norman. The other three were just ordinary, causing no turning of heads as they passed by. I was later described by the inhabitants of our village as a typical Englishman. When they said it I gathered from their tones that it was not especially a compliment. By that I think they meant, phlegmatic, unemotional, ordinary. But Norman, he was handsome. He caught everyone's eye. To give an idea how the girls took to him, he was once told at a certain brothel in Arras to pop in any time he felt like it and not to bother about paying. He was a Welshman, with dark wavy hair and fine, well-shaped features. He had too the breezy, self-assurance that went with the confidence that his appearance inspired in himself. To add to his charm he was the despatch-rider of the party and his clothes were dashing. He wore black, shiny leather gauntlets that reached halfway up to his elbows and jackboots. Most days a pair of goggles sat jauntily just above the peak of his hat. I couldn't blame any girl for falling for him. He breezed in and out of the village all day long and it was inevitable that he should become noticed and talked about. But that came later.

This first night we were on our way down the drive of the chateau to see what the village had to offer.

Coming onto the country road we turned left and along, passing the small cluster of houses on each side that made up the entire village. There was a small store (we noted this) and as the houses were almost about to peter out there was an inn, or estaminet as we were to call it. All the way along we had not seen a solitary person.

'How about a drink,' said Jim. And in we went.

Inside there were a couple of tables for the customers and a small bar, behind which were shelves stacked with bottles of drinks of all kinds.

We sat down at a table and waited. Then a door opened and Madame came out. She was an elderly lady dressed in black. Unpretentious and shy.

'Oui, messieurs,' she said, obviously feeling ill at ease.

215

This was a new situation to her. Strangers of any kind did not pop often into her estaminet, but four soldiers from overseas, settling in, obviously to spend the evening there, was something she was quite unprepared for.

We looked at Jim, our interpreter. He had learnt French at school and was eager now to make use of it. He gathered our orders together and passed them on to Madame. She went behind the counter, came back, served us, then went back to her room, plainly eager to be on her way, out of our presence.

The evening passed in pleasant enough fashion. We called 'Madame' when we wanted her and she came out of her room, unsmiling, took our order, served us and went back.

When we left that evening her manner had us puzzled. Did she dislike the English? Would she rather we weren't there? I think we had been harbouring secretly inside us a belief that we would be welcomed with open arms and this cool reception had disappointed us.

But Madame was old enough to remember well the coming of our fathers, and the devastation of her country that same memory would evoke. To her we were not harbingers of good tidings but rather reminders of unhappy days. Or it might be that she just felt very shy in our company. I don't know. All I do know is that rather gloomy looking face that she presented to us throughout that first evening was not a true reflection of her real self. We learned that later.

The second evening found us back at the same

216

table. There was nothing else to do in the village and there was warmth and conviviality (between ourselves, at any rate) in the estaminet. The drinks were cheap and we were enjoying the novelty of it all. Jim had to do all the talking for us for we others knew no French and the elderly lady knew not a word of English. The situation was both unusual and amusing.

Still Madame remained sedate and aloof. She served our drinks and retired each time immediately to the refuge of the other room. There were no village folk there, except at very odd times, for most of the men had gone off to the war.

Some time during the second evening the street door opened and in came a woman and her two daughters. One being about seventeen and the other around thirteen. These were the elderly proprietress's daughter, a widow, and her two children, Odette, the eldest, and Renee. They whispered, shyly, 'Bonsoir, messieurs' and passed into the other room. From then on things started to liven up. Every now and then the kitchen door would open and one or both of the girls would look out upon us, giggle, and draw their heads back. This, of course, would raise some comment followed by laughter from us. We went back to our straw palliasses that evening feeling that things were progressing a little.

By the third evening the girls had taken to serving us occasionally and now we started to fool around with them. There was also a young lady, Germaine, with a little baby. She was the wife of Madame's son. He was at the Front. In fact it soon became clear that the entire village had become almost denuded of eligible young men. We had the field pretty well to ourselves.

After about a week of spending every evening in the same position, all the time becoming a little bolder, a little more familiar, we had broken down the unsmiling Madame, who had become Marie, and we had managed to persuade her to enter into efforts at conversation. Then one evening she said, 'Ne restez pas la toujours. Entrez dans la cuisine chez nous.' This was interpreted by Jim as meaning, don't stay there all the time, come into the kitchen with us. A very welcome invitation. We picked up our drinks and wandered into the precincts behind the door. Here we were in a typical French, village-style living-room. There was a stove with an ever-simmering coffee pot resting on it. There was an immense, heavy-looking table in the centre and the floor was covered with blue and white stone tiles. But over all was the atmosphere, an atmosphere of friendly politeness and kindness. We had become the intimates of a group of the most gentle, the most refined, the most amiable people I have ever known. We were admitted into their circle. We had become their friends. For from that moment onwards we spent all our spare time in their company. The evenings were always passed in Marie's kitchen along with the other members of the family and during the day if one or the other of us was off duty we would be invited into their houses for

218

a glass of wine and a chat.

Slowly we learned to make ourselves understood and to form some understanding of what was being said to us. Although without Jim around this often had to be accompanied by much waving of arms or pulling of faces.

One night Marie asked us would we like to have supper each night. If so we could give her our order the evening before and the next day she would buy our requirements while she was at the market. This offer was taken up eagerly. So each night we would now tell her what we wanted for tomorrow night. 'Eggs and chips for me, please!' 'I'll have a piece of steak with tomatoes and chips, please.' 'Make mine sausages and chips, Madame, please.' There was only one stipulation — having ordered them we had to promise to be there to eat them the next night. This we were only too ready to agree to.

The weeks went by with us becoming more and more at home. Events happened, like the baby was baptised, or Renee's birthday arrived, to which we were always invited. We belonged. We were part of the life there. We helped them in some of their farm chores, for they all had farms, even old Marie. On one lovely summer day I can see myself as I turned the handle of a machine for Odette while she fed turnips into it, which came out the other side chopped up all ready to be served to the cows. Sometimes we helped make the butter. Life was idyllic.

Phyllis had now become little more than a memory. I had tapered off the amount of letters I was sending to her and one day they stopped altogether. She had found herself another companion, I believe, and I had lost some of my importance. But, in any case, Phyllis, and all things English, seemed a world away to me. I was caught up in this new way of life, where I was never just Syd. It had to be Monsieur Syd (which came out more like Seed).

By now young Renee had taken to bringing into the estaminet some of her little girl-friends to see the English soldiers. One evening she was sitting there with a friend just staring at us when all of a sudden (so Jim told us) she turned to her little companion and said, 'The English burned Joan of Arc, didn't they.' She could almost smell the fire upon us.

Marie's daughter was called Maria. She was the mother of Odette and Renee. One evening when she was not there her mother, Marie, told us that during the first World War, when Maria was a young girl of seventeen, some English soldiers had been billeted in the village and young Maria had fallen in love with one. This had lasted for some months and then orders had come for them to move on. There had been much shedding of tears and she had never seen or heard of him again. Marie said that this had been most upsetting at the time, and, in fact, Maria had never forgotten him. It would be natural to expect that our coming to the village had brought it all back to her.

And here nature played one more of its unhumorous tricks, for Odette, who was seventeen, the same age as her mother had been the previous time, fell in love with Norman. Perhaps this was inevitable. Yet it didn't have to be. But it became inevitable once Norman started showing an interest in her. Then she didn't stand a chance. She already had a boy-friend, young Leon, a gawky, immature, country lad who, I believe, considered himself her fiancé.

Norman could not let any opportunity pass and the moment he had seen Odette's eyes upon him one evening in the estaminet she was a goner.

Thereafter we all knew that there was something between them. She was in love, and could not hide it. Who can? While Norman, well he was pretty blasé about who knew about it anyway.

Poor Odette, I really felt quite sorry for her. She was so sincere. She would have been so easy for Norman to have handled her to suit his mood or fancy. And it was clear that she could only be hurt in the end. She wasn't beautiful. She was just an honest, quietspoken, unsophisticated country girl. She happened to be the only one there and that made her, for Norman, an irresistible object of interest.

One day her fiancé, Leon, told me that he would like to have a word with me. We went for a stroll and he told me (to this day I don't know how I understood him so clearly. But I know I did.) that he was in love with Odette. He said that she was his fiancee and that everyone knew that they were going to be married one day. And now Norman had come between them. He knew that she had fallen in love with Norman and that Norman was not in love with her.

'How was it going to end?' he asked.

'Could I help him? Could I have a word with Norman and ask him, please, to have nothing more to do with her?'

I promised that I would. He was pitiable in his misery. Poor chap he couldn't pit himself against Norman's handsomeness. Asking me to have a word on his behalf was all he could think of.

I spoke to Norman, but it was useless.

'No,' said he, 'I'm not promising not to see her any more. Why should I. I can't help it if she likes me better than him, can I?'

No, he couldn't help that, perhaps. Of course she would like him better than Leon. That was to be expected. But he could help encouraging her.

So everything went along as before, with Leon looking extremely glum, while Odette still had stars in her eyes. Norman seemed about the same as ever. He took these things in his stride.

Our work was minimal. The high-speed radio station that was now erected was to be the link between London and H.Q. in France in the event of the cross-Channel under-water cable being destroyed. In the meantime we were to maintain an almost continuous silence. We did open up, each day at a different time, and exchange signals for about five minutes and then close down again. But we also had to have someone constantly on duty just in case we were required to go into action. So it was little more than a case of having to be there, even though there was practically nothing to do.

Month after month went by like this. The war had started and yet it hadn't. It became known as The Phoney War. But this suited us fine. How different to the retreat from Mons with its hundreds of thousands of casualties, that had come at the beginning of the other war.

I don't know what we expected to ultimately happen but I know that inside me I harboured a hope that sooner or later both sides would realise the futility of engaging in open warfare and would decide to call the whole thing off.

Rumours of us being sent on leave began to circulate and I wondered whether I should go to Paris for mine, where a Leave Centre had been set up, or go back to London to see my folks. The idea of going to Paris appealed enormously. Paris the word has a magic ring to it. I had never been there and had always wanted to go. This opportunity to spend three weeks at the army's expense was golden. It was most tempting. Maria had said to me, 'If you go to Paris for your leave I can give you the address of a relation of mine who would be only too happy to take you around.' What a magnificent offer. Yes, it was most tempting, indeed. But against this was the fact that if I did not go home to England I might never have the chance again. Open hostilities could break out at any time and if anything should happen to me how wrong it would be to have denied my relations that last opportunity of us

223

all being together. And so when my turn came around for leave I opted for England.

It seemed at the time that I had thrown away for ever the chance of spending three lovely weeks in the one city in the world whose very name conjures up more attractions than any other that I know. Yet, life being what it is, I have been since, twice, and stayed for some time. And I even think now that to a very large degree I know Paris. I know it and I love it. But then, I chose to go on leave to England, entirely from a sense of duty.

Actually I didn't want to go on leave at all. I didn't want to leave my French family. We had no need of a change. Our work wasn't burdensome, and our surroundings were most congenial. However, I went. I spent three weeks back in England and in fact on arriving it was most pleasing to see again Arthur and Emmie, and Doona. It was then that they told me that Phyllis had found a boyfriend who seemed to be lending a much more receptive ear to her talk about marriage than I had. She later married him.

At the end of those three weeks I returned to France, to Marie, Maria, Odette and Renee. It was like coming home again. There was the coffee-pot still simmering on the stove and the same polite attitude of one towards the other was still there. They welcomed me back as though they were really pleased to see me. Strangely enough I had also missed the language, even though my understanding of it was so slight.

Nothing had changed, of course. Norman was

still chugging backwards and forwards to Arras, Odette was still obviously in love, while Renee in her schoolchild innocence still treated us all the same, just a bunch of foolish grown-ups.

That same evening as we sat around the big table in the centre of the room with a continuous flow of chatter and laughter passing from one to the other I felt glad to be back.

Nine months went by in this fashion. We knew others in the village. There was Mme Dupont with the pretty little daughter. In some way that I'm not sure of Jim had become friendly with her and used to be invited along to tea. As with most the husband, Monsieur Dupont, was away with the forces. Jim told me one day that Mme Dupont had suggested to him that he would make a fine husband for Louise, her little daughter. 'Would he wait?' The daughter apparently was very fond of him, but then, she was no more than a child. About thirteen. Jim said that he was so taken aback and in fact found the idea so attractive that he didn't like to turn it down. He had made some non-committal reply, at the same time hoping that he had kept the idea alive in the mother's mind. Louise was obviously going to be a beauty later on, and there was some suggestion too that the Duponts were slightly rich. They had one of the bigger homes in the village and were always dressed well.

Then there was the concierge and his wife, in charge of the chateau. They had become very good friends of ours and we spent many an afternoon in conversation over a glass or two of wine in their flat.

Altogether this village had become to us just like our own. Everyone knew us and we knew everyone. Some of the inhabitants we more than knew, we had developed an affection for. I felt as though I would be happy for life to go on this way for ever.

Then one day it happened. We were told by our genial captain to pack everything onto the trucks. The balloon had gone up and the German advance was coming in our direction. All through the night we worked, and in the early hours of the morning we mounted and moved off. The dawn was just breaking, there was a mist lying over the fields, all was peaceful and perfectly quiet. Not a soul was in sight. I imagined they were all as yet still abed, sleeping.

We moved away and I cast my eyes over the entire village as we left, our home for the last nine months. There they were, the homes of those lovely people. The estaminet, where Marie was resting, quite unaware of the fact that we would not be there that evening to eat the supper that she had brought for us. And a little way down the road would be Odette, who would awaken to the fact that Norman had left. This same thing had happened to her mother many years before. She would be sad and lonely for a long while to come for she was so much in love, and so sincere. As for little Renee, she too would miss us, but not for long, for she was young and the young tend to forget easily.

There would be others too, for we had left our mark all over the place. Nine months of constant association can be a long time.

All this and more swept over me as we moved slowly down the road, away, away from our precious village. As we passed the signboard with its name clearly marked it said, GIVENCHY LE NOBLE. Yes, that was it. I would never forget it.

I would carry the fond memory of this place with me through the years.

With the passing of time my memories became a little dimmer and I began to wonder at times whether perhaps I wasn't holding an exaggerated picture in my mind of the affection that there had been between us in that village. I had grown to think of those months as nine of the most charming months of my life. Always I hoped that I would be able to go back again one day. At times the chances seemed very remote. But thirty years after we moved off on that quiet, misty morning I went back. I went back with my heart in my mouth. What would I find? Well, let me tell of that later.

★ ★ ★

Right now our position had become untenable and we were on the road to Dunkirk, although this was unknown to us. All we knew was that we were on the move.

Within an hour, with the coming of full daylight, we were dive-bombed and one of our trucks was set on fire. Nobody was hit

227

on that occasion as we had all taken cover in a ditch alongside the road. After that it seemed that we were stopping and taking shelter every few minutes. Our progress was painfully slow, and costly. We lost two more trucks that day and had our first casualty. One of our comrades took too long leaving a truck during a raid and he was simply blown up. In the short time that we spent looking for him we just could not find him, so we moved on.

Three days later, begrimed, tired, and battered, some of our number left behind in eternity, we arrived at Dunkirk. Coming over a bit of a rise, with no idea where we were, all of a sudden there was the sea and there the rescue boats. There was a fine stretch of holiday sand with column after column of troops in various stages of sartorial disarray leading down across the beach and out into the water, many of the farthest out being up to their chests.

To their credit some of these chaps, to whom it must have seemed that the war was clearly lost, would still not give up their arms. They were holding their guns way above their head to prevent them being rendered useless by the sea water. And this was going to make their task of getting on to a craft and away to safety all that much more difficult. But somehow, these chaps (they were a minority, mind you, and I did not enter their noble ranks) just could not bring themselves to make this last token of surrender.

There was a majesty about the whole scene when one first came upon it. A sort of dignity.

There was no panic. Just a quiet, patient, quite orderly evacuation. Up to a point each one was taking his turn in the order in which it was due. No pushing others aside. No scrambling over one another. Until they started striking out in the water to reach nearby craft which could not come farther in, one could see to which column each man belonged.

I feel very tempted to say this patience, this acceptance of their lot, almost as though it was expected, this orderliness and respect for the rights of the chap alongside, even under the most nerve-wracking conditions (for planes were strafing at will all the time) was so British. Yes, why shouldn't I say it? For where else, among what other nation would one find it? I don't know whether to feel proud of them as I write, but I know this, it makes me feel very sentimental towards them.

We distributed ourselves among the columns and slowly edged forward toward the sea as those in front were picked up, picked off by enemy planes, or drowned through sheer inability to keep afloat. Later on, when I was in the sea myself, I was to see men dragged down by the weight of their waterlogged uniforms struggling to keep afloat as the movement of the water knocked them off their feet. I watched men drown here and there, no more than a few yards off, drown with a thousand virtual rescuers all around. One couldn't help, there were too many and our concentration was mainly centred on finding a vessel sufficiently close for us to swim to. For it must be remembered that with the constant danger that there was threatening from the skies the longer we hung around the more chance there was of us meeting one with our number on it.

I spent the whole of that first day swimming out to boats only to see them move off before I could reach them. It became a game of chance. One picked out a boat that looked not only near enough to swim to but also near enough to swim back from if necessary. Dusk came and I was still boatless. I decided to call it enough. Exhausted, cold, and sodden, to say nothing of scared, I scrambled back across the beach and lay down in the garage of one of the empty houses lining the sea-front. Many of these houses were on fire. It was an eerie sight.

The evacuation and the bombardment went on all night but I slept, I knew nothing of it. Next day it was once more into the water to try my luck again. In the distance could be heard the sounds of heavy guns as the advancing enemy forces came nearer and nearer. In the end those remaining would be taken prisoner. Catching a boat became almost a matter of life and death. But this didn't make it any easier and it was many hours before I was finally hauled on board a pleasure boat.

When the little craft that had picked me up arrived back at Margate I, along with the others, went ashore to the hand-shaking and patting on the back from the crowds who had waited to greet us. We were handed packets of cigarettes, bars of chocolate, cups of tea. Anything that they thought would help show their appreciation.

We looked like men just returned from hell. As indeed we were. The transition was too much. Back there we were in danger of death at any moment. In a world devoid of reason, Here, all at once, we were heroes, being fussed over by a whole nation that was falling over itself to make us welcome. Here we were with all the grime of war still upon us, with girls and women wanting to kiss us, grime and all. Here there was quiet, there was peace, there was sense. It was too much for a sensitive nature. I had to fight to keep from breaking down completely. We couldn't take all the things they wanted to give us, there were too many.

We were put into trains and despatched to different army depots. I went to Reading, and in the train, at every station that we passed, there were crowds on the platforms once again wanting to fuss over us. It was an ordeal. As far as I was concerned I had done nothing to deserve this.

At Reading we were all sorted into our various regiments and it was then that I found Jim again. He had got away from the beaches a few hours before me. It was good to see him and to recall our village days. Norman and Ginger I never saw again. I have no idea what happened to them.

Back home at Arthur's and Emmie's I was treated like a man returned from the dead. They feted me. They couldn't do enough. Both had watched the situation in the newspapers and had listened to every news bulletin on the radio. They told me they had cut out maps that the

231

papers had published and they were able to pin-point our position and the German advance with every day that passed. They thought there was no hope and had given me up for lost.

The feeling at this time, with which I fully agreed, was that the war couldn't possibly last much longer. But how wrong we were, for five more years were to pass before the war was finally over. Five years of constant air raids, of much destruction, of strict rationing and much loss of life.

After a short but happy spell with Arthur and Emmie it was back to Catterick again, where I very soon found myself attached to a unit that was to be leaving the next week for somewhere overseas. This turned out to be West Africa we learned later, where we understood we were to make a three pronged attack on the French Ivory Coast, from where repeated U-boat attacks were taking a heavy toll of our shipping. We were to be the land force.

We sailed from a Scottish port in the dead of night in convoy. On the way we learned from the usual unrecognisable source not to pick anyone up. The safety of the convoy as a whole was more important than any one ship. At sea, with the ship in total darkness, slipping silently through the night, one could not fail to be aware of the danger that there was all around us.

And so the days, and nights, passed dreamily on until one day our whole life was enlivened. We were sailing quietly through a smooth sea, the sun was shining benignly down, there was hardly a sound to be heard, when all of a sudden one of the ships on the convoy went up with a loud explosion.

I'd swear I felt our ship immediately speed up. Like an animal that has suddenly been startled.

There was a feeling in the air then of, who's next? but nothing further happened. We hastened on our way, while the destroyers veered off to give chase.

On we sailed until we came to Freetown. There a small number of us, myself included, disembarked and immediately went aboard a small ship which set off as soon as we were on board. From then on we were all alone. But I had a greater feeling of safety on this little craft. She was fast and small. Too fast for any submarine to follow and not a very big target to fire at. Also we hugged the coast all the way and this gave us a feeling that we weren't entirely cut off.

It was on this little ship, cutting through the water at a most comforting speed that one of the crew told us where we were going.

'You are going to the Gold Coast,' he said.

'What would we be going there for?' we asked.

'I don't know but you can have it for me. What a climate. You're bound to catch malaria, you can't dodge it there.'

This didn't worry me too much. Hadn't I recently spent five years in India. A malarial country. In fact I had a feeling tucked away inside me that I was immune from malaria. I'd seen one after another go down with it when I was on the Frontier, and heaven knows I'd been bitten by mosquitoes often enough. There must have been a malaria carrier or two among that lot. No, I wasn't worried on that score.

The voyage passed without incident and one day we chugged into Takoradi harbour. Ashore we were in the Gold Coast, later renamed Ghana. Our 'Speck' was really getting shuttled around now.

Very soon we were herded aboard a train and left for the interior.

Our train stopped or slowed down at several small stations. We were heading for Accra via Kumasi. At these small stations we met the Africa that one reads about. We became 'Massa'. It astonished me. I had thought that this sort of talk had died out years before, if it ever really existed. But here it was, as large as life. 'Hello, Massa, you buy bananas. Massa, Massa, you buy him this?' They all seemed happy and were all the time laughing. I felt enormously interested.

After passing through mile after mile of densely overgrown bush we came finally to Accra. Here we disembarked and were taken by trucks to our new home. This was a permanent, well-established army camp, but the troops were terribly raw.

I was directed to my 'giddah'. This was a pill-box shaped hut made of mud, with a thatched roof. At the back was a small outbuilding, which was the room for my 'boy'. Inside I had one largish room the shape of the building, with a bed with mosquito net in position, a folding chair, a table, a canvas type wash basin on a stand and a raffia rug. Altogether a very comfortable little home for a mere corporal. Especially when one throws in the servant boy as well. He, by the way, was paid by the army. His job was to do absolutely everything for me. He ran errands, he cooked all my meals, kept the place clean, did my washing and ironing. At night when I came back from duty he had a bowl of warm water waiting for me in which to wash down, alongside of which was laid out a clean towel. He had a cold drink ready for me after I had washed and then he was ready to serve dinner that he had bought and cooked for me. Another influence upon my character? Must have been. I was treated as though I were really someone. These servant and master relationships are no longer encouraged anywhere but, call them good or bad, call them what you like, I'm bound to admit that I did enjoy being treated as somewhat superior, and I'm glad that I got in on it before it eventually disappeared, which it did not too long after I had known it. In fact that war was to speed it on its way out.

One thing I will say in my defence to those who feel ready to criticise at this stage, I always treated my 'lesser' fellows decently. There might have been more than an element of condescension associated with this 'decent' treatment. I'll not deny that, but I did seem to acquire their respect. And in view of the general attitudes prevailing at the time, which were the immediate influence upon my way of thinking, I'm satisfied that I saw, from my own reasoning, that these characters calling me Massa, plus the forehead-touchers in India, were not there for me to enjoy and abuse. Also, they were always paid on the dot for any service rendered.

However, the nature of this story is not meant to be an apology in any way whatsoever. What I did I did because that was me and here I'm only concerned with events as they happened. If I were there now I've no doubt there would be a different tale to tell, for I am a different person, but it was then, nineteen forty-three, and I was a young man of thirty-three.

My job in this camp was to train a squad from scratch. They came in straight from their villages, from the bush, and I taught them to drill, to use a rifle. I taught them Army Orders and, finally, I taught them the Morse Code. When they left me they had passed from native village lads, who knew not the first thing about the duties of a soldier. Knew not even how to put on a pair of boots. They passed from that to well-drilled, smart-looking young men in uniforms who knew how to send and receive morse messages at a reasonable speed

This was most satisfying work. I could play the part of Corporal Dendy. Now I could see how much he had enjoyed it. Like him I would bring my men in off the hot drill square to the cool shade of a tree and there I would stand them at ease and proceed to tell them off at great length. But unlike Dendy I could not wait until they had passed out before telling why I was doing this. From then on I had their respect.

The trouble was they could not listen to me telling them off without a great big grin spreading across their happy faces. The situation was ridiculous.

After four months of this work I and three others were flown a thousand miles north to Gambia. It was from Gambia that our invasion would take place. Now my life became really native. I was given a small detachment of four African soldiers, three radio operators and a truck driver. We drove fifty miles into the bush and here at a selected site, in a clearing in the bush we set up a radio station. I was the only white man in the district. A walk of only a few yards in any direction and I was among monkeys leaping from branch to branch, chattering madly at my approach, while birds of the wildest, most garish colours were everywhere.

Here was I, where never in my most imaginative dreams would I have expected to be. And here I stayed for many months.

In this jungle clearing I contracted malaria. It just had to be. We were hemmed in by all kinds of undergrowth. The mosquitoes were our constant companions. One had to accept that they would be bitten over and over again. It was unavoidable. And as the disease is so prevalent among the natives it was also to be accepted that a high proportion of the malaria-carriers would be amongst the biters. So down I went. For several days I knew I was ill, but thought it might wear off. In the end I could take no more and sent a message off to the effect that I suspected that I had malaria. A truck was sent for me and I was taken back to Bathurst, the capital city of Gambia, and put into hospital.

In all I was in Gambia for a year and during that time I had malaria three more times. Like that seaman had said, 'You're certain to catch it.' He was right and I was wrong. One might dodge it in India but parked down in the very centre of the jungle there in West Africa for months on end one became a sitting duck.

Almost every evening one would hear the beat of drums coming from one direction or another. This was usually the sign that some village was celebrating. These beating drums were irresistible to me and invariably I would wander off, following the sound until I came to where a dance was in progress. Here I would stand around, a part and yet not a part, for my presence was always accepted, yet ignored. In the light of a huge bonfire which was their only illumination I would stand there fascinated.

Women in this part were to be had for a song, and they often offered themselves to me on meeting them out walking. 'Massa,' they would say, 'you want piccin?' This was short for piccaninny or baby.

Somehow this bland way of presenting themselves never attracted me. For one thing we had been very strongly advised not to have intercourse with the local maidens as a fair amount of disease was prevalent. This was enough to frighten me off, for I was still very health and strength conscious. But in addition I like my sexual experiences to come upon me a little more stealthily than in the 'You want

238

piccin' fashion. But this is not to say that these more forthright tactics didn't have any success. They did, and many a companion of mine had a spell in hospital for a disease not contracted from the bite of a mosquito.

At the end of a year there were signs that all was in readiness. That it wouldn't be long before that which we had trained so assiduously for would be put into action. We were ready for whenever the order came — it was now no more than a matter of fixing the date. Then, out of the blue, I was told that I was to spend three months leave in England. It was considered that eighteen months in that climate was sufficient and that after that one needed recuperative leave. And so once again I found myself in convoy on the high seas. Once more after another tedious zig-zagging voyage we reached England.

I spent a very pleasant three months staying at Arthur's and Emmie's and it was then that I saw how Emmie was standing up so bravely to the bombing. She refused to leave the house, no matter how severe a raid. Her argument was that once she started taking refuge outside, in the shelters or down the Underground stations she would be perpetually running away. She preferred to take a chance in her own home, she said. She knew of families who automatically, without waiting to see whether there would be a raid that night or not, took up their beds and went straight to the Underground. They had become panicky and the first signs of nightfall were enough to have them worried. This she refused to do. Rather than become frightened of her own shadow she chose to take whatever came her way. She went to bed, whatever, and she slept, sometimes right through a nearby air raid. She was a perfect example of how one can steel themselves to behave normally in the most abnormal of circumstances. And she would not accept praise. 'Don't tell me I'm brave,' she would say, 'I'm scared all right, but I just can't be bothered to pick up my bedding every night and go trudging through the streets with it and back again next morning. I just can't be bothered. I like the comfort of my own bed too much, bombs or no bombs.'

She saw no bravery in this. Well, I did, and I still do.

Once a bomb dropped only three houses away and the explosion threw her out of bed. She said that pieces of the ceiling fell on top of her and the room was filled with dust. She wondered whether the house would stand up to it. But she cleaned the room up, swept up the pieces of ceiling, went back to bed, and within ten minutes was asleep again.

This, odd as it might sound, I wholeheartedly believe. One because it was not the sort of thing that Emmie would say if it were not true, and two because she was renowned as a magnificent sleeper.

I suppose there were many mothers like that during the war. All praise to them.

At the end of my three months leave I was to report for onward transport back to West Africa. I wasn't feeling too good at the time but I didn't suspect anything. However, the medical examination that was required showed me to once again have malaria. I was put into a military hospital in London and downgraded to a medical category that prevented me from going back to my unit in West Africa.

I never did go back and have no idea what happened to my kit, or to several personal belongings that I had left behind.

For the next twelve months I was considered to be unfit for active service abroad, until a time came when I had had no recurrence of malaria for several months. Then I was upgraded and posted once again to India for service in Burma.

The trip out to India this second time was most unlike the first, in so far as I was no longer a starry-eyed youngster. I had seen all this before, over and over again.

Nothing much stands out in my mind except for one thing. On my mess table was a young soldier — rather nice-looking, with fair, wavy hair. A perfectly normal young man, but what made me remember him was the story he told at the table one day. He said that on the day of his enrolment when the officer had asked him what was his work outside he had answered, 'Crooning, sir, I was a crooner.'

'You mean that was your full-time occupation, you earned your living crooning?'

'Yes, sir, I was a singer, a professional singer.'

'Oh, and what is your name?' asked the officer, still looking somewhat astonished.

'Mercer, sir, Tony Mercer.'

241

He was a young fellow of about twenty-three or four at the time. His name meant nothing to me. Tony Mercer, never heard of him. But from now on I listened to hear him sing. I had a bit of a voice myself and only had to hear the latest song a couple of times and I had it memorised. So I kept this Tony Mercer, this professional singer under watch. I waited to hear him break forth into song. Then one day he did it, he started gently, quietly twiddling through a popular number. I listened. 'Hm,' I thought, 'not all that good. I think I could do as well as that myself.' I had a notion that most of these successful characters are only lucky, anyway. Any one of us, given the same chance, could do equally well.

Then, about half-way across to India a ship's concert was organised and, of course, Tony was roped in. That evening I learned a lot. In the first place he had taken such care with his appearance that he hardly looked the same fellow. He was so much more handsome. He had the knack of making the most of himself. Then there was his composure. On the improvised stage he was more than at ease, he was in his element. He was more than calm, he was revelling in it. This was his trade. And the song he had chosen to sing, none but a professional would have dared choose it. It was Drigo's Serenade. And he sang it beautifully. Then I knew that it was no mere chance that had enabled him to say 'Crooner, sir,' when asked what was his occupation. He could sing. He was an accomplished singer. I saw at once the difference between his rendering of a song and mine.

We became quite pally and he told me that when this blooming war was over if ever I saw his name outside a theatre I was to call in on him and he'd give me a couple of 'complimentaries'.

The years went by. I'd forgotten all about him. His name had disappeared along with so many others, until one day I saw for the first time The Black and White Minstrel Show. I was well into my fifties then, once again staying with a much older Arthur and Emmie, and onto the television screen came one portly gentleman, by name, Tony Mercer. The name rang a bell but the figure didn't. I searched back. Could this be the young fellow the Drigo's Serenade singer? Handsome Harry? It became even more impossible to recognise him with his black-faced disguise. I would tell people, 'I believe I knew him during the war. We were on the same boat going to India, I think.'

And so I had gone on believing, yet wondering.

Then Tony Mercer, now a well-known personality arrived for a 'season' in Auckland, New Zealand, where I was living. I wrote to him. This would solve the puzzle 'Was he the young fellow sailing out to India during the war who sang Drigo's Serenade at the ship's concert? Did he remember Corporal Metcalfe?

Nothing happened. I had made a mistake. Then one evening after I had gone to bed I heard the phone ring and my landlady answering

243

it. Shortly afterwards there was a knock at my door, 'There's a man asking for Syd on the phone.'

Yes, it was Tony. He remembered the boat and he remembered me. 'Unfortunately he was about to leave for England, but he would be coming out again next year and we must meet.' I looked forward to that.

A year passed and I waited to hear from him. But nothing happened. Then, sadly, I heard that he had died. Well, at least he had reached the top of his profession. He had had several years of success.

Talking of personalities (or perhaps rather personages) I met another in Auckland. One day walking along a side street I noticed a young man coming towards me on the other side of the road. If he had been wearing running togs and was going round and round the track at White City Stadium he wouldn't have been any more familiar to me than he was as we came closer to each other in that narrow side street. I crossed over. 'Excuse me, aren't you Gordon Pirie?' I asked.

His eyes lit up. 'Yes, I am,' said he, smiling.

'I've seen you run a few times in London,' said I. 'You've given me some pleasurable moments in your day.'

'Thank you. Do you know,' he said, with a tone of disgust in his voice, 'I walk around here all day and nobody recognises me. You are only about the second person. By the way what would your name be?'

'It not only would be, but it actually is, Syd

244

Metcalfe,' I quipped.

He laughed. And then I saw how each man's horizon is limited by the activities in which he is most interested.

'Metcalfe,' said Gordon, 'that's a famous name.'

'You're thinking of Adrian Metcalfe, the quarter-miler,' said I.

'Yes, he was a good un.'

Now, I don't suppose one person in a thousand would have heard of Adrian Metcalfe, an athlete of some standing in the early sixties, yet to Gordon Pirie his name came instantly to mind. Had the Prime Minister's name been Metcalfe I'm sure Gordon would have still thought first of the runner.

We landed at Bombay. So, here I was again, in India. Just as well I'd paid my debts.

Little did I think when I packed my souvenirs and left for England that first time that within a few short years I would be back again. Yet here I was once more amid all the old familiar scenes.

Now the medley of beggars and others wishing to sell me things recognised me for what I was, an old-timer. I had expressions that no new boy could have known. And I've no doubt there were other signs that told them too. I knew how to wear tropical kit, and I wasn't staring around me in wonderment.

But neither was I sorry to be there. India has something about it that makes one want to go back. Even now I would like to see it again. It is such a bubbling hive of activity. There is the

245

chatter of people around you, who are talking to each other long after they have passed out of ear-shot. There is music being played at some nearby bazaar. I call it music but to us it is no more than a weeping and a wailing. One would think the singer is in agony. Yet there is no denying the bewitching effect it has upon those standing listening. Then there are the perpetual urgings of the drivers of bullock carts as they pass ponderously by in the roadway. In the bigger cities there is also the continuous clanging of bells as the trams clatter by noisily on their way. To all of this there would today have to be added the din from the flow of modern traffic. For in my day it hadn't yet arrived.

From Bombay we were sent by train to Mhow, and here I lost trace of Tony Mercer. Where he went to I don't know but I went straight to Burma.

If we have any friendly spirits watching over us throughout our lives then I must say mine must be very influential in the spirit world for up to now I have passed right through the war hardly seeing a bullet fired. And it was beginning to be clear that if one could only hold on a little the whole thing would be over, for the Allies were now well on top in Europe. It had become little more than a matter of mopping up. And, of course, once the war in Europe was over and all attention could be directed to the Japs it couldn't possibly last much longer.

So it was a case of could my friendly spirit keep up the good work for just a few more months?

In Burma we were continually on the move but to this day I don't know whether we were chasing them or they were chasing us. I never saw an enemy soldier so I was unable to say whether they were coming in our direction or going away.

My impressions of Burma are all unassociated with acts of war. I was intrigued, for one thing, by the apparent tranquillity of the native people. On passing through a village, for example, we would be received in complete silence, faces a study in lack of emotion, all puffing away on a cigar. There would be mum, with baby in arms, gran'ma and gran'dad and a cluster of children, all, except the baby, with a cigar protruding from their mouth. It was an incredible sight until one became used to it. And the size of the cigar was in accordance with the age of the smoker. Little cigar for youngster, big cigar for gran'ma.

They eyed us as we passed with complete equanimity, as though we were not of the slightest interest. Whether they liked us or hated our guts I wouldn't have the faintest idea. Their look told nothing.

The villages all appeared to be comparatively well-to-do. Much more so than those of their Indian cousins.

Harking back to that question of whether we were retreating or advancing. I rather feel, on reflection, that we must have been doing the chasing for there never seemed to be any urgency about our movements. One day we had a very nice swim in the Irrawaddy and that wasn't very suggestive of an enemy hot on our tail.

It was soon after this swim, I was manning the radio station, when I was told that I would be returning to India to be trained in a new piece of radio equipment that nobody knew much about. So there, my guardian spirit had done it again. I was to leave the danger area for a course of training somewhere in India. This was good news.

The course was being held at an army school in Agra, the city best known for its proximity to the Taj Mahal. Actually the Taj is situated just on the outskirts of the city.

I became very well acquainted with this edifice, for I went there quite frequently.

What it was that drew me back again and again I do not know. Certainly it has a charm. And just as one never tires of looking at beautiful women so I found the pleasure that one derives from just standing and gazing upon this lovely building equally inexhaustible.

Standing before it, there in the forecourt, its presence has a remarkable effect. I'm sure others felt it too for there was always a silence. One never laughed in its proximity or made an unruly noise of any kind. To have done so would have been disrespectful and would have brought all eyes upon the perpetrator.

To me it conveyed a feeling of peace, of sublimity and humility. It overawes and makes the beholder feel small.

Remembering that it has stood in its present splendour for four hundred years and still brings thousands upon thousands to just stand and stare — this was enough to make one such as

I realise what a tiny speck I was alongside it.

It gives the impression of floating just above the ground rather than resting upon it. As for there being foundations under the ground to which it is firmly attached, I almost refuse to believe it.

I went up to the top of one of the four minarets situated one at each corner, from where I could look closely upon the huge domed top. It is reckoned to be perfectly symmetrical. That would have been calculated by some geometrical method, I suppose. As far as I was concerned such calculations were valueless. All that seemed to matter to me was the effect that it had upon the onlooker. What matter an inch or two here and there when one is gazing upon such beauty? By what does one measure that?

I took my boots off that I might wander inside and I gazed upon the tomb of the Mumtaz Mahal, that lady whose husband so loved her that he thought her worthy of such a tomb.

Thank heavens I saw all this at a time when there were no tourists. One strident note would have sent me away shattered, I'm sure. Instead of which there were never any but the Indian people who move over the ground in the way that the Taj rests upon it, as though their feet are passing just over the top.

From England came letters to tell me that Emmie's father Charlie was ill with tuberculosis. I was kept up with the course of his illness and then one day I read that he had died. He was a comparatively young man, being still in his fifties. So Charlie passed on and with him went a link with my youth. There would be no more Xmas parties that went on until the early hours of the morning. No more host and hostess who concerned themselves only with the enjoyment of everyone present, contemptuous of the mess being made, that they would have to clear up the next morning.

Yet although Charlie is no longer around, he is very far from forgotten, for Emmie once told me that she never goes to sleep at night without saying, 'Goodnight, dad'. And at that time she always sees his face looking at her, and there is always a smile upon it. Also, on the anniversary of the day that he died and on his birthday Emmie always enters a church and lights a candle for him. So Charlie has a few more years to live yet.

Letters also came to tell me that Doona had a little girl and had christened her Barbara and Emmie had also had a little girl whom she had christened Linda. So now I was twice an uncle.

Back in India we were listening intently to the news for the end of the war in Europe. This we knew would indicate that the war in our part was virtually over too. Their cause was lost and ours won, after all the years of hardship and disappointment. It was a wonderful feeling to know that in the foreseeable future we would all be home again, free, at liberty to choose how we wished to live.

Then came news of the terrible destruction at Hiroshima. This told all. The war could not continue now. With the power, plus the readiness, to destroy whole cities with one tiny bomb what nation could resist? Now the end must be near.

And so it came. While still in India peace was finally declared All fighting had ended, we were free to go home. It was an enormous sense of relief that engulfed us all at that time. To those of us who had come in at the beginning it had seemed a life-time. It had felt at times as though the war would go on for ever. At other times it had looked as though we could not possibly win. Yet here we were, safe and sound, but those many years and those several experiences older.

Now we could relax. Now we were superfluous. An army without an enemy.

I took one more trip to the Taj Mahal before I left India for ever. It looked just as beautiful.

So once again I sailed through the Suez Canal (this was getting to be monotonous) and into the Mediterranean.

Back home I was issued with my discharge suit and I presented myself at Arthur's and Emmie's for approval.

No more thoughts of travel were in my mind, I was thirty-six and it was time to create some sort of permanence around me. With this in mind I looked around for a steady job. A job with a future to it. I would be a nine to five man from now on. No more flitting from one place to another, let's have a little more solidarity associated with my life.

So, to this end I applied for a job as a clerk in the Civil Service. Then one day I was sent

251

for to attend for examinations. These took up an entire afternoon and we were to go home and await notification of results. When these came I had passed and was advised that I had been placed with the War Office.

What could be more steady or permanent than that — I was a civil servant. My future seemed assured.

And here my story could well have ended. At least the venturesome part of it. For as I settled down to the pleasures of peace-time I felt that it was so good to know that life held nothing more risky than the dangers associated with crossing the road. In time I even replaced my discharge suit with something more elegant, more tasteful and considered that the reflection that confronted me as I pretended to be looking at the goods in a shop window was not so bad after all. Getting a little thinner on top perhaps, but otherwise still reasonably youthful.

At work nothing would have distinguished me from any other office clerk. My particular job was to distribute Mentioned in Despatches certificates. It kept me going all day. Except for tea breaks. I would receive a list of new awards and would then write asking the recipient to where the certificate should be sent. Any correspondence on the matter came to me and I was free to answer but all my letters had to be approved and signed by the head of the department. It was a cosy enough job but the money wasn't particularly good.

After some months there I sat a promotions examination and passed. Then more months passed but no promotion came my way, and so, no extra pay. Being impatient to see something happening to this end I phoned the promotions department and was told that having passed the examination meant no more than that I was now eligible when my turn came. But that might be years away. And then it was that the little boy who told the manager of the electrical engineers that he couldn't wait for another year for a rise rose up from the past and took over. He told the War Office that he had no intention of waiting years for their promotion. They could work out how much they owed him in holiday pay, for he would be leaving at the end of the week. And that ended my twelve months as a civil servant.

But I was not satisfied. Life was not varied enough. This sitting at an office desk all day, coming and going at the same time, doing the same things was boring me.

At home there was every comfort. Emmie and Arthur were good company. I popped round on Doona and Mick at odd times, my little nieces had started to talk. But I wanted more. Now I realised that despite my travels there was so much more still to be seen. So much more that I would still like to see.

At this time too I thought I would like to learn French. The little that I had acquired whilst in France was now reduced to the merest smattering and so I bought a 'Teach Yourself' and began to learn grammatically. It seemed a pity to let it go to waste. And, who knows, one day I might manage to go back to my village again.

18

The Merchant Navy

On leaving the War Office and wondering what to do the thought occurred to me, 'How about the Merchant Navy?'

At thirty-seven years of age, instead of looking around for a marriage partner I was considering how to further my travels. This I feel was the first stage on the road to ending up the caretaker of a block of offices. Here I was, nearly forty, I had just given up a secure job with the government that would have enabled me to face the future, the economic future at any rate, with complete confidence. I had a job for the rest of my life under comfortable conditions with periodical promotion almost assured and a pension on retirement. Had I married at that time. Had I only had a girlfriend of whom I was reasonably fond, I would have stayed on in the job and could have been now a totally different character.

But something within us takes over at times. We don't always act according to what we know to be best. Certain urges that we have will not be denied, they convince us that their way is right and we find ourselves only too ready to believe them.

I went along to the Merchant Navy authorities that day under some form of compulsion. The thought of being on the move again meant more to me than anything.

I was seen by a gentleman who told me that the only vacancies that there were, were in the stokehold or the galley. And for either of these it was necessary to have some experience. I thought a moment. The stokehold? That held no appeal. Neither had I any experience. The galley? Yes, I could fit in there all right. There was my cookery course in the army. That could qualify me.

'Yes,' I told the gentleman, 'I've had experience as a cook.'

He took my word for it and gave me a railway ticket for Cardiff. There I was to report to the Marine Cookery School. It appeared that whatever experience one had as a cook ashore, no matter how expert one was, there were still things to be learnt about cooking at sea. There was, for example, the use of the safety bars which the cook fixes across the top of the stove in rough weather to stop the pots from slipping off. There was the conservation of water as one can't just turn taps on at random as they do on land. Then there is the need to be able to make bread. And further to this, the way in which to make the dough rise if there is no yeast available.

Cooking at sea, it appeared, was a separate art. Something almost apart from any land based cooking.

There were a number of us, we were the beginning of a new class, to last for six weeks. Now I was happy this was better than the War Office. Now the future was uncertain, with a prospect of the unusual associated with it. This was for me.

We were advised where to go to find lodgings and told to mention that we were from the School. That was the landlady's security.

The next morning there we were at the School door, waiting, eager to see what our new days were to be like. Inside there was one large room with several benches set up and alongside each bench was an oven. But there was only one instructor. He handed each of us a card on which was printed the item which we were expected to make. 'Don't start until I tell you,' he said. Then his practice was come along to each bench inspect our card and say, 'Oh, yes, well now, weigh up and sieve two pounds of flour, then rub in half a pound of margarine. I'll come along and see you later.' Then off he went to the next bench, and the two pounds of flour would be well and truly sieved and the margarine rubbed to death before he came back again. Then he would explain the next move and away he would go again.

Finally one had the whole thing, by easy stages all ready to put in the oven, but here once again the instructor took over. He insisted on doing all the oven work himself. It appeared that all these items that we cooked had to be sent somewhere to be eaten, and he was so afraid of them being spoilt. There was also a very strong rumour prevalent that he received a bonus on each person that he successfully turned out. Certainly he was more than reasonably concerned that we should eventually pass. So much so that he was afraid to let us handle anything ourselves.

Each day we went along and each day we watched while he produced that which was on our cards. We also took down several pages of notes.

Then came the day for our examinations. A body of examiners was coming along to inspect our produce and to grant certificates to the successful candidates. Once again our instructor went through the same procedure until we finally found ourselves standing before our benches with a neat little arrangement of produce in front of us. This was our test piece.

The examining party arrived and, of course, we all passed. Not only passed but were complimented. They tasted one piece of mine and liked it. The look they gave me made me feel quite ashamed. I felt like saying, 'I didn't make that, sir.' That look should have been directed at the instructor — it was his piece they were testing not mine. I had only followed his instructions.

It seemed very unfair to me, for, after all, we were going to have to go to sea and cook for a very discriminating table. If the seamen didn't like what we were giving them they were going to be very quick to say so.

One day I was told there was a ship in the dock wanting a Second Cook and I was to apply for the position.

I approached the chef and told my story — not much experience, never cooked at sea before, just had six weeks at the School — and he decided that I was not the man for the job.

257

He said that he wanted a cook for the crew and it was essential that they be given good meals, otherwise there could be trouble aboard the ship.

Then he came out with a suggestion. 'I am wanting a scullion,' said he, 'that's something like a galley boy. You'd have to do just about everything, peel potatoes, wash up dishes, keep the place clean, bring up the stores. It's a pretty busy job but you'd get some idea what life in the galley is like. Could be a good way of starting off.'

This suited me. I'd get my trip and I could pick up a few ideas at the same time. Yes, it could be just the thing. I took it.

The ship was the 'Kenilworth Castle', going all round Africa.

Strangely enough she belonged to the very company that had so many years earlier recommended me to join the Gravesend Sea School. So here I was after all, except that instead of being an officer I was to be the galley boy.

We sailed. And from then on I became the general factotum. At everybody's beck and call. There was a passengers' cook, a crew's cook, a baker and the chef, and each one was my boss. My day started early in the morning, I peeled all vegetables that needed peeling, I brought up stores from down below, sacks of flour for the baker and sides of meat for the cooks. I scrubbed the galley out three times a day and I stood at a sink full of hot water and washed one grimy dish after another — dozens upon dozens of them.

Then, when all other more important jobs were done I was free. Free to sit outside on the open deck and peel potatoes.

It was my job to see that a huge tub was kept constantly at least half full. Other vegetables had to be kept in good supply too. Like carrots, swedes, turnips and parsnips. My work was both arduous and endless.

Not only was it hard work, but, in addition, on reaching a port I was not able to leave the ship until all my work had been done. Always was I the last one to go ashore, as there were always those blessed dishes to wash up and the galley floor to scrub down. The place had to be left spotless.

But, no matter, however lowly my position, however dirty the work, nothing could take away the satisfaction that I felt when, after we had reached the sunny weather, passing once again down the West African coast, I found myself sitting outside the galley stripped to the waist with my tub of potatoes waiting to be filled. This was the job I enjoyed doing most. Sitting there in the warm sunshine with the sea passing quietly by, a cool breeze whipped up by the movement of the ship swirling around my body. One man in a mighty ocean. At peace with the whole world. This is one of the reasons why one comes to sea.

Our first port of call was the Canary islands. Here, no sooner had we tied up than the crews were overboard, ashore, in search of whatever they thought the most worthwhile thing to go in search of. They were a roughneck crowd and their idea of what man was most in need of after some days at sea was of very limited range. One never saw them at the Concert Hall, or the Art Gallery. They dodged the Museum like the plague and they only wandered into the Zoo by accident when trying to find their way back to the ship after a hard day's drinking.

In fact one could confine their activities in port to two spheres only. One was in the bars, where they would often stay until they were thrown out at closing time, and even then they left with enough bottles to enable them to continue drinking on their return to the ship. The second of their favourite pastimes on coming ashore also needed no more than a short walk from the dockside. This was to the brothels. There they would take up with the girl they were with the last time they were this way. Or they might fancy a change this time.

Then we would be off again with the crew exchanging their various experiences. Their talk was mostly of the merits of the different prostitutes they had been with, and they seemed to take great pride in speaking of the number of times they had managed to have intercourse in the one night. They also bragged of the number of times that they had had venereal disease. The sea either attracts the very worst types or it creates them, I'm not sure which, but certainly by the time they have wandered around the world a few times and rubbed shoulders with a few of the old hands they have said goodbye to every degree of refinement.

Later on I became second cook and baker on other ships and as such always shared a cabin with the second steward. Once I was lying on my bunk when the 'second' came running into the cabin and hurriedly locked the door. He was white with fright.

'What's the matter?' I asked.

'They're after me,' he mumbled.

He had no sooner finished than there was a disturbance outside. Then came the noise of someone trying to open the door.

'Open the door, you bastard,' someone yelled.

Of course he wouldn't open up. He knew what to expect if he did. Apparently some stewards had harboured a grudge against him for something he had said or done. Now they had been ashore and had returned rip-roaring drunk and were out to get him. They wanted his blood and they didn't care how they got it.

It was a frightening situation, for these men can be villainous. They would beat a man into insensibility and carry on beating him. They would smash a bottle over his head, or they would knife him. And these outside the door were obviously so drunk they wouldn't have known what they were doing.

Then they started bashing the door down.

I urged them to go away, but they weren't interested in what I had to say. They were the hounds, having cornered their quarry — now for their reward.

He, poor chap, was literally terrified.

Then the door started to give way and they swarmed in and took hold of him. He struggled,

261

but it was useless. They carried him away, beating him up as they went. They weren't men at that moment, they were animals. Wild animals.

Had it been merely a matter of fist fighting I probably would have tried to interfere but by that time I knew them well enough to know that they don't stop at fists. They'll use anything. And I knew too that to incur their enmity would have led to them lying in wait for me the next time that they were drunk, which would be the next time they were in port. So instead I rushed off to tell the chief steward, but I'm afraid that by the time he reached them the damage would have been done.

That second steward was badly hurt and too afraid to work in the same department again and so for the rest of the voyage he was put into another part of the ship.

When we left the Canary Islands en route for Ascension Island on that first voyage of mine I had no idea that these were the sort of men that I had joined forces with. I was happy. The skies were clear, the air was warm and we were going all round Africa. I could only see the pleasantness around me.

At Ascension Island we stood off. We had one passenger for the island, a radio operator, for there is there a Cable and Wireless station, and, I believe, nothing else.

From there we headed for St Helena. Here I would very much like to have gone ashore. Had it been possible I would have made straight for the house in which Napoleon lived during the years of his banishment. It is preserved as a Napoleonic Museum, I understand.

Some of the seamen went but I didn't hear mention of the house. At least not that house.

A group of the islanders came aboard and a more simple and friendly people there could hardly be. They had recently been visited by the king, George VI on his way back from his visit to South Africa. This was the islanders' main talking point. 'I saw the king. He looked straight at me.' This would be said with childish enthusiasm and obvious pride. 'Yes, I saw him, I was standing right close up to him.'

Much of their merchandise was made of a little red bean that grows on the island. There were table mats, tea cosies, belts and necklaces, all red beans. There was hardly anything else. A not very wealthy people, yet happy. Totally unsophisticated. Out-of-step with the rest of the world, speaking with an accent probably brought out by their early ancestors.

We left them in their splendid isolation and went on to Cape Town. My horizons were broadening. I was bringing in names that previously I had considered it interesting enough only to read about.

On this trip, in fact, which lasted for six months, we not only visited these places once but some twice, and even three times. We dawdled around this coast, unloading, leaving, then coming back to re-load. We went across to the island of Mauritius and back to Durban, where we had been already. We stayed at both Beira and Lorenco Marques in Portuguese East

Africa and then up to Tanga in Tanganyika. Then to Mombassa in Kenya. After that we rounded the north-east corner and into the Red Sea. Then home.

Arriving back at London Docks I paid off and left the ship, and this became my first day off from work since the day I had joined her. I had stood at that greasy sink, I had scrubbed down the galley deck, and I had carried up my sacks of vegetables from down below, come what may, day after day for the whole time that I was away. And usually the only hours that I had had ashore had been in the evenings after I had cleaned everything up. No wonder then that when I was asked, 'Are you coming back for the next voyage?' I had said, 'No, thank you.'

It had been most interesting, but once was enough.

By this time I had become aware of the crudity of my shipmates. I had realised the extent of their conversational topics and the colourfulness of their vocabulary. If I was ever going to sea again, at least I would like a spell ashore first, among what I would have termed normal, decent people. Besides which I had no desire to re-engage as a scullion. Despite the lack of ambition with which I am endowed I did aim a little higher than that. And so I said goodbye to my little spot on the deck and with a sizeable pay packet I caught a taxi to Arthur's and Emmie's. A taxi was necessary because we were allowed to make all manner of purchases on the ship of foodstuffs which were still in short supply ashore. Then there were the odds and ends that we had picked up at various ports of call.

After three weeks just lazing around, enjoying the leisure time that was now mine I felt that perhaps it was time to be on the move again. Let's see what else was on offer. It was interesting to be able to apply for work and wonder which countries it was going to lead me to.

'We have one wanting a second cook and baker going to the States, and we don't know where to from there.'

'Yes, that'll do me,' I said.

'The States. Hm, I like the sound of that,' and with this thought in my head I went off to the docks.

There she was, the 'Fort Lliard'. Not much to look at. About six thousand tons. A merchantman.

Up the gangplank I went and into the officers' dining room, where they were signing on the crew. Here I handed in my card and was struck by the note of relief in his voice as the officer called out, 'OK, I've got a second cook and baker.'

This seemed to me to be rather flattering, for even though I was described on the card as such, that was hardly how I would have described myself. But I kept quiet. Maybe they wouldn't have cause to think of me any other way. I hoped so, anyway.

We sailed with our nose pointed towards Boston, USA. That part was all right, I would like to see the States, but there were many miles to go yet and a hungry, fastidious crew to please all the way across.

Let me say right now that the Atlantic is a mighty ocean, especially on a not so mighty ship. And it was winter. Just before Xmas in fact. This was different to sailing into the sunshine. The skies were grey and so was the sea, and we heaved and rolled from the moment we were in the open. In addition our galley was no more than a little iron shed, right on the open deck. The seas came over the ship's side and rolled continuously up to just outside the galley door. There was a raised piece about eight inches high at the bottom of the door, over which we had to step, otherwise the sea would have washed right through.

In here I met the cook for the first time the next morning, and I put my cards on the table straight away.

'Look,' I said, 'I might as well tell you, this is my first ship as second cook and baker. I've never made bread before, but I think I'll be all right with most other things. If you would show me how the bread is made I shouldn't take too long to pick it up.'

Here I was, in the position that I had dreaded all along. All through that stooge of an instructor at Cardiff being so eager that each man should pass (for whatever reason). If only he had let us do it ourselves. Even if we did make a few mistakes. It was surely better to make our mistakes there in the School where the only person affected would be him rather than let us be faced with this present situation where we were already at sea and regarded as qualified men.

However, I had done the right thing, I had told the cook.

It was the right thing but unfortunately it didn't work out right, for he was no more of a baker than I was. Later on the crew were to question whether he was any more of a cook either, for he was in continual trouble with them. In the meantime I have thrown myself at his mercy.

'All right,' he answered, 'I'll show you how to make bread, but I don't want you arguing about it. If you want me to tell you you'll have to do it as I say.'

'Yes, yes, yes.' Anything, as long as I got out of this predicament. I promised.

But that afternoon when we settled down to make our first batch of forty loaves I very soon realised that he didn't know any more about it than me, for he was fumbling and hesitant. Either he had never known or he had forgotten. His methods were nothing like that Cardiff instructor's, and heaven knows that instructor certainly made a nice loaf.

He was a slap-dash cook. He was in all things and I can consider it was sheer bad luck that I should have to run into him on my first trip as a baker.

The batch that he turned out was very poor quality and several loaves were brought back. Of course they came to me, and I apologised. I couldn't say I hadn't made them. That could have been worse. After all I was supposed to be the baker. The situation was tricky, and it wasn't helped by the rolling of the ship and the murky weather outside. This was another aspect of life at sea. No sitting outside here with a cool breeze swirling around my torso. It was blowing like mad.

In fact the whole situation was pretty miserable.

The next day when it came time to make bread he had gone to lie down (this was his regular practice) and so I was able to experiment to a certain extent. But my bread was poor. It had large holes in it and it crumbled badly.

Naturally the crew brought them back and it was then that my natural willingness to see my own faults came to my aid. I told each member of the crew that came to me that I recognised that the bread was far from good, that I was new to the game ('We can . . . well see that,' they'd say.) and that I reckoned I'd get better as the days went by. They always took my apologies grudgingly, but at least they took them.

In all respects where I was able to make it up to them I would. It was my job to make all sweets and cakes, and all pastry. And every evening I had to return to the galley and cook a light meal for the watch coming up from the stokehold, and here I was able to win back some of their respect, for I spared no effort to give them something good, and plenty of it.

This stood me in good stead later on.

And so the days went slowly by with regular complaints coming back to the galley. Not only about my bread but about the cook's offerings as well. I never ceased to acknowledge the justification of the complaint when it applied to something I had made, but the cook hadn't the same capacity to sink his pride. He insisted that the men were complaining needlessly. They didn't know good food when they saw it. The officers hadn't complained, so there couldn't be much wrong with it. Burnt! Burnt! What did they mean burnt? It tasted all right to him. Not enough! Well that was all they were getting.

It was a hateful position to be in. The men were right to complain and I knew it. The food was terrible, and my bread was not improving at the rate at which I had hoped it would. It was more a case of them having to become used to it.

However, we reached Boston with no more than a not very happy crew, and there we stayed loading grain. We were two weeks there and it was like heaven not having to make bread, for this was purchased ashore while we were in port.

Coming from the shortages that there were back home in England, that we had become used to during the war, this that we were seeing in Boston was like another world. Shops were filled to overflowing with fancy goods of all kinds. This was opulence. I couldn't remember when the London shops had been similarly filled, it seemed so far back. There was an abundance of everything and everyone was well dressed with money to spend.

We made the most of our stay there. Each to his own taste. There were those who never did more than wander a few yards from the ship's side, drink themselves silly and totter back again. Then there were the womanisers. They too didn't stray very far. Why walk a mile when one can find what they want around the first corner? was their motto.

Then came me, our hero, the good boy, and a chap that I had palled up with. We called in at the bars, but at least they were in the more cosmopolitan parts of the city, frequented by a wider cross-section of the population.

One evening we were drinking at a table in one of these bars when a young paper-lad came around calling, 'Tribune, Tribune, Boston Tribune, sir?' He came to our table, got as far as 'Tri,' then stopped and said to himself, 'English,' then walked away. I rather wished at the time that this fact hadn't been so obvious. But I knew that it was. Our clothes were cheaper and not so up-to-date. We had just come from a country that had been hard hit by the war and the effects were still plain to see. The deficiencies that the war had left behind in England were showing in both our dress and our demeanour. But I would rather that it hadn't been a little paper-lad of about thirteen who had had to bring this home to us. He had walked away as though one couldn't hope to sell a Tribune to an Englishman. Did he think we couldn't afford one?

While we were there we saw a real blizzard. The snow came down so thickly that it was almost impossible to see through it. And the atmosphere was so cold that not a flake melted.

The roads were covered to a depth of over a foot in no time at all. This was a good illustration to me of how on those occasions hundreds of cars can become hopelessly trapped. All of a sudden they won't go any further. The snow is too thick and they can no longer plough their way through.

I took advantage of the opportunity to stock up with chocolate for my two young nieces, for this was a luxury hard to come by back in England.

Then the time came to leave. We had a ship full of grain and we headed back across the Atlantic.

The discontentment continued and the voyage back was no happier than was the one out. Until one day the English coast loomed up and it was with a feeling of relief that I saw it. Now we could sign off, go away and lick our wounds. It had been both embarrassing and precarious. The crew could have become violent, and it was not a pleasant thought when we were miles out to sea. However, here we were now, sailing along the English coast. We began to speculate as to which port we would arrive at. It wouldn't be Liverpool, we were past that and heading down the west coast. Then we rounded Lands End and were making for the English Channel. Through the Channel we went with no sign of preparations to call in anywhere, and then we passed where we should have entered the Thames Estuary had we been going to London Docks. This was a nuisance, we would now have to make our way back to London by train from somewhere like Hull, nor Newcastle. But before then we started to head away from England, into the North Sea. We had come home but we weren't stopping there. Where were we going? No-one knew for sure, so we could only wait and see.

Through the Kiel Canal we went, where we were offered cameras, watches, cigarette lighters, all manner of fancy goods in exchange for British cigarettes. This was not too long after the war and cigarettes, especially English, were at a premium. Some of us did all right out of it. The watch that I picked up is still giving good service today.

Out of the other end of the canal into the Baltic Sea. Here the waters were just one vast blue expanse, without a ripple to be seen, except that V-shaped ever widening pattern that we formed as our bow cut through the surface. Otherwise it was just a sheet of glass, and the air was crisp and clear, without the merest trace of a breeze. We passed islands floating, it seemed, on the top of the sea, bright green islands with little houses with white walls and red roofs. There wasn't a sound anywhere, other than the slight rustling created by our passage through the waters. This was a dream world. It was all so pretty.

I can remember standing on the deck in my vest feeling completely comfortable even though our rigging had icicles hanging from it and the deck was covered with ice. Someone advised me to put something on otherwise I could be frost-bitten. I did, but I hadn't felt any need of it.

We were going to Copenhagen. By now the news had got around. This pleased me, I would be able to see the Little Mermaid.

But there was more than the Little Mermaid in store for me, for it was here that some members of the crew became vicious drunk and came back to the ship to 'do the galley staff over'. And that included me of course. It all happened late that afternoon after we had been in port some five or six hours. The cook and I were just preparing to serve up dinner when three drunken sailors came a trifle unsteadily into the galley and said to the cook, 'Hey, bastard, we want you down in the crew's quarters. Come on.'

Now, fool as the cook was he was not fool enough to wander meekly off with them at that bequest. There was an implication in their voice and manner that no fool could have misunderstood.

'Get out of my galley,' he said, trying to adopt an air of authority.

But they weren't to be put off by any false show of bravado. They stepped forward, all three grabbed him and they carted him, struggling and yelling, off to the after-end of the ship, the crew's quarters.

I stood there quite helpless. So this was it. They would beat him up. He had asked for it and he would undoubtedly get it. I was sorry for him. After all I wouldn't wish that on anyone. But overriding my concern and sympathy for him was the thought that it might be my turn next. I would fight, but what chance would I stand?

For about twenty minutes I carried on doing what needed doing and then the cook re-appeared in the doorway. He looked like an apparition. He was completely dishevelled. His hair was awry, his shirt was torn, his nose was bleeding, his eyes were puffed and his top and bottom dentures were missing. But above all was the wild, excited look in his eyes. It was as though he had become completely and utterly mad.

He said nothing to me. He went straight to a bench, picked up the biggest meat knife he could find and went out again. He could have tackled an army with that knife, it was so big, and as sharp as a razor.

The next thing I knew there was pandemonium aboard. The crew were running everywhere. The captain appeared on the bridge, took one look at the scene on his ship and disappeared back into his cabin.

Within little more than seconds after that a dozen Danish policemen came on board and order was soon restored.

From then on, for the whole three weeks that we were in Copenhagen we had one policeman patrolling the deck and peace reigned.

The cook swore that he would sue the company for the cost of his teeth, but he was a very subdued man thereafter. He had had a nasty shock. And so had I. For I was expecting them to come for me all the time.

Later I learned why they didn't. Apparently I was on the list and I was to follow immediately on the cook, but three hefty 'firemen' — men from the stokehold — had stood up for me. They had argued that the baker at least does his best. And he does admit when he is wrong. And they had won the day. Otherwise I might have been carrying the marks of that day yet.

The day after this, with all meals served and my day's work done three of us went ashore for the evening. As we went down the gangplank onto the dockside two girls came towards us.

'Excuse me, are you boys English?' they asked.

'Yes,' said we, 'we're English.'

'So are we,' said the girls, 'may we talk to you?'

Certainly they could talk to us. We could hardly think of anything we'd like better. We wandered off, with the girls leading the way. They lived there.

Their story was that during the war their father had been killed and later their mother had become friendly with a Danish sea captain who used to regularly call at their home town — Newcastle.

Then she had married him and had moved with her two young girls into a flat in Copenhagen.

Now the two little girls were no longer so little and they each longed to find some way in which they could leave mum to her sea captain and her new baby and get back to England.

Apparently they visited each English ship that

came in to port in the hope that they might find someone who would like them enough to want to help them make their way back.

These two girls said they'd be glad to show us around for the whole of the time that we were in Copenhagen and that we must come home and meet mum and 'dad'. This was an offer that we jumped at. It is very seldom that a seaman is given the chance of being welcomed into one of the homes in a country that he is visiting. And in this case it was to be more than a casual visit — they were inviting us to be their friends for the whole of the time that we would be there. A very unusual and at the same time very acceptable offer.

'And we have a friend for you too, Syd,' I was told. 'Her name is Una. She is a Danish girl. Very nice. We'll be meeting her this evening.'

So I was to have a Danish girl.

Altogether we spent three weeks in Copenhagen and we saw our girls every evening during that time. And, in fact, a very affectionate relationship developed between all of us. I gathered that the English sisters were extremely co-operative in all things and they had certainly passed me on to a very 'friendly young lady, for Una was, like Danish cheese, very tasty. She made my three weeks stay in Copenhagen a most memorable one. I had hoped to see the Little Mermaid and instead I had been presented with a maid all of my very own.

Then there was the eldest sister: she had her 'boyfriend' a little worried. He told us that she seemed to be more amorous than he could cope with. And already she swore that she loved him. She had him wondering just what sort of scene there was going to be on the day when our boat sailed.

Una gave me none of these worries. In fact I had the idea that seamen sailing off and leaving her behind had become quite commonplace. She was making the most of my presence without showing too much concern for the future. But the eldest sister — she was all the time speaking of the misery that would be hers on the day when her lover left.

Then one day the truth came out, and everything fitted into place. Una told me that Judith (eldest sister) was three months pregnant by some Danish fellow and she had been haunting the English ships during the past three months hoping to find herself an unsuspecting English father for her forthcoming child. She was so afraid that if the baby was born before she could find someone then all hope of getting back to England would be gone.

Poor girl she must have been frantic. What a worry to be burdened with. Her young sister was in on the secret. They all three knew about it and were all helping her. But Una couldn't resist telling me.

Looking back on this incident I can feel dreadfully sorry for her, but at the time all I could think about was warning my mate. He, it seems, was already becoming very fond of Judith. There had even been talk of her coming over to England to be with him. But on hearing what I had to say his defences were up. 'Right, we're finished,' he said, 'I'm having nothing more to do with her. She'll be telling me I put her in the family way next. Thanks, Syd.'

I wonder what happened to her. Her situation was certainly very sad.

19

I Leave Ship In Australia

Altogether I sailed five times and spent three and a half years at sea as a ship's cook. How extraordinary that what I could not do as a young boy, when I rather feel that I could have been so much more valuable to an employer, I was now finding so easy to do. However, life likes to play games with us at times I think.

So, after the Copenhagen debacle it was with the greatest of haste that I paid off the ship, but not before receiving a severe admonition from the captain.

He had asked me into his cabin to say that although he was going to mark my book as having given satisfactory service I, in fact, was the worst baker he had met in over thirty years at sea. I didn't dispute this. It didn't really surprise me. Having heard already that he intended to mark my book as though I had given good service I felt it wisest to remain quiet and just listen to what he had to say. 'But,' I thought, 'he might just as well have taken my livelihood away,' for I didn't think I would ever have the nerve to risk going through that lot again.

But such is the lure of life at sea that after four or five weeks of just taking things easy, with the passing of time making my memories a little less painful, I decided that if I approached the next ship's cook and told him my case before actually signing on, instead of waiting until we were out to sea, maybe I could look around until I found one who was able and willing to teach me the ropes.

And it is just as well that I did for the next trip was the one that I would have hated to miss. I signed on as a second cook and baker again, but this time the atmosphere was just the opposite. Here I struck a cook, an elderly man, who had been cooking for all his life and had been a baker ashore. He was, into the bargain, a sensible person. On approaching him and telling him of my previous experience he had said, 'Don't worry, if you have any sense at all I'll soon have you making a nice loaf.' And so it was. In fact half-way across the captain, on a tour of the ship, said to me, 'You make a nice loaf, baker, keep it up.'

What a fine thing to be told coming right on top of the captain who rated me the worst baker he'd met in thirty years at sea.

This ship was going to South America. To Uruguay and Argentina, and the voyage was the smoothest, the sunniest and the happiest that I did. Each afternoon for two hours I would lie on a blanket laid across a hatch cover and with a gentle breeze playing over me I would listen to the soothing sound of the sea lapping softly against the side of the ship as we went calmly on our way.

My fairy-godfather, the ship's cook, knew this route well and he had said to me, 'At this time of the year there won't be a ripple on the water all the way over.' And he was right, if there was a ripple it must have passed by while I was still asleep.

On arrival we called first at Montevideo, where we spent a few days, and then further up the River Plate where we stayed for eight long, lovely weeks. The weather was glorious and it was a beautiful city. Every bar or cafe, no matter how small, had a live musician to entertain the clientele and where there were pavement tables and chairs the entertainers were often in the streets. It was music all the way. And lively, exciting music at that. Out there they have afternoon siestas which enable them to carry on with their entertainment until the early hours of the morning. And whenever I was wending my way back to the ship, no matter what unearthly hour it was, there was always music and lights and laughter all around me.

Yet even with a city as jolly as this, that simply begged you to come right in and be made merry, still the majority of our crew thought that the greatest pleasures were to be had within a few short paces from the ship. And even after a stay of eight long weeks there were many who had no idea what the centre of the city looked like. There was ample opportunity, and time, for all forms of amusement. I know, for I didn't miss out on anything. And while I would agree with the others that the girls there were highly enjoyable, with a zest for their trade that does them credit, yet I would also recommend anyone going to these cities to look around a bit. There's lots there of all kinds.

Yes, thinking back, if every tradesman did his job half as well as those girls did theirs the world would be a happier place to live in.

We sailed back in waters as placid as those going out and a ship's crew with not a complaint to make about any part of the cooking. By now I had become fully confident. I actually enjoyed experimenting with all kinds of fancy cakes.

And so the days went quietly by with my blanket still laid out on the hatch cover and a book to read until I fell asleep, which I almost invariably did.

We were cut off. In a world of our own. A world of sunny days and balmy evenings. Of smooth seas, flap-jacks for breakfast and accommodating hatch covers. Added to which I had the pleasure of paying-off a fully competent and confident second cook and baker.

The next boat took me to Nigeria and up a West African river. This was distinctive for the insight into the way some people live out their lives in the most peculiar circumstances. Their houses were built on stilts perched just above the surface of the river. When they came out of the front door it was to enter their canoe and to paddle away up or down stream. As our ship passed them they waved and shouted and generally gave one the impression of being most happy with their way of life. Certainly the only troubles they would have would be very local ones, for they would know very little of what was happening away from their precious river.

Then came my last trip as a merchant seaman. Not that I knew that it was to be my last. When it started it was to be just another voyage. One more among the many that I was hoping yet to do.

One day the clerk at the bureau from where we obtained our berths said, 'Second cook and baker, let's see, yes, I have one here, going to Australia. How would you like that?'

I liked it. And so I signed on for an approximate six months voyage.

It was to be eleven years before I saw England, Emmie and Arthur, Doona and my two nieces again. I was to go from thirty-nine, in the full vigour of my life, to fifty, and I would be struck down by a very severe illness during that time. And this was to have been just another trip!

My Seaman's Discharge Book tells me that I joined the Fort Miami on the twenty-ninth of March, nineteen forty-nine. She sailed, a vessel of seven thousand tons, from Victoria Docks the day after that and the second cook and baker was one Sydney Metcalfe. It also tells me that on the nineteenth of August, some five months after we left England I was allowed to sign off in Sydney, Australia. That is all it says. For the rest I shall have to rely on my memory.

We had a comparatively uneventful trip out, calling at ports down the African coast again and from Durban across to Fremantle in Western Australia. This ship had another unruly crew and at Fremantle the cook was chased off the ship by some vengeful seamen who had been seen in town in a state of high dudgeon and a high state of drunkenness who had said they were coming back to do the cook over. The seaman who had heard them say this had hurried back to tell the cook and he, having seen men 'done over' before, turned quite white. Then without having uttered one word went down to his cabin, hurriedly changed into his 'shore' clothes, walked down the gangplank without even stopping to pack a suitcase, and was never seen again.

He had left behind everything he owned and all the money that was owing to him for the voyage out from England. He had thought none of these things were worth risking waiting around for.

As soon as it reached the skipper's notice that the cook had left I was asked would I run the galley alone until someone could be found to assist me.

What could I do? I had no choice. And so it was as a one-man organisation that I continued around the Australian coast doing everything that needed doing in the way of cooking and baking for forty men. It became hard work and left me very little free time, but there was little I could do about it.

And so we came to Sydney. After three weeks discharging our cargo there our ship left for Tasmania, and here it was that I was bitten by the 'leaving the ship' bug. We were moored alongside a small jetty up a river and into a lake and it looked for all the world as though we were completely land-locked. There we were, at the edge of a lovely lake surrounded by beautiful green hills with no apparent way out. At the end of the jetty was a small township where there was but one small pub and where when the pub closed the inhabitants of the township insisted on taking us into their homes to finish off the evenings with a friendly chat and a bit of supper.

This seemed the most idealistic spot I had known. There was beauty all around, there was peace and quiet, and there was the most friendly of people. What more could one wish for? I longed to stay on, and I couldn't get the idea out of my mind. I had no wish to go back to England yet. Not for a while. The thought of spending a year here among these friendly people and the sunshine seemed most appealing. Then, when I had had enough, I could always sign on another ship going home. Second cook and bakers were not easily come by.

And so I approached the captain. Would he kindly pay me off? He was not interested. My reason for wishing to leave the ship, 'I like the look of the place,' only made him smile. 'Couldn't consider it,' he said, in a manner that simply dismissed the whole matter. I retired to think over what my next move should be, for I was determined to leave the ship here one way or another.

For two weeks we were loading apples and timber here in this delightful spot and then it was off down the River Tamar and back to Sydney. Here we had barely tied up when I was waiting outside the captain's cabin once again.

This time I was more aggressive.

'Skipper,' said I, trying to appear more

determined than I really felt, 'I would like to make one last appeal to you to pay me off. If not then I'm afraid I shall have to go about it my own way. I shall have to jump ship.'

And it worked.

'Hm, all right,' he said, apparently quite unperturbed, 'but if I allow you to sign off will you wait until I find someone to take your place?'

Certainly I would wait. In fact I promised to help him to find someone. And so one fine day in August nineteen forty-nine I was handed my pay and my Seaman's Book and I said goodbye to the Fort Miami. Little did I know that I was also saying goodbye to a way of life, for I would not make another voyage except as a passenger.

Immediately on leaving the ship I boarded a plane for Hobart, Tasmania.

I could not go to my little lakeside township, there would have been no work there. Hobart, being the capital and largest city in Tasmania became the logical place in which to look for a job. Yet it was not as a city worker that I spent my twelve months in Tasmania. For I answered an advertisement for a 'Milkman/Gardener' on a property some sixty miles out into the countryside. The special attraction being that it offered accommodation, and I got it.

The owner of the property came to town to interview me and took me back with him.

My work involved milking seven cows every morning and evening, killing, skinning and cutting up into joints for the families on the farm two sheep each week, making butter, feeding the pigs and maintaining a large-sized vegetable garden. In between times I would be put onto various jobs around the place, such as repairing fences or perhaps a bit of tractor work, but always, no matter what I was doing, everything had to be dropped when it came time to milk my seven cows.

This was a very far cry from the life I had been living at sea during the last three and a half years. But perhaps not such a far cry from the life I had once contemplated when as a lad I had tried to emigrate to Canada. Here I was, after all, on my farm, mending fences, killing sheep. Out in the open spaces, as far from London as it was possible to get.

I was given a whole house to live in and told that during the shearing season the house would be filled with itinerant shearers. In the meantime, however, it was as near an experience to living in a haunted house as I ever hope to come by. To get there it was necessary to walk about a quarter of a mile across a field to this house standing all alone on the edge of a river. It was in total darkness and on opening up I would then have to grope my way to my room by the aid of a torch, given to me by the farmer. In this room was but a bed and a chair — no floor covering, no curtains — and here I would undress by the light of the torch. All would be quiet for some time after the disturbance that I had created on my entry, so quiet that the silence was eerie, but within minutes of going to bed the rats, with whom I shared the house, would have regained their confidence and started running around on the other side of the ceiling just above my head. I suppose a rat sleeps throughout the day, for you can take my word for it he spends the best part of the night running around.

It is not the best atmosphere in which to fall off to sleep, with what sounded like a hundred or more rats free to wander where they pleased once you had gone off. And I hated every night that I spent there. Except during the three weeks when the shearers were in occupation. For then the house took on character and came alive with their chatter and laughter. For the whole of those three weeks I did not hear one rat. They were lying low, or had gone back to the river, but the very first night I was alone again out they came in full force. They seemed then to be worse than ever. Whether because I had become a little unaccustomed to them during their absence or whether because they were making up for their enforced three weeks of inactivity I would not know.

For twelve months that was my life — a farmer's boy.

But it was a loveless life on this property. My work went on for every day of the week, even through holiday times, when the rest of the hands were off duty for a few days. This meant that I never went anywhere, never met anybody. No girls came my way, no nothing, and I think it was largely this that induced me at the end of twelve months of abstention to feel that it was time I moved on. My love of the peace and quiet had been satisfied and now it was to somewhere a little more up-to-date, a little more boisterous that I looked. One has to be born, or accustomed in early life, to the quiet of a rural atmosphere. Once the sounds and sights of the city have worked their influence upon a person it is hard to shake them off. So it was a case of, 'to which city shall I go?'

Both Melbourne and Sydney I had already seen so this time I opted for Adelaide, South Australia.

Twelve months had gone by since I had left my ship and in answer to enquiries from home as to when I would be coming back I had already started what was to become a long chain of letters saying, 'I can't afford to come back yet, I haven't enough money saved. Maybe in another year's time.'

And with the passing of each year I, in fact, never did save enough money to enable me to confidently spend the amount that it would have cost in fare with enough left over on arrival. For one thing the farmer in Tasmania owned two racehorses and he had led me to think that it was only a matter of backing these whenever he told me 'they were going' to be able to make my fortune. Not only did his horses continually run contrary to how he had thought they would but in addition I was now left with an affliction which it has taken me much time and money to overcome. I became a regular racegoer. A guarantee of remaining constantly hard-up. My hopes of ever saving enough for my return to England lessened with my ever increasing absorption in the search to find an infallible racing system.

In Adelaide I became greenkeeper to a large tennis club and each Saturday found me at the races diligently disposing of my week's wage packet. It went on week after week, month after month, year after year. But, and this was what I had really left Tasmania for, I did meet people, I did have female friends, and there was now some variety to life.

One girlfriend I acquired in somewhat unusual circumstances. She was something of an intellectual (I was reaching out now) and was librarian at the University, where I was now attending evening classes for French. My French was now improving. So much so that one year I decided it was time I took another language and ventured into Italian. But back to Marion, the librarian. She came into my story in this fashion. One day I saw a notice to the effect that a delegation was to be sent from Australia to attend some conference or other in Red China and a meeting, at which the South Australian delegate would speak, was to take place at such and such a hall. The purpose was to raise funds. It was to be held on a Sunday afternoon and as there was nothing else on I went along.

And there I heard Marion speak. She was our representative. I recognised her as the librarian and thought how small and how very brave she looked up there on the stage. Her whole manner suggested to me that this was something she was not at all used to doing. She had to force herself to stand up there with the eyes of the entire hall upon her and hers the only voice being heard. It was a test of her courage and she came through it beautifully, both scared and determined. Neither did she seem to me the type that would congratulate herself afterwards. She would walk away just glad it was all over. I felt both sorry for her and proud of her. If only I had the same guts.

Nothing would have got me up there in the same position. The most I would dare do would be to phone her up and congratulate her, and I would think that was bold.

She wouldn't know who I was, of course, and would probably not care either, but it would do me good to tell her how I had felt as I sat listening to her that afternoon. I admired her and I would like her to know it and I hoped she had a really enjoyable trip.

She was delighted to hear what I had to say and wondered did she know me? I didn't think she did. She had little occasion to have even seen me, even though I was attending the University in the evenings.

Somehow we got around to making an arrangement to meet, and from that moment onwards she was my girl. And she it was who introduced me to a whole new circle of interesting friends. There was one couple that we used to visit who had a home set right amid the foliage in the hills overlooking Adelaide. They were a couple who had a complete disregard for all convention. They wouldn't be at all unusual today but they were then. They liked to serve up food that was different, always with wine, whenever the fancy took them and considered that if they were interested in whatever we were discussing or the music that we were listening to we should not stop just to eat. Meal time to them was when one felt like eating. And neither did the husband believe in the wife getting up and going to the kitchen to prepare something. If she was enjoying the company she had every bit as much right to stay as had he. This sort of behaviour made them a strange couple in those days. They were Communists. But only as a result of giving the subject some thought. They did nothing unless they believed in it. They were utterly sincere and it was that as much as anything that made them so interesting. For complete sincerity isn't so readily come by as we would like to think.

There was always a select variety of good wines to hand in their mountain retreat and it was most gratifying to sit on the verandah of their home overlooking the lights of the city of Adelaide down below with a glass of good vintage wine alongside, a radiogram playing softly behind in the house and interesting company to boot.

Imagine how this compared with the foul-mouthed, single-track minds that I had had for company at sea.

Marion introduced me too to a young woman whom she had known for some years who for the whole of her life had trained to be a concert pianist. She was living with a young fellow who was ten years her junior. But I was now mixing in a crowd that considered that this was no more than one was entitled to do it they wished.

But what holds this young woman fast in my memory is her playing of the piano. Somewhere along the line she had realised that she would never make the concert platform and she now played only for her own and her friends' enjoyment. But this still left her the finest pianist by far with whom I have sat in the same room and watched their hands weave their fascinating magic. She might have failed to become a concert pianist, but it would have taken a far greater authority than me to have recognised why. As far as I was concerned she was faultless, without peer, but that was because she was there in that very room, ready to play my wish at my command. In what concert hall could I achieve this? There she was, a young woman who had spent years practising the piano for four to six hours every day, playing to us, an audience of four. Once Marion and I spent an entire weekend at her place in the country when our evenings were taken up by listening to her for hour after hour. We were extremely lucky.

This was a most satisfying period of my life, my job was pleasant and there were people to meet and things to do outside my work.

But Marion and I were not made for each other. I believe we both wanted to love one another, for we were neither of us young and we were enjoying having a congenial companion to share our activities. But love would not come and towards the end we argued far too much. And because we were not sufficiently fond of each other there was nothing to draw us back together again wishing to make up. We remained dogged in our views and our arguments began to drag out, causing us to wonder whether we perhaps wouldn't be happier apart. And so we parted.

Afterwards, on looking back, I saw the danger of having an intelligent girl for a sweetheart. Very often, when in company I had given an opinion, Marion would say, 'What Syd really means is . . . ' and then she would go on to explain in words an idea far superior to what I had just used. Sometimes I would think 'Hm, was I really meaning that. Aren't I clever?' But surely, any man could only stand so much of that sort of thing.

So Marion went on her way looking for someone rather more intelligent and more informed than I, while I went off in search of someone a little more dumb than her. At any future public meetings I would confine my appreciation to clapping from the seat in which I sat rather than rushing to the nearest phone to offer my congratulations in person.

20

Murder In South Australia

One year, for a change, I took Literary Criticism as a subject at the evening classes. These were being conducted by a university professor who was a Doctor of Literature. An eminent title.

At the very first evening there were so many pupils present that he advised us to bring in some extra chairs from the classroom alongside. He watched us bring them in, then with a feigned look of concern on his face he said, 'Whatever you do don't forget to put those chairs back after we have finished, otherwise you'll have the night cleaners after me. The cleaners run this place. After all, they can always get another professor but they can't always get another cleaner.'

We all laughed at the mock fear that he put into his voice, but at the same time we recognised that he was more than a little serious.

It was also at Adelaide that I appeared in a murder trial.

It came about in this way. I was a member of a migrants club. It was after Marion and I had parted and my evenings had become a little hard to fill in. We were migrants from all around the world and one of our group was a young Hungarian. He was a quiet young man, rather serious, dreamy-eyed. He never had much to say for himself and I never really understood him. But if there was one thing about him of which I would have felt sure it was that he was a gentle type of person.

Imagine my surprise then when I picked up the paper one day to find that a young prostitute had been found strangled in her flat and that a Hungarian, who I recognised as the member of our group, was charged with her murder. Everything pointed to his guilt. He had even admitted being in her flat that night, but he swore that she was alive when he left. However, there were other incriminating factors and the case dragged on for several days. At the end of that time he would be found not guilty and discharged. But the general feeling was that had she not been a prostitute he might have found it rather more difficult to obtain such a verdict.

Then one day, shortly after his discharge I met him coming towards me. As I went to speak to him he walked straight on, apparently not seeing anything or anyone, lost to all around him. My immediate feeling was that his stay in prison, when he didn't know whether he was to live or die, had so affected his mind that he wasn't in a fit state to be set free. I honestly thought this as he went past me and I turned round and followed him for a while. All his movements bore out what I believed. He staggered a little and he crossed the road regardless of the traffic.

'Good God,' I thought, 'he should be having treatment somewhere, not wandering around the streets.'

That night he ran amok and murdered again. This time he attacked a young couple lying on the grass alongside the river that runs through the city. One he left dead and the other injured. Then he went back to where he was living and attempted to strangle one of the household, who only escaped by jumping out of the window. He was berserk.

The police came, he was taken inside and once again he was charged with murder. Clearly he was not normal. As such it seemed unfair to treat him as though he were. In my opinion he was insane. I know I am not qualified to say this with any authority, but I know how he looked when I saw him that day, and I know how I felt as he went by. I also know what he did that same evening, and putting all three together I am perfectly satisfied in my own mind that he did not have control over his actions. And I am astonished that this wasn't recognised before he was released. This is how I see it now and this is how I saw it then. And feeling that way I felt obliged to go forward and put my views to his solicitor. He was interested and asked me would I be prepared to make my statement in court, which of course I was. A man's life was in the balance and if they were going to try him as though he were perfectly aware of what he was doing then he didn't stand a chance.

I was called into the witness box and I told my story. The prosecuting counsel pooh-poohed it and the judge ridiculed it. I believe the judge thought I was some sort of publicity seeker.

The young Hungarian, seeming to barely

understand what was going on around him, was found guilty and he was hanged.

On the day that his execution took place I felt terrible.

The whole business has left me with a sorry feeling that murder trials are wrongly conducted. It is not the object of everyone there to arrive at the truth. The prosecuting counsel, for example, does not go into court with the thought in mind, 'Let's see if we can find what really did happen.' Instead his aim is to prove that the accused party is guilty. And being a man highly skilled in delivering his arguments he often makes out a very good case against him. But if he approached the case less eager to emerge the winner and more concerned with establishing the facts would he still advance the same arguments?

It is that matter of approach that appals me. In my own case I was perfectly sincere in what I did. I told the truth as I saw it and I was made to look silly. What was gained by that? Well, I'll tell you what was gained — they scored a point and demolished a witness favourable to the defence. But should this be their aim?

So I felt on the day that he was hanged, and I have seen no reason to feel differently since.

21

I Join The Cancer Clinic & Am Taken Ill

For four and a half years I stayed in South Australia and my age advanced from thirty-nine to forty-four. Not much of the little boy left now.

Still letters from home asked the same question, 'When was I coming back?' And still I parried them with the same, 'I haven't enough saved, but I would think perhaps sometime next year.' And so not only the days but the years went by, until it occurred to me one day that I would like to see another state. So I packed my bags, caught the train and landed in Melbourne for the beginning of a five-year stay.

Still our letters flowed back and forth and one day I opened one from Doona to find that she had given birth to a little boy and that she had named him Philip. She didn't say why, but Prince Philip was a great favourite of the ladies about then and it was probably on account of this that my nephew was so named. If so he couldn't have been more aptly christened, for young Philip has turned out to be a real prince of a boy. Sincere, honest, devoted to his mother, he wants nothing more than to become one day a real man. To this end when he was still a child he used to punch the wall or the door with his bare fist. When we, all solicitous, would ask, 'Philip, Philip, why do you do that? You'll hurt yourself.' He used to answer, 'I want to be tough.' He, in fact, wanted to be everything. On another occasion we had been watching high-diving in the Olympic Games on the Telly. Little did we realise the effect it was having upon young Phil, but later in the evening he took to standing on the kitchen table when he thought no-one was looking and with arms outstretched before him he would lean forward until at the very last moment just when he was about to over-balance and pitch straight onto his face he would jump. This called for precision timing and was no frolic for a child. Needless to say we stopped him as soon as we spotted him. 'What are you trying to do?' we asked.

His answer was so plaintive and child-like. 'I want to be a high-diver.'

Today, as I sit her writing my notes Philip is fifteen. A butcher's boy. Not a high-diver, neither is he particularly tough. Neither is he any of the hundred and one other near impossible things that he aspired after from time to time. But whatever he is not there is also very much, of a highly commendable nature, that he is. Highest on the list comes his eagerness to please his mum, and his devotion to his sister.

In later years he had taken to doing little jobs outside, for which he received payments. These he saved until at Xmas time he had quite a sizeable sum. Then this he proceeded to demolish by buying presents for everyone that he could think of. Sometimes when he felt dissatisfied with a particular present he had bought a friend or relation he would buy them a second one. If after that he saw something that he thought that that person would especially like he would buy them a third present. And so he went on until all his money was spent.

I was home one year when Doona was remonstrating with him over this.

'Phil,' she said, 'you must stop buying people two and three presents at Christmas time.'

'But I only do that for the ones that I like the most,' he said. He was about twelve at the time. I think this just about sums up his lovely nature. This tells better than I could what a fine kid he is.

Back in Melbourne I continued as a rabid racegoer and saw many a Melbourne Cup run. My bank book testified to the fact that I still had not solved the problem of how to consistently back winners. It was keeping me broke. I wasn't getting anywhere.

Then came a spell during which I achieved some status in a job and came nearer to marrying than I had ever done before.

The job first, for it was on account of that that I met the girl I so nearly married. I had answered an advertisement for a porter at the Cancer Clinic in Melbourne and it turned out to be work that I thoroughly enjoyed doing, despite the sinister sound of the place. We were treating the patients with radio therapy and as this was a long drawn out process we often became quite familiar with them. Indeed a most friendly relationship very often sprang up between us. This made for a real pleasant atmosphere and gave one the feeling that they were doing something worthwhile in life.

Of course there were sad, even distressing moments brought about by the very closeness that we had ourselves helped to create with the patients, but after a while one felt they wouldn't have changed the job for any other. This was a general feeling for everyone there felt the same.

We were a team, a happy team and this atmosphere of friendly helpfulness was felt by everybody who came into the place, including the patients.

Then one day after I had been there about a year I was asked would I like to give up my work as a porter and, with a little office of my own, establish a small Statistical Department. This was to entail transferring the particulars that were written on the card that each patient had onto a punch-card. To do this one needed to know something about anatomy and physiology. And as certain items regarding the patient's illness had to be taken from their medical history it also involved some understanding of what we were treating and the medical jargon that is used.

I explained that I was totally ignorant of all these things but it was thought that with the passing of time, after some reading up of the necessary subjects I could be just the man for the job. So another porter was taken on and I moved into my own little office. In time things worked out just as they had said they would — I became quite familiar with terms and expressions and parts of the body and the job held no worries for me. Then came a further request upon my services which was to lead to me doing the most prestigious job of my life. I was told that the Victorian State Government was wanting to curtail their grant to the Clinic and had asked us to interview each patient on their first arrival to decide what they could afford to pay. 'Would I do this in conjunction with my punch-card duties?'

Now, one never refused to do anything in that institution. One only wondered how they would fit it in. So I became Interviewing Officer. Two extra chairs were put into my office opposite my desk and I found myself doing a job that I had always wondered about when I had seen other men doing it. That is, interviewing people, with apparently all the time in the world to laugh and joke, or reminisce about something they had both known in the past. I used to think to myself, 'How does anyone ever get a lovely job like that?' And now I had one.

My instructions were not to hurry, to take my time and primarily make the patient feel at ease.

Really, I can see now, they couldn't have chosen a better man. This job was designed for me, every bit as much as I was designed for it. It placed me, for the first time in my life ahead of everyone I met. I was the authority, I was confident, I knew the answers, I could help them. They were worried. They didn't know what was going to happen to them. They looked to me for whatever comfort I could offer them. I was 'Mr Metcalfe.'

Faced with a husband and wife, eager to hear anything I had to tell them I felt like a teacher with an obedient class, or an actor with an enraptured audience, or a pianist with a grand piano. I felt so in command of the situation.

Gone was the inferiority complex, gone any timidity or repressive tendencies — I could be myself, shorn of all artificiality. Any shyness came from the other side of my table. Quite frequently a person seemed ill at ease in my presence, and then it was for me to make them comfortable. I could even dispense charity. If I thought a person couldn't afford to pay anything I would tell them so. 'Look,' I would say, 'I don't think you should pay anything at all.'

'Oh, but I want to. You are all so good to me here,' would often be the answer.

'Very well then,' I would reply, 'if it would please you, when you have finished your treatment we would be happy to receive a small donation. But don't make it too big.'

What a happy position to be in!

All correspondence relating to patients' payments came to me. This involved quite a bit of communication between the Medical Benefits Associations and the clinic and I became the expert on these matters. I did all my own typing, having learned the teleprinter during my days in the Signals. So there I was, one of those characters that we meet from time to time, comfortably installed in a nice office with apparently not a care in the world. I had reached the pinnacle of my working life. Never would I be such a respected member of society again.

This went on for five years, and might have been going today, for the situation was too happy and satisfying to leave. I had too many friends. But I was taken ill. For ten weeks I lay in hospital and at the end of that time I was discharged, but still very affected by my illness. It seemed fitting that I should go back to England. This I did. Just when I had steadied down and was prepared to remain a permanent member of the one organisation fate stepped in and said, 'No, not just yet, there are still a few other things in store for you to do.'

My interviewing work tied up very closely with the young lady on the reception desk. Every day I would give her a list of patients I was wishing to see and as they arrived she would pass them on to me. Also, on arranging what payments they were to make I would bring them back to the reception desk and tell Noreen what they were to pay. This they would give to her each time they came for treatment.

In between times I would frequently chat to her about matters outside our work. She was a very lovely girl and I was soon attracted.

Very soon I was to learn that she lived with her mother and had never had a boyfriend but she had once had a girl with whom she used sometimes to go to the pictures. But mother had discouraged this. So it was plain that Noreen, although a woman of thirty-nine, was very much under her mother's thumb.

When I asked her if I could take her out one evening she said that she would have to think of some reason to give her mother for not coming home straight from work. She thought of a reason and we had dinner out and saw a picture show. But of course this couldn't happen too often if mother first had to have the wool pulled over her eyes. She was a very suspicious woman.

There followed an extraordinary period during which I courted that young woman while faced with every impediment imaginable. Noreen told mother of my existence in the hope that she would accept the inevitable, but this was not how her mother's mind worked. She didn't see it that way, and, instead, ordered that my name should never be mentioned again, and she forbade her to see me.

This sounds ridiculous, even as I write it, but there it was, this was what I had become entangled with.

But love, and other associate emotions connected with it, will find a way and we arranged that through the week I would be on a certain corner where Noreen would pass when she took the dog out for his half hour in the evening.

So that was our quota during the week, a half hour each evening, with the dog all the time trying to draw his mistress's attention away from me. Then at weekends she was a night sister at a private hospital, and then I would spend the night with her until the early morning buses started to run, when I would wend my weary way back home to fall into bed to sleep the best part of the day away.

Life became topsy-turvy in this mad desire

to maintain our relationship against near insuperable odds for mum apparently had Noreen terrified.

Yet, despite all handicaps we decided to marry and I was taken along to the local priest to obtain a special dispensation to be allowed to marry in a Catholic Church. Noreen was a fervent catholic, while I was a non-believer, a heretic. But at this stage nothing mattered — we wanted each other above all else. Mother had been told of our intentions and Noreen was being bombarded every evening by all manner of arguments as to why she should not go through with it.

We found a flat, we partly furnished it and the wedding date was only two weeks away. I had gone to bed one night when I was told by my landlady that I was wanted on the phone. It was Noreen.

'Can I see you, Syd?' she asked, almost sobbing, 'I've something awful to tell you.'

I think I knew what was coming.

We met half an hour later.

'Syd, dear, I can't marry you,' she said, in the most sorrowful of tones, 'mum has brought my brother home from Sydney where he was working and the two of them have been at me all night long. They say they will never want to see me again. They say I will never go to heaven. Oh, what am I to do? I don't want to give you up, but I don't want to lose them either.'

There was lots more that she said. She was nearly out of her mind. All I could do was to try to console her. If they had managed to talk her out of wanting to marry me it seemed best not to try to change her mind.

I accepted the situation. It seemed best, for we were marrying against the most bitter of opposition, anyway.

And so we called the whole thing off. But had she held out against her relations I would have married her a fortnight later and been most happy to do so. But it was not to be.

Then I was taken ill. Some who knew us both have connected the two events, for the illness followed very soon after our breakup, because by that time I had become fully aware of the dreadful hold that her mother seemed to have upon her. The flat that we had taken was not very far from where the mother was living and I had a feeling that mama would still be able to work her influence upon Noreen from that short distance.

Even now, looking back upon it from this dispassionate point in time I feel that Noreen would have found it impossible to break clean away from her mother, and if the mother had had any contact with her at all I'm afraid we could not have been happy.

But reactions are not the result of reasoning and what happened to me then was not at a dispassionate point in time. I had been looking forward most eagerly to us being married, so maybe what happened next did have some connection. Anyway, that I will never really know, but one day, on my way to work, as I stood up from my seat in the local train that I used to catch, I noticed myself stagger. Only a little, and I took no notice of it then, but from that moment on things happened fast.

Before I left work to go home again that day the back of my throat had become numb and there was a slight pins and needles effect in the fingers. By the next morning, at breakfast, my vision would occasionally split — an object would appear as two images, and the print on the paper was too blurred to read.

When I left the house the slight stagger of yesterday had grown to something quite disturbing, and my head was beginning to ache. While at work I arranged to see the doctor that evening and he referred me to a neurologist, to be seen the next day.

By now my speech had become somewhat slurred and my headache was becoming quite intense. I wondered what was happening to me. It was all so sudden and without any apparent cause.

The neurologist put me straight into hospital, and once I was put to bed, as so often happens, there seemed to be a general collapse. I felt completely exhausted, my head was now splitting and I could only move my limbs with a great effort.

When the next day I went to walk to the toilet no sooner was I out of bed than I fell straight to the floor. My legs would not hold me up. I had to be lifted and put back into bed. And it was ten weeks before I would get out again.

When I fell to the floor I wasn't to know whether I would ever walk again. In fact I was losing the use of all my faculties so fast that

I felt quite frightened. Nobody seemed to be doing anything to help me. There was a lot of discussion about my case but nothing was actually being done. What did it all mean? I hadn't felt ill at any time, yet here I was slowly becoming paralysed. And that's how it was — I became slowly and relentlessly paralysed, and there I lay, just one big headache. If I attempted to call out for anything words would not come — I could not fashion them. If I were lying uncomfortably I could not change my position. I could not have a motion. I could not swallow. They gave me only liquids and had to pour them down my throat.

To make matters worse the neurologist did not know what was wrong with me, and, consequently, didn't know how to treat me. Once when I was well on the road to recovery I thanked him for all he had done for me. He seemed most affected and said, 'Please don't thank me, I haven't known what was wrong with you and haven't been able to treat you.'

Whatever it was it reached its zenith and passed slowly on its way, for one day I could tell that some power was coming back into my body, and from that day on it was just a matter of watching myself become a little bit stronger day by day.

While I was there everything possible was done to find what was wrong with me. I had numerous X-rays, four lumbar punctures, cortisone injections, and drugs were administered that would have certain effects if I had a certain complaint. But nothing showed. I was ill for no known reason, and just as mysteriously I recovered.

One night I was lying in my hospital bed when I heard the night sister and someone else going from patient to patient. At each bed the sister told her companion who was the occupant, what was their illness and what progress they were making.

As she came to my bed I had my back towards her. It was the early hours of the morning and she had no idea I was awake.

'This is Mr Metcalfe,' she said, 'he has a brain tumour.' No more. Nothing about progress. Then she passed on her way. But what a bundle of concern she had left behind.

Now, I had had five years at the Cancer Clinic at this time and I had seen many tumour of the brain cases. They had sometimes sat opposite me in my little office. Always they were accompanied by someone who did the talking on their behalf. I saw them when they came for what was known as 'post operative treatment.' They had had all their hair shaved off and a flap had been cut into their skull which was now sewn back. The stitch marks would be quite plain to see. Big and red. There was always a vague, distant look in their eyes, as though they found it hard to concentrate on matters close to hand. Whenever one was sitting there on the other side of my desk I always felt sorry for them, and as they went out I would think, 'Poor blighter.' Now it was time to extend a little of that sympathy towards myself. 'This is Mr Metcalfe,' she had said, 'he has a brain tumour.' Nothing about progress, and I thought I knew why.

She had passed on now and I was left with the knowledge of just why I was lying there paralysed. I was now in possession of information concerning myself that the doctors had chosen not to tell me.

There had been times in the past when I would have wondered how I would react to being told that my end was near. I would have said that I would not take it too well, but here I was — depressed, feeling extremely sorry for myself, but in no sort of panic.

Slowly the idea became acceptable; so, I had come to the end of my life. Well, let's have a look at it. What kind of life had it been? I was fifty. Not a young man. Not particularly old, but many died younger. What had I got out of life? I suppose the most that I had achieved was to manage to do a pretty considerable amount of travelling after once trying so desperately hard and finding all opportunity closed to me.

I had seen, after all, so much more than had at one time seemed even remotely possible. And I had finished up by working these last five years in the Clinic, where I had felt that I had been able to give a degree of comfort to some people there.

Now it was my turn to be as courageous as some of those that I had known during those five years in the Clinic.

Well, first, I determined, I would write to everyone at home and I would make them see that it was not such a terrible thing to know when the end had arrived. I would make it easier for them to accept by letting them see how well I felt about it. But I did wish it had been something a little less horrifying that I had finally been afflicted with.

And so, with thoughts of this nature passing through my head I fell asleep.

In the morning I awoke feeling at first that it had all been a horrible dream, but then it came to me that, in fact, it was all true. Too sadly true. That night sister had come around and she had said that I had a brain tumour. But the reasoning of the night before stayed with me and I felt low, but calm.

When the doctor came to do his rounds I determined that I would tell him what I knew. Then he could speak to me more frankly in future. It would even make his job easier.

So, when he arrived at my bed I said, 'Doctor I would like you to know, I know what is wrong with me.'

He looked at me quizzically and said, 'What do you mean? Why even I don't know that.'

'But I heard the night sister tell someone on her rounds last night that I have a brain tumour.' I said.

'No, that's not so,' he replied, quite emphatically. 'It was thought of as a possibility, but if she had looked more closely she would have seen there was a question mark alongside. No, we X-rayed you for that. You can get that idea right out of your mind.'

This meant then that I wasn't going to die. Once over this silly business of being paralysed and I could start living all over again. It was marvellous news.

In time I was well enough to totter around the ward all on my own and one day I was told that I could leave. And so I left, very weak and very easily made tired, but now it was just a matter of taking things easy until my full strength returned.

All the time that I had been in hospital Noreen had called on me fairly regularly. She told me that she had left the clinic as she felt it would be embarrassing for us two to be there in such close contact. But there was no further talk of marriage or what had happened in the past. Surely there is nothing more dead than a dead love affair, and so it was buried, along with the others, in a communal grave.

From then on Noreen went her way and I went mine and I have never heard of her since. Yet she might so easily have been my wife, even as I sit here writing. The events of life seem to turn on such slender threads. One extra turn or one less and our whole life is changed. Yet through it all our nature remains basically the same. And so it was very much the same character who on leaving hospital had already decided that he would go straight back to England on the first available boat.

Actually I had decided this in hospital. It had seemed to me that my illness could very well have been an indication that I was not getting any younger. Had I not recovered I would have been given an Invalid Pension and that would have meant that I would have had barely enough to live on, let alone save up for my return to 'the old country'. No, it was definitely wisest to go now, straight away, before age caught up with me and I became compelled to see my days out in a 'foreign land'.

My letter home to say that I was coming back brought back a welcome beyond all my expectations. Arthur wrote to say that he and Emmie had now bought a house in North London and that they had a spare bedroom, which they called 'Syd's room'. This was the room that it was thought I would eventually return to when I had had enough of Australia, when we could all be together as the years rolled by.

Emmie wrote a separate letter in which she said that if I was unable to work then she would leave her present part-time job and go out full-time in order that they should have enough coming in to keep me. What a magnificent gesture!

There were no stipulations placed upon my coming to stay with them — 'Come on home and we will look after you for as long as it is necessary'. I have said before that we remained all three friends, what more proof could I have had than this?

22

Back To England

I took to haunting the shipping offices in Melbourne asking them whether they had a cancellation they could offer me. Now I wanted to get back as soon as possible.

Then one day while waiting to be seen I heard a passage cancelled there and then, right under my nose. It came over the phone. 'Was that a cancellation?' I asked.

'Yes, it was,' I was told.

'Right, I'll take that, if I may.'

And so there and then I was booked onto the Ormonde, sailing via Ceylon, Red Sea, Suez Canal, Mediterranean, Home.

This was my first trip as a passenger and I revelled in it. Life was luxurious. Meals were superb, in high-class surroundings. We had tea and biscuits brought to our bedside before we arose, we had ice cream handed to us as we sat lazing in deckchairs watching the flying fish skim over the tops of the waves. We played games or we simply watched others playing, we attended ship's concerts, we fell asleep to the gentle rhythm of the ship's movement. We made friends with those around us and generally felt that there was a quality about this way of life that we, most of us, were quite unused to. My feeling was, 'let's make the most of it'.

Letters that I received en route told me that Emmie would meet the boat train at Waterloo and take me back to their 'new' home. So, that was all arranged. All I had to do was to look out for Emmie when the train pulled in.

But eleven years had gone by, and, in addition, Emmie had decided to undertake a crash diet in an attempt to lose weight. She had always been a biggish girl, but that was her, and when one thought of Emmie they saw in their mind a biggish girl.

So when I alighted from my train that day at Waterloo Station it was for such a person that I looked. All the way along the platform I walked, with my eyes scanning the crowds lining the barriers. But Emmie was not there. There was only one person remotely like her but I dismissed her almost at once, she was not Emmie.

And so I reached the end of the barrier and was heading towards the exit, thinking, 'That's strange, it's not like her not to be here when she has promised.'

Then there was a tug at my elbow and I looked round to see the young woman who had reminded me of her a little but was definitely not her. This person was about ten stone. Slim, with another face even.

'Don't you recognise me?' said this other person, and of course I knew at once, this must be her new self. I had heard about the slimming course but my mind had not kept pace with it. My reasoning had told me to look for someone more slender but my memory still prevailed and compelled me to look for the girl I had last seen eleven years before.

It took quite some hours to accustom myself to this other Emmie, but with Arthur it was quite different. I sat at the dinner table as he entered the room and it was as though he had just been round the corner to buy a paper since I last saw him. And we immediately fell into natural and easy conversation.

I was introduced to 'Syd's Room' and saw at once that my comfort had been well attended to.

Linda came home from work that night, a girl of sixteen, a complete stranger. To make her more difficult to identify she had dyed her naturally fairish hair jet black and so I had to start right at the very beginning getting to know her.

The same evening I called on Doona. A little thinner but little altered. There was a little boy there named Philip whom I had never met, but he was very easy to get to know, and there was a young lady named Barbara, Doona's girl. I could still see traces of the child in her, even though she had gone from six to seventeen in my absence. Then there was Mick, always quiet, perhaps a little quieter.

That was my family circle (could one be smaller?) and we were all re-acquainted in no time at all.

Now, from the days when I had turned down the opportunity to spend three weeks leave in Paris in order that I might pass that time with my relations I had always had a longing to see that great city, and I had been so near yet so far. I knew it well, or certain aspects of it from films and books, and the more I saw of it the more I wished to go there. During the whole of my eleven years in Australia whenever I saw a film set in Paris I always thought 'What a fool I was not to have gone there when I was in England. It would have been so easy. Now I'm here on the other side of the world.'

So, before looking for a job my first move was to be a trip to Paris. I was not going to miss out this time. But I had no wish to go alone. Would either Emmie or Linda accompany me? The matter was discussed and it was agreed that Linda would have other chances later. Also it was felt that she might enjoy it more in younger company. That left Emmie.

A few letters around the place and I came up with a booking into a small hotel along the Boulevard St Michel, on the Left Bank. That sounded Frenchy enough. A good start.

Came the day and we sailed from Newhaven to Dieppe. I was agog, for not only was this to be my first trip to Paris but I was also going to try out my hard-learnt French. For I was determined that I would get by with their language or bust. But, at the same time, I was confident that the proprietress of my hotel would speak English (hadn't she sent me a card printed in English, French and German?) and it was my intention to relax my rule to the extent of asking her each morning in English how I would make my way to wherever we were going for the day.

At Dieppe we passed through the customs and on to a waiting train and away to — Paris.

On arrival at St Lazaire Station I can remember the feeling yet that engulfed me as we stepped down from the train and walked along the platform, each with our suitcases, towards the gate and its ticket collector.

Once through the gate and this was it. This was Paris. I was there. It was a wonderful feeling. Before leaving London I had studied the plan of the Paris Metro and I knew which station I was to go to for our hotel. But where was the nearest Metro station? Nothing for it but to call upon my humble knowledge of the language. Boldly I stepped before a workman, obviously hurrying home, and I said, 'Excusez-moi, Monsieur, mais où est le Metro, s'il vous plait?'

And it worked, for not only did he understand me, but I also understood him. 'It was at the bottom of those stairs that he pointed out.' And so it was. I was not only in Paris but I was talking. It was a great thrill.

Emmie and I spent two happy weeks there, during which we saw everything that one associates with this lovely city. We even spent an evening at the opera, although while there my vision split and I was unable to watch it any further. Apparently my eye muscles were not yet strong enough to stand up to an entire evening focused on the one object.

But just being there was sufficient to me. There is an atmosphere about Paris that one cannot find elsewhere. It is like an exclusive scent associated with a pretty lady, it is her, it belongs and one cannot attach it to any other. Paris has this exclusiveness. I am sure that if I were deposited there blindfolded, by just sniffing the air I would know exactly where I was.

There was one momentary disappointment. At the hotel I found that not a soul spoke English, I had to sink or swim by my own resources. But it did ensure that every word that I uttered whilst there had to be in French, which was perhaps a good thing.

Each morning on leaving for our day's sightseeing Madame the proprietress would say, 'Bonjour Monsieur, Madame.' My reply was, of course, Bonjour Madame.' But Emmie would insist upon saying, in tones as broadly of London as was her wont, 'Good morning.' I tried for almost the entire fortnight that we were there to induce her to relax to just this extent. 'Won't you just say bonjour as we go out of the door,' I would plead.

'No, I'd feel silly if I did. She'll have to get used to me, the other doesn't make sense.' and so each morning it went on, 'Bonjour Monsieur, Madame.' 'Bonjour Madame.' 'Good morning.'

When we came back a job had to be found, for I was now to settle down to the steady routine of living out the final years of my life. One of us had spoken of us 'all growing old together'. And in this mood I became a Waste Inspector with the Metropolitan Water Board. Waste Inspectors are uniformed men who go around the districts of London looking for leaking taps, burst pipes, overflowing overflows; in fact anything that constitutes a waste of London's water. Apparently an enormous quantity of London's water supply is just allowed to leak away through faults that no-one would bother to repair if there weren't someone such as we to compel them.

We had our own way of detecting these faults and then we would hand to the owner of the premises, or perhaps the tenant, a notice to have it repaired within a certain time, after which we would return to see that it had been done.

This was another job that would have lasted me until eternity. A semi-government position. Pensioned and secure. But these jobs, by very virtue of their security are anathema to me. They attract and breed a certain type of individual who delights almost every evening of his life, when he has a few moments to spare, in working out how much his pension will amount to come retirement time. I used to listen to them. It was as though today counted for nothing. All their hopes and plans lay in the future — when they would be sixty-five.

I never bothered to work out my pension, for I knew I wouldn't be there then. In fact, it took me no time at all to realise that this was not for me, and within six months of being home I was already wondering whether 'all growing old together' was exactly what I wanted. And as my health improved so did the old urge to be going somewhere, anywhere, reassert itself. I left the Water Board, it was too permanent, and I took a job as a greenkeeper with a bowling club. This offered me a little more freedom of movement and allowed me to make my own decisions.

But niggling away at the back of my mind all the time was the longing to be off overseas again. Somewhere new, somewhere different. New Zealand came to mind. Once, when living in Australia I had been advised to go to New Zealand. 'You would like it there,' I was told.

There were features of life in England that I was finding most disturbing. It had changed vastly in the eleven years that I had been away and whereas people such as Arthur and Doona had had these changes creep up upon them slowly and surreptitiously, to me they had come in a flash. When I had left England to pay off my ship in Australia it was still very much the country that I had known throughout my life, but in the eleven years that had passed so much had happened, and when I came back and found these new features of English life suddenly thrust upon me I could not readily accept them. Maybe I had had too many forehead-touching encounters in my youth, or too many locals calling me Massa later on. Certainly these things cannot happen without leaving a trace of effect behind them. That is not possible. But, whatever, it may have simply been that I felt footloose once again and was using these other reasons as an excuse, both to myself and to my relations, but the fact is I felt an irresistible urge to be on my way.

That is why once again the shipping offices began to be haunted by my burly figure. But this time the urgency was not so great. I could wait a few months and so I took a booking for

Auckland, New Zealand, to sail in some seven months time.

Now I was happy again. Now I could settle down to enjoy life, because it was impermanent, it was only for a while. This seems to be the sauce with which I have to garnish any job or any way of life that I'm taking part in. It has to have an end to it. I have to regard it as only for the time being. Maybe that is why I have never married, for, after all, by design at any rate, there is nothing very temporary about that.

I told Arthur and Emmie and there was obvious disappointment. In some ways I was disappointed with myself. Here I was now fifty-three — would I ever settle down?

Arthur asked me why New Zealand? 'Why the other end of the earth? Why couldn't I move down to Devon or Cornwall? That would take me away from London, which I was professing to find irksome, but we wouldn't be so cut off from each other.'

But no, it had to be a clean break, I had to get right away. A move to Devon or Cornwall would not have excited me. There is an uplifting that comes from walking up the gangplank of a ship and watching her pull away and out to sea. There is a complete change comes over one when some two or three days later they find themselves in a totally different climate. And then there is the feeling of wonderment that comes from going somewhere one has never been to before. I had been to Devon, and Cornwall. No, it had to be somewhere miles away, and I liked the idea of taking a long while to get there. So it was to be New Zealand.

When the day came to leave England Arthur came to the boat at London Docks to see me off. When he left he went down the side of the ship onto the quay side, then he walked, all alone, to the gates of the docks. There he stopped and turned around. He looked in the general direction of the ship and he waved. He couldn't see me, so he couldn't see me wave back. But I did, Art, I waved back that day. I've never told you but you looked a most pathetic figure then. I couldn't see your face but your very gesture told me how miserable you felt. And so did I.

This trip out to New Zealand took me by a route that I had never done before. We went across to Curacao, a Dutch-owned island in the West Indies, then through the Panama Canal and into the Pacific. This was the first time I had been into the Pacific and it opened up to me new names, like Tahiti, Fiji and Raratonga. We passed atolls and other small South Sea islands and here I was presented to a part of the world hitherto unknown to me. In Tahiti I went ashore and was sitting alone on a seat by the beach when an elderly man sat down alongside me and immediately entered into conversation.

'Big ship,' he said, pointing in the direction of ours.

'Yes,' said I, realising his English was limited.

Then he said, pointing to another, 'Little ship.'

Now, I realised that his language being French we could do much better than this if we switched over to his tongue, and so I spoke to him in French. From then on I was his friend for life. He wouldn't leave me. He took me home, introduced me to his wife and three sons, insisted on me taking wine with them and persuaded me (not that this required any great effort on his part) to stay for dinner. He took me to a friend on another part of Tahiti and, generally, gave me an insight into the life of the island that would have been quite hidden to me had I been left to my own resources. He came down to the ship and saw me off and made me promise that should I ever be that way again I would look him up. Eight years later I was that way again, on my way back to Europe, and I did call at his place, but he had died. Eight years can see many changes.

In New Zealand I quickly settled down. It is not a hard country in which to acclimatise oneself. More English, in speech, behaviour and thinking than Australia, with a kinder climate. One feels on landing there that they have come right to the other side of the world to something only slightly different to that that they have left behind.

My life became reasonably pleasant for here I took to making the most of the nearby beaches and could feel myself swimming better than I had for many years past.

My first job was as greenkeeper with a Women's Bowling Club with a membership of two hundred women. I was the only man associated with the club, and as I set out to give them the best bowling greens in Auckland it was natural that I should become a bit of a favourite around the place.

Still I frequented the races and now trotting came into my orbit. A popular sport in New Zealand.

Then, one day while pushing the heavy roller over the greens I felt suddenly completely exhausted, and from that moment on my condition deteriorated. I was so weak I could barely walk home after my day's work. A trip to the doctor was inevitable and he said that my previous illness had left my nervous system weakened. I must take lighter work.

It was this search for lighter work that led me to the job of caretaker.

So the trend was towards a quieter, more sedate life. Not so often now did I think of being up and away. I had the most comfortable lodgings with an elderly lady. There were just the two of us. She had been a nurse all her life and if I as much as sneezed it was all I could do to stop her from ordering me into bed where she would very soon have me propped up with six or seven pillows behind my head. She had a remedy for every minor ailment that came my way. The slightest of cuts were treated as though gangrene had already set in and if I dared belch I was immediately assailed with the appropriate medicine.

We became company for each other. We watched the telly at nights, we bought a budgerigar and a fish tank with seven or eight fish. I made a small vegetable garden at the back and my lodgings became like my

327

own home. If I dared mention anything that I had a particular fancy for in the way of food, sure enough that would be my dinner for the next evening. She was good company, being interested in most things and having learnt well in her younger days the gentle art of listening. We did crosswords in the evenings together and my life now became almost that of an elderly man.

The bird I taught to talk, which he did with a broad cockney accent. He raised many a laugh with, 'It's turned out nice again, me old darling'.

The comforts of home life began to take on some importance to me. Not that my evenings were spent entirely at home. That would be far from true, but I was finding the pleasures of a well-furnished home most enjoyable.

Now I was taking German as a language at evening classes, and the idea was beginning to take shape in my head that I would like to go to Europe. There were so many countries there with such fascinating names that I had not seen. Switzerland, Austria, Germany, Belgium. These were no more than places on the map to me. I would love to visit them. To think of myself in a situation where I could put some of the many evenings spent learning French and German into use seemed to me so attractive. I must go. I would go. It became my goal, but how to achieve it? At the moment I had not enough money, even though I was saving steadily. But now I was edging along towards sixty (if I have speeded up in the telling of the latter part of this story it is only what happens in life — the early years seemed as though they would never go, while the later years will not linger long enough. Also so much less worth writing about happens in later life.), I couldn't wait too much longer. Yet neither could I now afford to give my job up, in case I could not get another on my return. This was the reasoning of an older man, I wasn't throwing up a job now and taking a chance on what happened next.

In association with the desire to get into Europe was also the thought that maybe I could go back to my French village at Givenchy le Noble. How wonderful that would be. To see again Odette, Renee, Leon, Marie and all the others. That is if they were still there. For I had no idea what changes had taken place. In all these years I had never had a word from them. The thought intrigued me — yes, it had to be done, even if it proved a disappointment, for I had harboured a belief all my life that there was something special about the relationship that existed between us all in that village during those early months of the war. I had never forgotten them and had thought of my stay there as one of the happiest times of my life.

I must go back, and risk a disillusionment. And so with this in mind I would occasionally check my resources to see whether I could afford 'my trip to Europe'.

My landlady, (I had now taken to calling her Kath) would ask, 'When are you going on your trip?' and never did I feel that I had enough saved to enable me to confidently go.

It remained but a dream. Then the shares that I had bought with my savings started to increase in value. There was a boom and in six months I had made a thousand pounds, if I chose to sell. This seemed the time to move — I sold, and altogether my account showed three thousand pounds. Good, I could spend two thousand and still have a thousand safeguard to come back to. If anything should happen to cause me to lose my job while I was away I would have the thousand to tide me over until I found another.

At this time I had a friend (we had met at the evening classes) who was only too pleased to take over my job until my return. All was arranged. Home via Pacific, Panama, Trinidad. Back via Cape Town, Durban, Australia. Now it had become almost impossible to travel without calling at places that I already knew.

So I left, to spend as long in Europe as I chose and to come back when I had had enough. I was fifty-nine. Six years from the time when Arthur had waved vaguely towards the ship as he stood looking back at her from the gates at London Docks.

Up the gangplank once again, to be confronted by another horde of stewards, plus all the familiar sights and sounds that go to make up life on the ocean wave.

This time it was felt that there was hardly room to accommodate me at Arthur's and Emmie's and so Doona stepped in and offered me a room at her place. Mick had died while I was in New Zealand (the first of our intimate circle to go) and she had a room to spare. Not only had Doona lost Mick but Barbara had married and had moved into her own flat. But she still called round once a week.

Barbara's marriage was to the very first boyfriend she had had. It came about in this way. When she left school, at fifteen, her first job was as an office junior. On the day that she started work she was just a nervous, little, just-out-of-school kid. Little more than a child. That same day she would periodically have to go into the workshop, alongside the office, for some detail or other and there worked Bill, a young man of twenty-two. He saw this youngster come in and recognised her as the new office junior. One glance in her direction was enough. She was of no consequence, just left school, no figure, no idea how to wear her clothes, nothing. He took no further notice. And for three years she remained in his eyes a little girl. Then one day he looked at her and he realised that that little girl no longer existed. That in her place was a most attractive young lady. Not a bad figure either. Hm. He looked again, in fact he stared. So much so that she noticed him and remarked upon it. That was it. That was their introduction. They were married within two years, and it looks as though I could add, 'and they lived happily ever after,' for theirs is a very well-founded marriage. They are ideally suited and Bill can thank his lucky stars he took that second look.

They treated me to a very pleasant evening at their place in Winchmore Hill, where I was able to see what a happy couple they made.

Back at Doona's young Philip was treating me as though I was someone from outer space. He brought his mates around to see me and he told me that all his school knew that his uncle was home from New Zealand. It was then that I saw how much he adored his mother, with his sister running a very close second. The last idealist in a day of extreme materialism. I hope he isn't let down too badly.

Two weeks I spent with Doona, part of which time was necessary while I was writing to find accommodation in Paris. I would start my European tour there I thought. However this wasn't easily found as it was now the 'High season', and, of course, Paris in 'High season' becomes inundated.

Eventually I came up with a certain Madame who had an establishment called Le Home Fleuri (The Flowered Home). She had a house full of students, she told me, but they would be going on their vacation in ten days time. 'Could I wait that long?'

'Yes,' I decided, 'I would wait.' In the meantime I would go over to some other part of France until such times she had a vacancy.

So I packed a small suitcase and a duffle bag and I moved off from Doona's. I was going to Calais and I was going to stay there until Le Home Fleuri could take me in. This was my move into Europe, the Continent. I had no plans beyond Paris. After that I would play it by ear.

The idea behind the duffle bag and suitcase was that into the duffle bag I would place all the things that I would have immediate need of, such as shaving gear, slippers, any book that I was reading, etc. That meant that on arriving at a station I could put the suitcase into a luggage room and with duffle bag slung conveniently over my shoulder I could go in search of somewhere to stay. If I had to wander far from the station before finding somewhere to put up then there would be no need to retrieve my suitcase until the next day. This often worked out to be the most practicable arrangement.

At Calais I landed into the most dismal setting imaginable. The skies were heavy with what looked to be an inexhaustible covering of rain clouds. The gutters were running inches deep and there was hardly a soul to be seen. It was as though the whole population had been washed away. I had nothing booked in advance and it was clearly impossible to go looking for anything in this rain. It was then that I spotted a taxi standing with the water swirling around its wheels. I rushed across, peered into the driver's cabin and asked in my best French if he would take me to a small, not too dear hotel. I got in and we drove off. I might just have well stood on the running board, for we simply went around the corner and stopped outside a dingy looking cafe. He tooted a few times on his horn and a most miserable looking Madame came to the door. Then followed a short burst of conversation across the sodden pavement from cab to cafe. He was asking her did she want a client? I heard him say 'Anglais'. This left her if anything a little more miserable. However she agreed to take me. I'd swear it was against her better judgement. So the cabby and I made a wild dash across the pavement through what had now become a torrent.

'How long did I wish to stay?' asked the misery.

'A few days,' I replied. I preferred not to be too specific in case I wished to move on.

By now the taxi driver was receiving his commission, a free glass or two of wine. Then he charged me the biggest fare for the shortest journey on record and drove off. I felt as though I had been trapped. He had driven me to this unpretentious looking place to suit his own ends. This wasn't a small hotel.

Madame Misery showed me to my room and left me. My Continental tour had begun.

23

Five Months A-Wandering In Europe

Each morning I came down to the bar and sat at a table, waiting for my breakfast. Madame would come across and serve me without seeming to see me. She had no need to talk for it was always coffee and rolls. She didn't have to ask me what I would like, I had no choice. Then one day she came to my table, looked as me, smiled, said 'Bonjour Monsieur' and something to the effect of it being a nice day. She looked a different person when she smiled.

On the day that I left to go to Paris she came over, shook hands with me and hoped I would look her up if I passed that way on my return.

What there was about me that had her looking so depressed she never did say. Maybe I reminded her of someone who had done her wrong.

Now began something that has had an extreme effect upon almost every day of my life since. I began writing descriptive letters to Kath, my landlady. There was so much to say and I wanted so much to say it. Each night on returning to my hotel I would write my impressions of the day and I allowed myself to be quite effusive. I knew that she would enjoy reading about every little thing I was seeing and doing, for My Trip had been spoken of for so long. Now it was here. I say I knew that she would enjoy any eulogising that I might do, but what I did not know was that she would transcribe my letters into exercise books, thereby producing a near narrative effect. Neither did I know that on my return she would convince me that I had in my letters excellent material for a full-sized book. However, that was quite a way off on the day that I emerged from the Gare du Nord in Paris carrying my suitcase in my hand and my duffle bag over my shoulder.

I knew that Le Home Fleuri was just a walk away. It was simply a matter of following the plan of the city that I had bought whilst in London. So off we went, a little surprised to find that the streets were laid out exactly in the order in which the plan said they would be. After ten minutes walking, taking each turning with complete confidence, there standing before me was my Beflowered Home, but it was not at all as I had pictured it. I had visualised an apartment with a flowering creeper all over the front. This one was at the end of a courtyard with a few modestly attractive plants in flower pots on the ground just outside the entrance. It was most unimpressive. For one brief moment I was tempted to go on and look for something a little more inviting. However, I thought of the lady of the house sitting there awaiting her latest arrival and I knew that I had to go in.

Once inside the shabby exterior was soon forgotten. The proprietress was a character and the house, while old, was clean and comfortable.

Each morning the few tenants that were there would come down to the dining room and from a huge cauldron-like affair they would ladle out a large cup of coffee, already sugared and milked. Then they would sit down at a large elongated table where eight or nine inches of a crisp, crunchy French loaf would be lying on a plate with a small bowl of fresh, tasty butter alongside. This was invariable. It even looked the same each morning. Yet I can honestly say it never became boring. In fact, like an old friend, the more we became acquainted the better we got along together.

This is what I wanted. This was what I had come to France for. The remaining tenants were French, with one young fellow from Belgium, and Madame spoke no English. No waiters coming to me asking 'What will you have for breakfast, sir?' in impeccable English. I only hoped my tour would continue this way.

At this modest apartment house I stayed for three weeks, finally extending my stay for a few days to enable me to see Bastille Day while still in Paris. This is France's National Day. It commemorates the storming of the Bastille at the beginning of the Revolution and represents to all Frenchmen the symbol of the day they won their freedom.

While in Paris I did two memorable trips. One was to Dunkirk and the other was to my village.

Dunkirk came first. It was but a day's run from Paris and was going to be for me a return to my younger days and a link-up with some of my former comrades. I knew not what to expect for I had read nothing concerning it during the years that had passed.

The day was gloriously sunny when I caught the train, the train that would speed back through the years and land me up on that occasion, so far away, when I had been one of that milling crowd caught up in a situation that we didn't even understand, let alone know how to deal with.

The latter part of the journey I did by bus and as I looked around me I saw that there wasn't one other person doing a pilgrimage such as I. It was just a local bus running from one small town to another and most of the people aboard were village folk going to the nearby market town. Theirs was a journey of today. They were travelling along the road of kilometres, I was going along the road of time. As we came to each market place so a few travellers would descend. I stayed on. My destination was yesterday.

At Dunkirk we ended up in the town square. Yes, I remembered this place, there had been a statue in the centre. There it was, it was of a former son of Dunkirk who had defended the city against the Dutch heaven knows how long ago. His name — Jean Bart. He stood, as he stood when I first saw him, his sword held on high in an attitude of defiance. But for the rest — it had disappeared. The entire square had been rebuilt with every solitary building completely new. There was not one thing to remind me even that this town was

338

French. What had once stood there had been destroyed to the last brick and they had set about refashioning their town with no more than a few skeletons of buildings remaining to tell them what was there before. Except for Jean Bart. He stood just where he always had, defying all. I read on this second occasion that he had stood in his present position surviving bombardments from three wars. During the first World War Dunkirk had been shelled daily by a long-range gun called Big Bertha. Innumerable inhabitants had been killed and many fine buildings destroyed. Jean Bart had stood unscathed. Then in the second World War the whole town had tumbled around him, yet, even then he remained unblemished. No wonder when it came to the reconstruction of Dunkirk they decided to leave him just where he was, waving his defiance to the world.

I wandered around the town, realising that there was very little left of what had been there the first time. Then I went down to the dockside, where we had landed and been forced to take shelter that night. It was distinctly familiar. It was old. More in the fashion that I remembered it to be. I struck up conversation with an old cafe proprietor. 'Yes, he was there at the time.' He agreed that he would have been there on the day that I landed. He left later, when things got too bad, and didn't come back until after the war.

There had been some brothels there where we had spent one evening. I remembered the card that my girl gave me. Her name was Louise. The card had said in poor English that the house was 'for amusing'. Well, yes, that would be right. We had spent part of the evening drinking and laughing with the girls while all the time a gramophone was kept constantly scratching away in the corner. They would never let this thing stop and in the end we were hearing the same records over and over again three and four times. Yes, it was an amusing evening all right. But it was no longer there, and, as with all the best places that are pulled down today it was replaced by something completely without interest. The new building was dealing in insurance. A necessary and useful enough service, but not for amusing.

Then I decided that it was time to go down to the beaches. At least they couldn't change them much. They would still be beaches whatever they did to them.

They hadn't changed. There were the houses along the promenade, many of which had been burning while I was there and one of which had sheltered me in its garage during the night of my two-day stay.

Right along this promenade they have erected the flags of every allied country engaged in the war. And for as far as the eye can see these flags stand colourfully fluttering in the breeze, for when they ran out of different countries they started again, and again, and again. There is at the end of the prom a simple monument speaking of the occasion and commemorating the dead. So far so good. I was quite impressed. It was lovely to be here.

But then I decided to sort out as near as

possible the spot where I had stood previously and I found it, to my satisfaction at any rate. I stood there on the beach and I let my mind drift back. It was easy. There away on my left were the smoking oil tanks, behind were the burning houses. Out to sea were hundreds of small craft busy pulling men out of the sea. I saw and heard the aircraft coming over and I saw the men fall onto the beach pressing themselves into the sand. Our cook was alongside me again, his face frightened as ever. I saw other faces that I knew I would never see again and I felt dreadfully sad. I stood awhile like this, a man from the past, and then slowly I allowed the sounds of today to creep back, and it was all over. It was a remarkable experience. One I shall never forget. But I don't think I would want it again.

Then I saw all around me children playing in the sands, with mothers chatting and the sounds of a fairground just a little way off, and I went away to enjoy myself.

The next trip was even more memorable, for this one brought back people I had known. This was more than a case of standing there and evoking memories. This next one was alive.

It came only a few days after my trip to Dunkirk. I had deliberately delayed it because I wanted to become as much accustomed to the language as possible. I wanted to be able to speak to and understand my village folk, for I knew they hadn't one word of English between them. I had worked for this and nothing must spoil it.

To get to Givenchy le Noble from Paris means a train to Arras, then a bus from Arras to Avesnes le Comte and then another bus from Avesnes le Comte to Givenchy. Quite a performance, but provided these all linked up reasonably well it wasn't as bad as it sounds.

Anyway, I had booked a train to Arras and I intended to catch the last train back from there to Paris the same day. That would leave me eight or nine hours in my village. Lovely.

When I set off I was wearing only a sports shirt and carried no luggage. I didn't need any, I was only going for the day, and it was beautifully sunny and warm.

The trip to Arras over I looked around for the bus to Avesnes. This left in half an hour. Good. Arriving at Avesnes I wondered where I should now catch the small local bus to Givenchy. On making enquiries I was told that the bus only ran every second day and today was not one. That meant a walk of five miles. This was, of course, not beyond me, and in fact I almost welcomed it. It was a walk that I had frequently done when we were billeted there at the start of the war.

Imagine if you can my feelings at this time. Here I was in Avesnes. Givenchy was five miles away along a quiet country road. We used to go to a house in Avesnes for a bath. A woman ran a public baths for the troops in her own home. She had two zinc baths in a room and she kept a constant supply of hot water from huge pots that stood steaming on her stove throughout the entire day.

Avesnes had hardly changed. I knew it well. Jim and I had come here together in those far off days. This was thrilling stuff. Within an hour or so I would be back in my village. What would I find? Would they remember me? Would I recognise them?

Although this village had cropped up in my memory from time to time right through the last thirty years I had really never in my wildest dreams envisaged myself walking back there unannounced one day as I was just about to do.

So I set out, feeling on air, to walk the last five miles of my pilgrimage. The road was vaguely familiar but there was nothing about it that I truly recognised. After about a mile I came to a figure of the Virgin Mary set up on a plinth on the side of the road. I crossed over. Surely I would remember this? I must have passed it dozens of times before. The dates upon it showed it to have been there at that other time but it did nothing to my memory. I had no recollection of ever having seen it before. This was most disappointing. Don't say I was not gong to remember anything. I passed on.

I felt gloriously happy. There was no traffic, it was idyllic, I began to sing. What mattered, there was no-one there to hear me. But with each mile that passed still there was nothing to remind me of those other days, until the chateau came into view. This was right on the edge of the village at the other end of a long drive. It had not changed in the least. If my memory had not been stirred during the long walk, it was here. For this was our old home. We had lived in this building for eight delightful months. A little further on and I was in the village. There were changes but they were only slight. It had had something of a face-lift. Been brought a little more up-to-date. What had been a rough, unsurfaced road was now smoothly sealed. Along the sides of the road ran a real kerb where there formerly had been nothing. There was too a modern inn, or estaminet. Did this mean then that ours no longer existed? I continued along the road to where I believed ours had stood but there was nothing there. In all this time I had seen no-one. All was quiet. Then around the corner came a tractor. I put out my hand to stop it. I had to find out what had happened to my people. The driver alighted. 'Excuse me,' I said, 'but didn't there use to be an estaminet here?'

'No, not just here,' said the driver, 'a little further down the road.'

'Was it run by an elderly lady named Marie?' I asked.

'That was my mother. The estaminet isn't used any more. It is my home.'

Then he stared at me a while and suddenly burst out, 'Seedney.'

'You know me?' I asked.

'Yes, of course, I am Marie's son. Don't you remember me? I came home on leave while you were there.'

Yes, certainly I remembered him. But there was no further time for reflection for he had burst into life, 'Maria, Maria, Seedney has come back,' he yelled.

And in a flash Maria was at the door of the house just alongside. There she was, I would have known her had I met her walking down the Strand. Older, heavier, greyer, but as much Maria as the day we had moved away with that light early morning mist hanging over the village.

She broke into a happy smile and came forward, arms outstretched. I was about to be kissed.

'Why have you been so long coming back?' These were her first words, 'Come in. Come in.'

I was told later that through all the years they had waited, expecting one or the other of us to call back on them and a little puzzled when no-one came.

Inside Maria's house the wine bottle was dragged out and glasses set up all round.

There was a scuffle at the door and Leon and Odette rushed in. They had married and had two children. I was embraced and bombarded with questions. I felt deliriously happy. This I had dreamed about. This was a dream come true.

Then there was the screeching of a car coming to a sudden halt and Germaine dashed in and threw her arms around me. She had gone from twenty-one to fifty-one in my absence but to remind me of those earlier days she had brought along with her her twenty year old daughter who was the original Germaine all over again.

By now the whole village had been alerted. A man in his early forties came excitedly up to me and said 'Hello, Seedney, do you remember be?'

I looked, hard, but as far as I could tell he was a complete stranger.

Seeing the lack of recognition he jogged my memory, 'Louis, Louis, remember you used to play football with me in the chateau courtyard?'

But no, it had gone.

'Just a moment,' he said and he ran out of the room. In a flash he was back holding a photograph before him. 'Look, look,' he said, 'you remember me,' and he showed me a photograph of himself when we used to play football together. He was about ten or eleven, and wearing that little smock that both the boys and girls wear to school in France. No wonder I hadn't recognised him, he was well past the little smock stage now.

By afternoon I had drunk so much wine that I couldn't stop talking and with all inhibition suppressed I found that my French flowed quite freely. All work was stopped while the village celebrated the occasion. Odette asked me on one side, 'Did I ever see anything of Norman now?' I told her that I hadn't seen him since soon after we left the village.

'What was his other name?' she asked.

I had forgotten.

Then she said, 'Bartlett, wasn't it?'

It was. It came back to me then, but I was amazed that she had remembered it through all these years. He must have had a very great impression upon her. Or would it be more simple to say she must have been very much in love?

I had brought with me a photograph taken with us all standing in an old-fashioned attitude outside the estaminet. In it Germaine's little child was sitting in a baby chair. This child, Germaine told me was now a married woman of thirty-one with two children. She was at the moment in the hospital at Arras recovering from an operation for appendicitis. They were going to visit her this afternoon, 'would I like to go?' So off we went, a very happy party.

At the hospital the thirty-one year old baby was shown the photograph and we all had a good laugh.

Soon it came time for me to consider catching my connection back to Paris but the idea was immediately squashed.

'You are not coming back after thirty years and only staying for one day,' said Odette, 'You can stay with Leon and I, we have a spare room.'

'But I have no shaving gear, no warmer clothing (the evenings were quite cool), I hadn't come prepared to stay.'

No matter, I could use Leon's shaving kit. As for the rest, it was dismissed. Odette would not be denied.

That evening Odette and Leon took me to see sister Renee. Little Renee had been thirteen when I last saw her. A slender little thing, shy, and still believing that we were the villains who burnt Joan of Arc. Now she had grown to be a woman of forty-three.

They said, 'You won't recognise her.'

She had married a school teacher and lived in an adjacent town.

It was evening when we arrived there and quite dark. We knocked at the door, Odette, Leon and myself, and we waited. Then the door opened and a plumpish woman stood there lit by the hall light, bearing only the very vaguest resemblance to the little girl I had last known.

'We have brought someone to see you,' said Odette, and we stood there, big grins all over our faces.

Renee looked hard at me for a while and said, 'Do I know him?'

Then almost immediately afterwards, 'Seedney.'

This thirteen year old child, grown to forty-three knew me within seconds of looking at me in the light from her hall on a dark night. And this without the slightest warning that I might be arriving. I thought it was marvellous.

We had a wonderful evening, with more wine, a room overflowing with animation and laughter. I asked Renee if she had forgiven us for what we did to Joan of Arc and she smiled and said, 'I have, but it all seemed so very serious at the time.'

That evening was one of the happiest I have known. I cannot remember once being stuck for the right word to say, but then, so much wine flowed that had I made all the mistakes in the world I don't suppose I would have realised it. That was my reunion with Renee. She still seemed shy and somewhat quiet.

Soon after my Continental tour was over and I had returned to New Zealand I had a letter from Odette in which she told me that a terrible sadness had overwhelmed them — Renee was taken into hospital on her forty-third birthday for the removal of a benign tumour and within a fortnight she was dead.

This was a tremendous shock to me. She was the youngest of us all, looking as though she had years and years ahead of her. Yet, on that night when we were all so hilariously happy she had but a few short months to live.

How extraordinary that I should have called round on her that night just in time to find her alive.

My stay lasted three days before they would allow me to leave and it was a very worried landlady that I met up with on my return to Le Home Fleuri. She had been thinking of going to the police.

Now I was free to leave Paris — the two main reasons for staying on there had been attended to. I had been back to Dunkirk and my village.

My journeying now took me into Switzerland, where I stayed wherever the fancy took me and then on to Austria. Now my French was of no use and I had to call upon my slender knowledge of German. But even then I still pushed myself into little gasthouses where it was a case of speak German or perish. Across Austria I went until I came to a name that spells magic to me — Vienna. Was ever a city more beautifully named?

By now my letters to Kath were flowing over with my enthusiasm.

Here I would like to remark on the fact that at one stage of my wanderings it occurred to me to compare my present circumstances with the average lot of my father. He, poor devil, had worked hard all his life, much harder than had I, for a miserable wage that just allowed him to live, at a most modest level. He saved up the whole year for his annual holiday, which was never more than one week. At that time there was great excitement as preparations were made to spend that week as far afield as Bournemouth.

The idea of having seven months off from work while he flitted across Europe would have struck him as uproariously comic. Yet here was I doing just that. It seemed so unjust and for a moment made me feel quite sad, and extremely lucky.

In Vienna I stayed eleven days, for the oddest of reasons. It seemed about time to have my trousers cleaned (they were the light drill type which shows the dirt very readily) and I confidently expected to be able to pick them up the next day. However, on calling for them I was told they would not be ready for another ten days! This was a set-back at the time. I hadn't intended to stay so long. But now I'm glad I did. I love Vienna.

When I finally retrieved my trousers and was free to move on I was faced with the problem of where to go to next. I would not retrace my steps, and I wished to come back through Germany. The only way to reach there was through Czechoslovakia. All right, but it was

350

the exact anniversary of the occupation by Russian troops the year before. The newspapers were speaking of uprisings, 'foreigners were not being allowed out of the country,' 'two young men had been killed in skirmishing in Brno.'

If foreigners were not allowed out even less would they be allowed in. Barbara had written to me begging me, 'Please, uncle Syd, don't go into Czechoslovakia, dreadful things are happening there.'

But, and this sounds awfully heroic, what was happening only made me all the more eager to go in. To see a country in a state of turmoil, under the surveillance of a foreign power, with troops parading the streets, was not on offer every day. I would like to see the reaction of the people. At the same time I was completely confident that nothing would happen to me. I wouldn't go asking for trouble. At Thos Cook's office in Vienna I was told that they thought they could arrange it for me. 'Where did I wish to go? To which city?'

Pilsen was my choice. And the reason being that I knew this to be a fair-sized town. It would, I thought, be much more representative of the general life of the country, the average Czech's life, than would be that in Prague. So I reasoned, and this was put down on my visa — 'to spend five days in Pilsen.' I was going. But first of all an appeasing letter to Barbara.

On my return to New Zealand I wrote at some length on my tour. A book which I entitled 'By Duffle Bag and Suitcase'. For this I was never able to find a publisher, although I am not without some slight hope that my manuscript will even yet one day find someone willing enough to encase it in an eye-pleasing book jacket.

For that reason I do not feel inclined to go into any great detail here concerning my impressions of all that I saw. But I would like it to be clearly understood that in Czechoslovakia I was distinctly shocked by the miserably poor conditions under which everyone seemed to be living. Actually I passed a while in two other small towns besides Pilsen. One was called Ceske Valenice and the other was Ceske Budejovice. Now I realise that these names mean little or nothing to the average reader, but there could be others who would wish to know on what I based my judgements. In all three towns the living standards were pitifully low. There were such intense shortages. Of course one cannot judge a country in a few days and I am not trying to do that but the lack of goods in shop windows, the poor quality of those that were there. The miserable utility styles. The lack of colour or fashion, or ornamentation, these things didn't need a lifetime's residence to realise.

Coming direct from Vienna, as I did, and having just passed through three other European countries on the way enabled me to make some comparison and it was this that made all that I saw in Czechoslovakia look so cheap and dowdy.

And it was not that I went there with an abhorrence of Communism. On the contrary, as a relic from my poorer days as a youngster, I had gentle leanings towards any system that promised the worker a fairer deal. I was fully prepared to find there that the 'system' was working a whole sight better than our Western press would have us believe. I was, in fact, wanting to approve of what I would find. Maybe that is why it was such a profound shock to me to see a country so apparently run down, so hard up, with a people appearing to be stunned into a state of resigned acceptance.

There was not one redeeming feature that I could put my finger on. If there are advantages to living that way they were completely beyond my vision, I saw nothing but squalor and neglect.

When I left, after five days searching in vain for something anything, that I could commend it was to go in a flash from poverty to opulence, for in Nuremberg I found a city almost in a state of festivity. Here was a fine well-lit, bustling, wealthy city with a people reflecting in their faces the satisfaction that comes from a way of life that provides not only a freedom from want but leisure time, and the resources with which to enjoy it.

Nuremberg looked twice as wealthy by reason of me having come from the shortages of Pilsen. For five months I was wandering around Europe, all the time trying to get by entirely in the language of the country. It was an exciting experience that sometimes led me into odd situations, like when, in Innsbruck, I had started to ask a young lady the way to the station and she had hurried away without waiting to hear me out. As she moved off I watched her retreating figure feeling highly amused. The whole incident struck me as some sort of a compliment. But when I saw her go straight up to a policeman, speak to him, then turn round and point in my direction, I reckoned it might be time I was on my way. Heaven only knows what she thought I was about to say.

Eventually I boarded the cross channel boat at Boulogne, filled with regret at the thought that I was saying goodbye to all this, perhaps for ever.

On board the boat I spoke English as my regular language again for the first time since I had left some five months before. Somehow I found this displeasing. There was no thrill to speaking my own language.

Back in London there was a month to go before my boat would leave. Once again I put up at Doona's and once again young Phil carried the news to school that his wandering uncle had returned.

Barbara and I had one lovely day at Bath. We had neither of us been there before and the sun shone benignly down upon us for the whole time that we were there.

Then once more it was a case of committing myself over to the captain of the ship for safe disposal to my destination, Auckland, New Zealand.

But fate had one more card to deal to me, for on this same ship she had also installed a widow of forty-one and a daughter of eleven.

The significance will be foreseen, we become emotionally involved. She was going to Brisbane, in Australia, and when the time came for her to disembark we were a very disconsolate pair for it marked the end of a very enjoyable though short relationship. Little did we know then but it wasn't to be the end of anything, for we began writing to one another. At first once a week, then twice a week, then sometimes without waiting for a letter to reply to. We fell in love by post.

And so a year passed during which time we had developed a complete understanding of one another. So much so that we were now afraid of a possible let-down when we met again. We took to now telling each other of our faults, to make it all the easier to take when they became apparent to the other later on.

At the end of a year in New Zealand I became eligible for two weeks leave and I flew straight over to Brisbane. Those two weeks were supremely happy. On the boat our friendship had been strictly formal. We had both been on our best behaviour, as one always is with no more than half-acquaintance, but now our year's correspondence had made us feel that we knew all there was to know about each other. We met as more than acquaintances. We had all the lovely things that we had written about one another behind us and being together was but a continuation of our letter writing. We were both caught up in a regard for each other that would not allow us to see things in their true light. We had a mist over our eyes, a fluffy, pink mist that prevented us from seeing anything sharply outlined. Everything was blurred.

In this slightly bemused fashion at the end of the fortnight I came back to New Zealand but now our letters dealt with only how we could be together for all time. It was planned that I should find somewhere for us to live and she would come over with her daughter, who by now I was thinking of as almost my own. That way we would be together FOR EVER.

I found a place, only a matter of yards from the beach and my new lady-love came over. We moved in together and settled down to spend the rest of our lives happily. Five days later during one of our constant heart to heart talks we agreed that the whole thing was a mistake. We had both grown too used to being independent and there were obligations, on both sides, associated with this living together which we were neither of us willing to accept.

So, right to the end, those characteristics that were the part of my character that would not allow me in the past, in my young days, to marry have once again won out. Now I have accepted the fact that marriage is not for me, I must remain a crabby old bachelor. Not that I don't enjoy the company of women. I do, enormously, but only at a distance that I can focus at. When they come too close my vision becomes affected.

In Conclusion

Life is subject to a whole range of ifs and buts. If, for example, Arthur had signed as my guardian and I had gone to Canada as a young fellow of sixteen nothing that followed would have happened. It is futile to attempt to imagine what the consequences of that move would have been — it remains one of life's reservoir of ifs.

Then there is the possibility of what changes would have been effected to my story had Chink been but a few years older. Undoubtedly I would have wanted to marry her. And what a sweeping change that must have created had it happened. But it didn't.

Later on had our ship not tied up alongside that most friendly of townships in Tasmania I might never have wanted to pay off in Australia. Does that then mean that I would never have had that illness in which I lay paralysed for ten long weeks? How are we to know? Life will answer our questions only provided they are framed in the one fashion: 'And what happened then?' 'And what would have happened then?' produces only a tantalising silence.

So, having lived our life, on looking back, maybe we can best feel satisfied by regarding it as that which fate had in store for us, the good and the bad.

Yet, is this the time for reflection? Could there not be something else, even now?

When I was young I would have seen a man in his seventies as someone very much at the end of his life. It would have struck me as odd that he should have any desire to squeeze anything further out of living. I would have seen him as incapable of having the same emotions as myself. He had no right to want to travel any more or show a keen interest in events going on around him. They were not for him. They were exclusively for such as I, the young.

But now that I am the object of that disdainful regard, now that I am seventy-plus, I find that my hopes for the future are not quite yet fully extinguished. At the back of my mind is a half belief that I might be able to end my days moving around the world at my leisure, selling the odd article here there for a living. It is a remote hope, I know, but it is good that I should have it. And it is not entirely without some foundation, for recently I have sold in all over thirty articles on a variety of subjects. For which I am indebted to Kath for arousing my interest in the first place.

In the meantime my situation is reasonably comfortable. Kath having given up her house and entered an Old Person's Home has led me to renting a small flat. And in doing so I find that that friendly spirit who guided me so safely through every danger during the war has once again installed himself upon my shoulder and is still watching over my welfare, for he has given me as a next door neighbour a handsome young woman of forty-one who, for reasons that she chooses to keep to herself prefers to remain unmarried. Why this should be doesn't worry me in the least. All that matters is that she should not have a change of heart, for as things are I spend three or four evenings every week with her in conversation and watching the telly over the occasional cup of coffee.

She is charming company and the moment she decides to offer herself to the world at large my privileges will cease, for she will be snapped up in a matter of hours.

At present she is happy to have me pop in from time to time as she sees in me no cause for concern. My presence breaks the silence of her empty flat. She can air her thoughts to me. And I have learnt the value of agreeing with those one wishes to please.

Were I a little younger she would not risk having me there. So, you see, I am now putting even my negative qualities to advantage. In fact I am finding that my age is now my virtue. Provided one can use their experiences discreetly their company can still be found interesting and even appreciated, and any lack of romance associated with one's loss of looks and figure is compensated for by, as with my young neighbour, the trust they are now prepared to place in you.

And, speaking of lack of romance due to advancing years, Kath hated the Old Person's Home for several weeks after she first went in. She, in fact, reached a pitch where she even decided she couldn't stay any longer and was on the point of leaving. Then all of a sudden her discontent disappeared overnight and she found the place quite acceptable. She had made friends with one of the residents, an old chap of eighty. A most companionable old fellow. With him as a friend apparently the whole place was transformed.

Now I understand they have decided to marry.

So, it seems, despite the different appearance that we present to the world as the years work their change upon our shape, yet, within, the little boy dwells basically almost unchanged right to the end.

Why Weymouth?

Many people have asked me why I chose to stay in Weymouth. Well, in the first place I do like to live by the seaside. But to be precise I will explain.

When I decided to leave New Zealand after thirteen years there it was because Arthur, my brother, was approaching seventy years of age. I was only two years younger, with Doona another two years behind me. So it was clearly time we lived closer to one another.

Therefore, I obtained a nine-month re-entry permit from the immigration authorities and booked a passage on the next available boat. The re-entry permit would give me nine months to decide whether I preferred to live in England or New Zealand. Ample time, surely.

On arrival back in England I stayed with Doona in Camden Town, a district in North West London.

In no time at all my mind was made up. I could not continue to live there. It was not the

England I had dreamed of when I was on the other side of the world. So many changes had taken place. My England had disappeared and a new one, a motley collection of peoples had taken its place. Arthur had warned me of this in his letters: 'You won't like it here,' he had said. He went on to say, 'If I could live in New Zealand, like you, I'd be out there like a shot'. How right he was — New Zealand was a very pleasant place to live. But of course, I had a special reason for wanting to come home.

However, it was not to be and, with regrets all round I booked my ticket with a shipping company for my return to New Zealand. This meant, of course, farewell to Arthur and Doona, for I would never come back again.

There were a few weeks before my ship was to sail and I decided that I would take advantage of this to see a bit of England I had never seen when I lived here. That was the South West — Gloucester, Bristol, Cheltenham, Weymouth. So off I went to make a tour, by train. This also was to be my farewell to England. All went well. It was (1976, the year of the drought), the year, when the sun was in its heavens all day and every day, and the countryside looked truly beautiful. I loved it and was glad I was making this journey. The memory of it would be with me all the time I was back in New Zealand.

Then I came to Weymouth. I was on my way back to London.

Weymouth is a moderate sized town on the Dorset Coast, a holiday town, full to overflowing in the summer time. There was an atmosphere

361

there. People had come there to enjoy themselves and it could be felt. In addition to a lovely wide-sweeping bay and the finest of soft sands there was Punch and Judy, there were the donkeys giving rides to children on the beach, and, wonder of wonders, a sand artist, the like of which I had never seen before. His models were all life-size and all splendidly coloured. I stood, fascinated, watching him assemble his figures and I went back time and again to see what progress he had made. (I might mention here that I have since written his life-story in booklet form which he sells at his model site.)

After two days in Weymouth I went on to Bournemouth but was so curious as to what changes my sand-artist had made that I came back to Weymouth for another two days. I was captivated, so much so that on my arrival back in London I knew where my future lay. It was there, back in Weymouth. There I would have my little bit of 'Old' England and there too I would be near enough to Arthur and Doona should anything happen.

I recovered the booking fee from the shipping company by saying that an illness in the family prevented me from sailing and I came down to Weymouth to live.

Both Arthur and Doona have died while I have been here, leaving me the last of the line.

To say I lived happily ever after is, up to this moment, true. I have a council flat. I have been here eighteen years and am convinced I made the right choice.

We do hope that you have enjoyed reading this large print book.

Did you know that all of our titles are available for purchase?

We publish a wide range of high quality large print books including:
Romances, Mysteries, Classics, General Fiction, Non Fiction and Westerns.

Special interest titles available in large print are:
**The Little Oxford Dictionary
Music Book
Song Book
Hymn Book
Service Book**

Also available from us courtesy of Oxford University Press:
**Young Readers' Dictionary
(large print edition)
Young Readers' Thesaurus
(large print edition)**

For further information or a free brochure, please contact us at:
**Ulverscroft Large Print Books Ltd.,
The Green, Bradgate Road, Anstey,
Leicester, LE7 7FU, England.**
Tel: (00 44) **0116 236 4325**
Fax: (00 44) **0116 234 0205**

DAWN

Kate Alexander

Madeleine Ardingley is shocked to learn that her beloved father is a liar and a cheat. The innocent, convent-educated girl is swept into the Parisian demi-monde and finds it not to her liking, though it appears to her cousin, Lord Janus Chilcote, that she is very much her father's daughter. Two years later, Madeleine is forced to appeal to the charity of the family in England she barely knows. Her quiet dignity and gentle manners soon win their affections, but Janus is as cynical as ever. However, Madeleine is to discover that he is a truer friend than she had ever imagined . . .

FROM ONE WORLD TO ANOTHER

Rita Rogers with N. Garnett

Rita Rogers is a medium of Romany origin. She inherited her gift, and a 400-year-old crystal ball, from her gypsy grandmother. But as more and more clients come to her from all around the world for readings, so do people seeking to understand her special gifts of communication with those who have 'passed over'. This is the first book by a psychic to attempt to explain her powers. It explores the strands of her extraordinary life and her own philosophy of the spirit world, with first-hand accounts of remarkable encounters.

LIGHTNING

Danielle Steel

As a partner in one of New York's most prestigious law firms, Alexandra Parker barely manages to juggle husband, career, and the three-year-old child she gave birth to at forty. Then lightning strikes — a routine medical check-up reveals shattering news. Almost overnight, her husband Sam takes his distance from Alex, and they become strangers. As lightning strikes them again, Sam's promising career in Wall Street suddenly explodes into disaster. With his future hanging in the balance, Alex must decide what she feels for Sam, if life will ever be the same for them again, or if she must move on without him.

THE QUESTION

Jane Asher

It all starts with a chance remark on the telephone, just a casual conversation, but it leads Eleanor Hamilton to an appalling and deeply disturbing discovery: John, her husband of twenty years, has been leading a double life — a life of unbelievable duplicity. Feelings of jealousy, anger and confusion follow, driving Eleanor to extraordinary limits. Only one thing is clear: she wants revenge, for the mockery John has made of her existence and for the happiness that she has missed. Then fate intervenes in the shape of a terrible accident . . .

STORY OF THE
WRECK OF THE TITANIC

Marshall Everett (editor)

This is a graphic and thrilling account of the sinking of the greatest floating palace ever built, carrying down to watery graves more than one thousand five hundred souls. The story is set forth clearly, giving the facts about the ship and the voyage, the passengers, and the pathetic details of the wreck. There are first-hand accounts of the survivors, telling of exciting escapes from death and acts of heroism not equalled in ancient or modern times.